95

Stories and Tales of Old Lancashire

CONTAINING ALL THAT APPEALS TO THE HEART AND THE IMAGINATION IN THE LANCASHIRE OF MANY YESTERDAYS

BY FRANK HIRD

n, N.21   Cat. No. 1208   DG 02242/71

PRINTWISE PUBLICATIONS LIMITED
1991

© Published 1991 by PRINTWISE PUBLICATIONS LTD.
47 Bradshaw Road, Tottington, BURY, LANCS, BL8 3PW.

Warehouse and Orders —
Unit 9C, Bradley Fold Trading Estate,
Radcliffe Moor Road,
Bradley Fold,
BOLTON BL2 6RT
0204 370753

'Stories and Tales of Old Lancashire' have been selected from
'Lancashire Stories' 2 vols.
Published about 1911, written by Frank Hird.

This compilation and edition
© PRINTWISE PUBLICATIONS LTD.
Reprinted   November 1991
             January 1992
             February 1993

Prints and text chosen, researched and edited by

Cliff Hayes

ISBN No. 1 872226 21 3

Printed and bound by Manchester Free Press,
Unit E3, Longford Trading Estate, Thomas Street,
Stretford, Manchester M32 0JT.

Front cover illustration: Warrington Market Place (T. Allom) 1834.

ACKNOWLEDGEMENTS

Thanks once again to Tony Gibb for introducing me to the original book.

Foreword

The first thing I checked when I was asked to write the foreword for this book, was that it featured my home town, Warrington. To my delight, it has gone one better, it has a Warrington picture on the front, as is only proper given that Warrington has for centuries been the gateway to the Finest County. You may have gathered by now that I do not give an ounce of credence to the sacrilege, perpetrated by politicians, of bending the boundaries to put us in Cheshire. The best word I ever saw that summed it all up was invented by an acquaintance of mine for a *"Lancashire Life"* competition: *LANCASTRATION.*

Lancashire, for me, is a wonderful mixture. We have the finest arable land in the world, and yet led that same world in the Industrial Revolution. Our buildings range from the elegant town hall in Manchester, the magnificence of the Grand Theatre in Blackpool and the proud and almost pompous stone in Lancaster, to the simple terraces in virtually every mill town and pit village. No county can boast of more beautiful villages than Wrae Green, Skipool Creek or Wray and for town hall gates, nothing beats Warrington for sheer extravagance with its real gold. Markets? Well you can buy anything you need, and quite a few things you will never want, on the market stalls of Lancashire, and we have got museums fit to bust. If you want pubs you can pick from one with thirty-six television screens playing unbearable disco music, to another with oak beams and cast iron tables and they all sell bottled beer for bellies, fizzy lager for lads, and real ale for men with beards, one or two of them even sell the odd cocktail, a sort of fruit salad with a paper umbrella in it.

Lancashire has got everything, but most of all Lancashire has got me. It is in my bones, my brain, my blood and my soul. I never want to leave it and damn the politicians who tried to take it from me.

Allan Beswick — August 1991

Original Foreword

FROM whatever point of view it may be approached—topographical, archæological, commercial or romantic — no county possesses so varied a history as Lancashire.

Lancashire has had many historians, such as Whitaker, Baines, Harland and Whatton. There is a literature, dealing with the county from every aspect, which fills many pages in the British Museum catalogue. But, although the greatest pains in research have been taken to ensure historical accuracy, *Lancashire Stories* does not claim to be a history. It may be described as the result of a consideration of the history of the county entirely from the human point of view; and, that there should be variety and constant change of interest, no order of dates has been followed. Human nature is the same to-day as it was in the days of the Normans; the story has been the one object of the writer, not the period.

It has been suggested that a bibliography should be printed with this work, but in a publication destined for the general reader, rather than for the historian and archæologist, such a list would be out of place. The authorities are given in the text wherever it has been deemed essential to the interest and value of the story.

Ready and most courteous help has been extended to me by the Lancashire libraries in the search for material and for illustrations to these stories. All the books, old prints, etc., in their possession were freely placed at my disposal, permission at the same time being given for photographs to be taken of anything germane to my purpose. My warm thanks are therefore due for this valuable assistance to Mr. A. E. Sutton, of the Manchester Reference Library; Mr. George T. Shaw, of the Liverpool Reference Library; Mr. R. J. Gordon, of the Rochdale Public Library; Mr. Charles Madeley, of the Warrington Public Library; Mr. Charles Leigh, of Owens College Library, Manchester; Mr. J. N. Dowbiggin, of the Public Library, Storey Institute, Lancaster, and to the Harris Free Library, Preston and Mr. James Brockbank, of the *Manchester Courier*, and Mr. J. L. Edmondson, of the Manchester *Daily Mail*, for their valuable suggestions.

My acknowledgments are specially due to the London Library and its assistants.

FRANK HIRD.

Introduction

I have, for a long time, tried to find a book of stories, tales or myths of Lancashire. A book that was not a long history or just the bare facts, but one of the unusual, and of the characters of what is the most fascinating county in England. After much searching and help from the Second Hand trade I came across a 900 page bulky volume "Lancashire Stories" by Frank Hird, written about 1910 and very popular at the time. It was just right, it had just the story tellers feel that I was looking for. It was informative, and factually correct but not over long. Tony Gibb first showed me the book and it was on his suggestion I first read it.

Liverpool Post & Echo

Having costed out a reprint of the 2 volumes, even in paperback it would have cost £10 to print, so it was reluctantly put on a shelf and left in abeyance, although I still found myself dipping into it on many occasions, as I found it fascinating.

I then decided to try again and approach the project with the same plan as with "Lancashire 150 Years Ago" and split up the county into three. I took the book again, and for weeks was up at the crack of dawn and every weekend, and read and re-read the 900 pages. Each Saturday morning I would listen to early morning radio while I edited and made notes to check out some of the facts. The news items and features reminded me of this book. Books like this were the radio of the time.

So may I present to you the Heart of Lancashire section, edited, just a little, but I hope still with the style that Frank Hird wrote them, informative, interesting and a good read.

Very little is known about Frank Hird and even enquiries to the usually helpful Lancashire Library didn't bring up any personal details. But I for one am grateful he did write it and I hope you agree we have produced an interesting and informative book.

Cliff Hayes

P.S. Please remember that they were written in approximately 1910, so if it refers to 40 years ago, it refers to 1870. If the story states 100 years ago then it means 1810 etc...

Contents

RUSH=BEARING AT ROCHDALE

RUSH-BEARING was a festival celebrated every year in many Lancashire parishes, but it reached its greatest splendour at Rochdale. It had its origin at the time when Christianity was introduced into England, Pope Gregory IV., in A.D. 827, directing that on the anniversary of the dedication of the Christian churches wrested from the Pagans, the converts to Christianity should "build themselves huts of the boughs of trees about their churches, and celebrate the solemnities with religious feastings." But when Christianity became firmly established, the annual rejoicing over the gain of the churches from the Pagans ceased to have that special significance. The festival, however, remained and served not only as a village festival but as a means of supplying rushes to be strewn on the church floor during the winter—hence it came to be known as "Rush-bearing."

In Anglo-Saxon times and far into the Middle Ages, the floors, even in royal palaces, were covered with rushes in place of carpets, and as the floors of the churches were either of stone or beaten earth, they were bitterly cold during the winter; the villagers therefore, in strewing the floor with rushes, were providing for their own comfort. It was the custom for the young men of the village to gather rushes when they were at their full length, and piling them high up on carts, sometimes to the height of ten or twelve feet, take them to the church. The carts were gaily decorated with ribbons; the procession to the church was headed by music, and the day was given up entirely to merry-making. In the course of time the decoration of the rush-carts became more and more elaborate, as will be seen from the following description of the Scarsdale rush-cart in the latter part of the eighteenth century—

"On the bowling green behind the house a booth had been built, with ribs of timber covered with canvas, and a floor of rough boards to protect the smooth sward. Here, to the accompaniment of a couple of fiddles, flageolets and a fife, about fifty couple were in the full excitement of a country dance, while many country lads and lasses were looking on. Through the garden behind the green wandered other groups. In front of the inn stood the rush-cart . . . . . . One of the larger carts, used in Lancashire either to carry manufactured goods or to bring harvest from the fields, had been heaped with rushes to the height of about twenty-four feet from the ground. The rushes were skilfully arranged in a perfectly smooth conical stack, rising to a sharp ridge at the top. From this centre four hedges, formed of rushes woven in a neat pattern, and each hedge about two feet high, descended to the four corners of the cart. On the summit was a bower in the form of a crown, made of holly, laurel, and other evergreens, round which were twined garlands. An immense wreath of large flowers encircled the base of the arbour, and a smaller one decorated its top. On each of the smooth sides of the cone, between the boundary of rush hedges, were inscriptions in brilliantly coloured flowers such as 'Colliers and Weavers,' 'Fear God,' 'Honour the King,' etc. Spangled flags of various bright hues hung from the sides of the crowning bower. A large silver salver from the Hall, with some silver tankards, hung on the front. About thirty young men, with white shirts down to the waist, profusely adorned with gay ribbons, and with wreaths of flowers on their heads, were yoked in couples between two strong new ropes. Each couple held a stave gaily dressed young men, similarly yoked between ropes, to hold the cart while descending any steep hill. A bugle

THE SCARSDALE RUSH-CART

fastened at either side with a knot in the rope, and they were engaged in practising some dances with which their entry into the principal streets of Rochdale was to be celebrated. A strong horse was in the shaft, and behind was a band of other sounded to summon the dancers from the booth, the revellers from the club room, and the wandering groups and whispering lovers from the garden. Some miles of road had to be traversed, and all the rush-carts from neighbouring villages were to meet in Rochdale at noon. There issued from behind the house the whole united band with a big drum, two bugles, two trumpets, several other brass instruments, with fife, flageolet, etc. They were the heralds of an immense banner, held in the air by four men, two on each side, who grasped long slender poles supporting a transverse piece, from which swung this mighty achievement of the house of Scarsdale. In the centre were the Scarsdale arms, which had never been so fiercely emblazoned before; on the top was a view of Scarsdale Hall, painted on paper mounted on cloth. There were masonic devices, emblematic monsters, wonderfully shaped spangles, roses, wreaths and other caprices of the imagination of the Scarsdale artists. The result was one of barbaric splendour, of colour and tinsel. This marvellous group was heralded by a deafening clamour of the band, which did its worst against rival sounds, even almost drowning the frantic shouts with which the phenomenon of the banner was greeted. . . . . Before the cart started for Rochdale, however, a country dance was formed on each side of the road, it being the privilege of the young men yoked in the cart to choose their partners from the prettiest country girls—nothing loath for such distinction. The band struck up loudly, the banner stood grandly at one end of the two sets of thirty couples, and at the other the cart. Half an hour was devoted to this dance, when the bugle again sounded, the dance at once ceased, the young men kissed their partners and took their places, and amidst the shouts of the crowd, and the wildest efforts of the band, the Scarsdale rush-cart started for Rochdale.

"About the same time a similar fête was in progress at Hurstwood, at Martinmere, at Eastleton, at Milnrow, at Smallbridge, at Whitworth, at Spotland, and other villages; for it was the glory to assemble at its rush-bearing . . . . . . at least eight and sometimes a dozen rush-carts from the neighbouring villages. Meanwhile the gala of the rush-bearing was in the delirium of its frenzy, the rush-carts having assembled in the street opposite the Butts, each with its band in front, the order of procession extending over the bridge across the Roche, and a considerable distance up Yorkshire Street. Every band played, with stentorian energy, 'Rule, Britannia'; the young men drawing every cart vied with each other in the vigour and picturesque character of their dances; the flags in every bower on the top of the rush-carts were waved triumphantly; the spangled and decorated banners carried before each band glittered in the bright noon; from every window hung flags of coloured draperies, handkerchiefs were waved, and loud huzzas broke to swell the exulting torrent of acclamation. The main thoroughfares were crowded by multitudes of folk in their gayest dresses; in side streets were stalls with Eccles cakes, Everton toffee, and Ormskirk gingerbread; and booths with shows of every kind frequenting a country fair. Conjurers stood on their stages watching for the passage of the procession to attract a crowd of gazers by their wonderful tricks. Mountebanks and clowns were ready to perform, when the streets were clear from the grand pageant of the day. There was a bear on the Butts, growling defiance at the dogs by which it was to be baited, and climbing at intervals to the top of the high stake to which it was chained. Then a pilot balloon of gay colours floated gracefully from a garden of 'The Orchard' near the river, and the roar of guns boomed on the ear at short intervals as the pretty phantom rose on the still air to a great height, and then floated away in the tide of an upper current.

"When the twenty-first gun had been fired, the procession commenced its progress through the town, amidst the wildest shouts and gestures of the crowd. Yorkshire Street, especially at its steepest and most tortuous part, in the heart of the town consisted five-and-thirty years ago" [this would be about 1780] "either of quaint stone houses, with mullioned windows, gothic doors and peaked gables, or of white and black timber houses projecting over first a low-browed shop, then with an overhanging storey, containing often a wooden oriel, and higher a gabled storey, whose bolder projection invaded the upper area of the street. . . . . . . In this narrow and tortuous lane of ancient houses the procession of rush-carts almost brushed the projecting gables. The men on the crown of each cart were covered with flowers flung by fair hands from the highest windows, just too far off to be reached by a friendly grasp. Overhead, webs of coloured flannel and calico stretched across from the peaks of opposite roofs, but little above the flagstaff of each crown. There was barely room for the great banners to pass. Every window was decorated and crowded. The bray of the bands resounded in the narrow steep street. There was a confusion of gay colours, an agitation of bright forms, a tumult of rude joy, the transient frenzy of a carnival, as each long train of white-shirted ribbon-covered men straggled its cart up the hill, pausing and dancing at intervals amidst the exultation of the crowd."

At one time a dozen of these carts from different parts of the parish entered Rochdale on the annual celebration, but in 1832 they had dwindled down to two or three—now the custom has ceased to be observed; but its memory is retained by the annual fairs and holidays which still go by the name of "rush-bearing." The introduction of wooden floors into the churches did away with the necessity for rushes.

In former days the "sermon taster" was a prominent figure in most Lancashire congregations; a self-appointed critic of the parson's discourses, and a veritable thorn in his side. It is related of one of these "sermon tasters" that he never missed a sermon for years at the church he attended, and that regularly, every Sunday, he lay in wait for the parson at the church door after the conclusion of the service, in order to "speak his mind" upon what he had heard. His opinions were given with uncompromising frankness. One Sunday the parson, seeing his critic waiting for him, and a little weary of the weekly complaints and comments, thought he would carry the attack into the enemy's country. "How is it, John," he asked, before the "sermon taster" had time to speak, "how is it, that although I displease you week after week you still continue to attend my church? Why don't you stay away?"

John's mouth fell open with astonishment. "Me stay away?" he gasped. "Me stay away? Why, if I stopped away there's no telling what sort of stuff you'd be preaching!"

PUNISHMENTS FOR UNRULY TONGUES

OUR ancestors had a ready and effective way of silencing the tongues of inveterate scolds. When a woman had been convicted of abusive language, or brawling, she was ordered by the magistrate to wear the "Brank," or Scold's Bridle. This consisted of an iron band that went round the head on the level of the mouth, with another iron band which went over the top of the head; in the lower band was a piece of iron that pressed down the tongue. The brank was fastened upon a scold's head with a padlock at the back, and, thus effectually silenced, the offender was led through the streets of the town by the beadle, an object of derision to all her neighbours.

In some parts of Lancashire this punishment continued until close upon the nineteenth century—this was the case at Warrington, where Cicely Pewsill, inmate of the workhouse and a notorious scold, had the unhappy distinction of being the last person to undergo the punishment.

The Brank or 'Scold's Bridle'

Every town possessed its scold's bridle and its ducking-stool. Writing of the former, Dr. Platt says, "This artifice is much to be preferred to the ducking-stool, which not only endangers the health of the party but gives liberty of tongue betwixt every dip." The ducking-stool, which was the alternative punishment to the bridle, was a chair, fixed at the end of a long pole placed upon the bank of a pond in the manner of a see-saw. The scolding woman, being securely fastened in the chair, was ducked in and out of the water by the beadle and parish officers raising the end of the pole on the bank. As the ponds over which these ducking-stools were fixed were not remarkable for their cleanliness, the ordeal of ducking was not only extremely unpleasant, but there was always the risk of lifelong injury, if not of death; for if the scold was dipped at all deeply, she came up half suffocated with mud, and as the dipping was repeated several times, she was lucky if she escaped complete suffocation. Sometimes they were deliberately held under the water till they were drowned.

The ducking-stool had its origin in a Saxon superstition—or perhaps the word feeling might more accurately describe their point of view—against the maiming or cutting of a woman's body. Women, therefore, who were guilty of crimes punishable by death, were drowned, and the ducking-stool consequently was a direct inheritance from those times, and for eight centuries was in use in every parish, and in every market town, not only in Lancashire but all over England. As late as 1799 it was used by the authority of the magistrates in the House of Correction which formerly stood on Mount Pleasant at Liverpool, and in 1695 there is an entry in the parochial expenditure of that year which runs: "Paid

Edward Accres for mending the duck-stool, fifteen shillings." There was a ducking-stool at Ormskirk at the south end of the town, "but from the improvement in female manners or refinement in modern taste" it was removed in 1780. In the Pendle district the part of the river Calder, locally known as Pendle Water, was used for ducking the scolds of the neighbourhood, and a ford across the river still bears the name of Duck Pit Hippings. Burnley had its ducking-pit on what is now called Brown Hill. Manchester had its ducking-pond where the Flags now are; after the abolition of the ducking-stool the pond was called the Infirmary Pool.

This mode of punishment for the misuse of unruly tongues seems to have lingered on to a later date in the Fylde after its abolition in other parts of Lancashire, for, writing in 1837, the Rev. W. Thornber says : " Different persons now living well remember that formidable machine, the duck-stool, once the dread of scolds, standing in Great Carlton. The stool or chair was placed at the end of a long pole, balanced on a pivot, and suspended over a pond of water, in which the offender was ducked. At Poulton a few are still living who remember the remains of the chair fixed over the duck-stool at the Breck for the punishment of scolds. Poulton must surely have been infested with these scourges of domestic happiness, for no less than three ponds there all bear the name of duck-stool."

The ducking of scolds was apparently a matter of frequent occurrence; there are constant allusions to the practice in the literature of the sixteenth, seventeenth and eighteenth centuries, of which this by the poet Gay is an example—

" I speed me to the pond where the high stool,
On the long plank, hangs o'er the muddy pool—
That stool, the dread of every scolding quean."

RACING BY NAKED MEN

THE following is taken from *Notes and Queries*—

" During the summer of 1824 I remember seeing at Whitworth, in Lancashire, two races, at different periods, of this description. On one occasion two men ran on Whitworth Moor, with only a small cloth or belt round the loins. On the other occasion the runners were six in number, stark naked, the distance being seven miles, or seven times round the moor. There were hundreds, perhaps thousands of spectators, men and women, and it did not appear to strike them as being anything out of the ordinary course of things. It is in reference to this usage, no doubt, that the Lancashire riddle says—

" As I was going over Rooley Moor, Rooley Moor shaked,
I saw four and twenty men running stark nak'd;
The first was the last and the last was the first."

The answer is—the twenty-four spokes of a wheel.

So late as 1882, says Mr. Harland, races by nude men still continued in many parts of Lancashire, notwithstanding the vigilance of the county police.

FAIR ELLEN OF RADCLIFFE

This is a very old Lancashire ballad, and Radcliffe Tower, where the horrible tragedy is said to have occurred, is still supposed to be haunted by a black dog, the spirit of the wicked stepmother.

THERE was a lord of worthy fame,
    And a hunting he would ride,
    Attended by a noble traine
Of gentrye by his side.

And while he did in chase remaine
    To see both sport and playe,
His lady went, as she did feigne,
    Unto the church to praye.

This lord he had a daughter deare,
    Whose beauty shone so bright,
She was beloved both far and neare
    Of many a lord and knight.

Fair Ellen was this damsel call'd,
    A creature faire was she ;
She was her father's only joye,
    As you shall after see.

Therefore her cruel stepmother
    Did envye her so much,
That day by day she sought her life,
    Her malice it was such.

She bargained with the master-cook,
    To take her life awaye ;
And taking of her daughter's book,
    She thus to her did saye :—

" Go home, sweet daughter, I thee praye,
    Go, hasten presentlie,
And tell unto the master-cook
    These words that I tell thee :

" And bid him dresse to dinner streight
    That fair and milk-white doe,
That in the park doth shine so bright
    There's none so faire to showe."

This lady, fearing of no harme,
    Obey'd her mother's will ;
And presently she hastened home,
    Her pleasure to fulfil.

She streight into the kitchen went,
    Her message for to tell ;
And there she spied the master-cook,
    Who did with malice swell.

" Nowe, master-cook, it must be soe,
    Do that which I thee tell :
You needes must dress the milk-white doe
    Which you do knowe full well.

Then streight his cruell bloodye hands
    He on the lady layd,

Who quivering and shaking stands,
    While thus to her he sayd :—

" Thou art the doe that I must dress,
    See here, behold my knife ;
For it is pointed, presentlye
    To ridd thee of thy life."

" Oh then," cried out the scullion-boye,
    As loud as loud might bee,
" Oh save her life, good master-cook,
    And make your pyes of mee !

" For pitye's sake, do not destroye
    My ladye with your knife ;
You know shee is her father's joye,
    For Christe's sake, save her life."

" I will not save her life," he sayd,
    " Nor make my pyes of thee ;
Yet, if thou dost this deed bewraye,
    Thy butcher I will bee."

Now when his lord he did come home
    For to sit downe and eat,
He callèd for his daughter deare
    To come and carve his meat.

" Now sit you downe," his ladye say'd,
    " Oh sit you downe to meat ;
Into some nunnery she is gone,
    Your daughter deare forget."

Then solemnlye he made a vowe
    Before the companie,
That he would neither eat nor drinke
    Until he did her see.

Oh then bespake the scullion-boye,
    With a loud voice so hye—
" If now you will your daughter see,
    My lord, cut up that pye !

" Wherein her flesh is minced small,
    And parchèd with the fire ;
All causèd by her stepmother,
    Who did her death desire.

" And cursèd be the master-cook,
    Oh, cursèd may he bee !
I proffer'd him my own heart's blood,
    From death to set her free."

Then all in blacke this lord did mourne,
    And, for his daughter's sake,
He judged her cruell stepmother
    To be burnt at a stake.

Likewise he judged the master-cook
    In boiling lead to stand ;
And made the simple scullion-boye
    The heire of all his land.

CONCERNING CHURCH BELLS

OUR forefathers held many superstitions and beliefs with regard to the powers of church bells. It was firmly believed that thunder and lightning could be driven away by their being rung, and also that evil spirits could be chased from persons and places by the same means. The passing-bell was rung for two purposes, one to bespeak the prayers of all good Christians for a soul just departing, the other to drive away the evil spirits which were supposed to be standing at the foot of the bed or about the house, ready either to seize upon the soul, or else to molest and terrify it in its passage. It was firmly believed that the spirits were kept aloof by the ringing of the bell, and that the soul, like a hunted hare, thus got the start, or had what sportsmen called "law." A high charge was made for tolling the big bell of the church, as, being so much louder, the evil spirits were compelled to go further off to be beyond the reach of its sound, by which the poor soul got a much better start of them; and since it was heard at further distances than the ordinary passing-bell, the dying person gained a larger number of prayers. In many parts of Lancashire it was the custom to ring a merry peal upon the church bells immediately a burial was over, the quaint belief being that the greater the clang of bells, the further would be the flight of the fiends waiting to seize upon the departed soul. The use of bells is set forth in this old monkish doggerel—

"Men's death I tell by doleful knell;
  Lightning and thunder I break asunder;
  On Sabbath all to church I call;
  The sleepy head I raise from bed;
  The winds so fierce I do disperse;
  Men's cruel rage I do assuage."

In some Lancashire parishes it is still customary in ringing the passing-bell to conclude its tolling with nine strokes of the clapper if it has tolled for a man, with six for a woman, and three for a child.

Before the Reformation, the great bell of the parish church was rung on Shrove Tuesday to call the people together for the confession of their sins, or to be "shriven"; hence the name of the day. This bell is still rung in some parts of Lancashire, and is called the "Pancake Bell," being now regarded only as a signal to the people to begin frying their pancakes. In some villages a bell is rung as the congregation is leaving church after the morning service. This is known as the "Pudding Bell," it having been firmly believed for many generations that it is rung to warn those at home to get the dinner ready. The origin of the ringing of this bell is not known, but, like many other old customs, it still lingers in remoter parts of the county, announcing to the village that the service is over and that "pudding-time has come." So late as 1870 the curfew bell was rung at Burnley, Colne, Blackburn, Padiham, and in many other towns and villages. This, perhaps, is the most remarkable instance of the persistence of an old custom centuries after it has ceased to have any reason. Owing to the number of fires which were constantly breaking out in the wooden hovels, of which the towns and villages were then for the most part built, William the Conqueror made a law that at the ringing of a bell, called the *couvre feu* (cover fire), at eight o'clock all people should put out their lights and fires and go to bed. The French words developed into the English word "curfew." For over eight hundred years this bell has been rung every night in many Lancashire steeples; in latter days even its original name has been forgotten, and it is called "the eight o'clock bell."

MURDERS DISCOVERED THROUGH DREAMS

DREAMS very rarely are of prophetic value, but there are two authentic cases in Lancashire, one in the seventeenth and the other in the nineteenth century, in which murderers were discovered by visions appearing to people in their sleep. The first case is that of the murder of John Waters of Lower Darwen, a gardener, who "by reason of his calling was much absent from his family." During these absences his wife seems to have become on too friendly terms with Gyles Haworth, who also lived at Lower Darwen, and together they conspired to murder her husband. This is the account written on April 17, 1663—

"They contracted with one Ribchester, a poor man, to kill this Waters. As soon as Waters came home and went to bed, Gyles Haworth and Waters's Wife conducted the kind Executioner to the said Waters, who seeing him so innocently laid between his two small Children in Bed repented of his enterprise, and totally refused to kill him. Gyles Haworth, displeased with the faint-heartedness of Ribchester, takes the Axe into his own hand and dashed out his brains: the Murderers buried him in a Cow-house. Waters being long missing, the Neighbourhood asked his Wife for him; she denied that she knew where he was. Thereupon publick search was made for him in all pits round about, lest he should have casually fallen into any of them.

"One Thomas Haworth of the said Town, Yeoman, was for many nights together much troubled with broken sleep and dreams of the murder; he revealed his dreams to his Wife, but she harboured the concealment of them for a long time : this said Thomas Haworth had occasion to pass by the House every day where the murder was done, and did call and inquire for Waters as often as he went near the House. One day he went into the House to ask for him, and there was a neighbour who said to Thomas Haworth, 'It's said that Waters lies under this stone' (pointing to the Hearth stone), to which Thomas Haworth replied, 'And I have dreamed that he is under a stone not far distant.' The Constable of the said Town being accidentally in the said House (his name is Myles Aspinal) urged Thomas Haworth to make known more at large what he had dreamed, which he related thus : 'I have (quoth he) 'many a time within these eight weeks' (for so long was it since the murder) 'dreamed very restlessly, that Waters was murdered and buried under a broad stone in the Cow-house; I have told my troubled dreams to my Wife alone, but she refuses to let me make it known. But I am not able to conceal my dreams any longer, my sleep departs from me, I am pressed and troubled with fearful dreams which I cannot bear any longer, and they increase upon me.'

"The Constable, hearing this, made search immediately upon it, and found as he (Thomas Haworth) had dreamed the murdered body eight weeks buried under a flat stone in the Cow-house. Ribchester and Gyles Haworth fled and never came again. Anne Waters (for so was Waters's wife's name) being apprehended confessed the murder and was burnt."

The more modern instance is given in the *Mirror* of June 1, 1844—

"A gentleman of veracity, the Rev. H.

Alexander, lecturing at Lancaster, stated a remarkable fact which had occurred some years before. An amiable young man, named Horrocks, had been robbed and murdered. He was found with his head beaten in, apparently by bludgeons. For many months vigilant search was made for the perpetrators, but all in vain.

"One night an individual who had been on very friendly terms with Horrocks, awoke much disturbed, and told his wife his conviction was that God had revealed to him in a vision that Samuel Longwith of Bolton was the murderer of his poor friend. Longwith was a person with whom the dreamer had no acquaintance, and whom he had scarcely ever seen, and lived twenty miles off. His wife told him to think no more about it, but go to sleep. He did so, but again woke from the effects of the same dream. He resolved to set out for Bolton instantly, and apply for a warrant against Longwith.

"He acted upon this determination; but the magistrate to whom he applied refused to grant one upon such evidence.

Passing the market-place he met Longwith, whom he immediately desired to go to a public-house with him to hear something he had to communicate. There, locking the door, he charged Longwith with the murder. The man was seized and faintly denied the accusation. In his confusion he said he was innocent, for he did not strike the blow. 'Then you know who did,' replied the friend of the murdered man; and Longwith was taken up and examined. He prevaricated in his statement and was remanded for three days, at the end of which, after many hours' prayer, he confessed that he had been induced to join three men in a robbing expedition, when, meeting Horrocks, who made some resistance, his companions murdered him. This confession came out before the grand jury, and Longwith was brought to trial. The dream was, of course, not offered in evidence; the jury felt satisfied, and Longwith was cast. He was doggedly silent after being found guilty, but again confessed his crime just before his execution."

SPIRITS AND SECOND SIGHT

PERSONS born during twilight were supposed to have the gift of seeing spirits, and to be able to foretell the death of their friends and acquaintances. Some believed that these powers also belonged to those who were born exactly at midnight.

The spirits of persons about to die, especially if they were in distant lands, were supposed to return to their friends and thus predict the calamity, but only if they had been thinking of their friends and desired to see them.

Second sight was also firmly believed in, and a man named Cardwell, at Marton, near Blackpool, who foretold deaths and evil happenings from the visions he declared he saw, had a large following. He was visited by people from far and near. Cardwell had so strong a faith in the reality of what he saw—the wraiths or ghosts of those about to die—that, having a vision of his child, he concluded that it was about to die, and so convinced was he that the child's days were numbered that he carried sand to the churchyard in readiness for its grave. But the child did not die, at least not until many years afterwards.

THE LEGEND OF BEWSEY HALL

IN the ancient days the Butlers of Bewsey Hall were lords of the manor at Warrington. Originally the family name had been Pincerna, but an ancestor acting as butler to Ranulph, Earl of Chester in 1158, had taken the surname of Butler from his office. The position of butler to so great a nobleman as the Earl of Chester was not a menial office, but was equivalent to that of a Comptroller, or Master, of the Household, in a royal household of our own time, and could only be held by a knight of good family. In later generations the descendant of the first Butler married the heiress of Matthew Villiers, Lord of Warrington, and so became possessed of Bewsey Hall and its surrounding property.

Amongst the many rights appertaining to the lord of the manor of Warrington was that of a ferry across the Mersey, which was the only communication between the Lancashire and Cheshire sides, a monopoly which brought a goodly number of groats each year to the Butler coffers. This monopoly continued until the reign of Henry VII., and was the actual cause which led to Sir John Butler's murder. Henry VII., being about to pay his historic visit to his stepfather, the first Earl of Derby, at Latham House, it was found that the

royal party would have to cross the Mersey by Sir John Butler's ferry, a passage that would not only cause many hours' delay, but which was not unaccompanied by danger, seeing the large number of horses and heavily laden sumpter mules. The Earl of Derby, therefore, being desirous of removing any possible inconvenience from the journey of his royal stepson, conceived the idea of building a bridge. He owned the land on the Cheshire side of the river, but was compelled to buy a piece of ground, belonging to one Norris of Warrington, on the Lancashire side. Immediately the purchase was effected he " builded a bridge at Warrington on both sides, being his own land," to the great disgust and annoyance of Sir John Butler, whose ferry was now rendered useless, and he himself deprived of the good income it had produced.

Sir John expressed his opinion of the Earl's action in building the bridge in no measured terms, and consequently a fierce quarrel broke out between the two. But when the King was approaching Warrington the Earl, apparently anxious to bring the quarrel to an end, sent a request to Sir John Butler that he should make one of the train of Lancashire noblemen and gentlemen who were accompanying him to meet the monarch. Sir John sent a contemptuous and most discourteous refusal.

The Earl of Derby—by reason of his relationship by marriage to Henry VII., and his vast possessions—was then all paramount in Lancashire, and such an affront to his high dignity could not be passed lightly by. Whether the Earl himself had any part in the dastardly means taken to avenge the insult is not known, but the name of his son, Lord Stanley, is given by the old chronicler as the instigator of the crime. "Sir John Butler, knt., was slaine in his bedde by the procurement of the Lord Standley, Sir Piers Leigh and Mister William Savage joining with him in that action."

The legend runs that, having bribed the porter at Bewsey Hall, the latter, in the dead of night, set a light in one of the windows to serve as a guide to the murderers across the broad moat, which they crossed in a "coracle," or leather boat.

" What hideous thing comes swift and dark
   Athwart that flickering wave ?
A spectre boat there seems to glide,
   With many an uplift glaive.

"The bolts are unslid by that grim porter,
   And a gladsome man was he,
When three foemen fierce strode up the
     stair
   All trim and cautiously."

The traitorous porter led the three murderers to Sir John's sleeping chamber, but at the door they found his chamberlain, Houlcroft, guarding his master's slumbers. In vain they parleyed with him, but the faithful servant would not give them admission, and after a desperate resistance was hewn to the ground. The noise of the combat, the clashing of swords and the cries of the devoted Houlcroft had awakened Sir John, who, leaping from his bed, was fallen upon and hacked to

pieces by the murderers before he could defend himself.

Lady Butler was sleeping in the same room, together with Sir John's infant son and heir. The miscreants spared her life, but, having dispatched the father, rushed to the cradle with the intention of killing the child. Nothing less than the destruction of the line of Butler would apparently satisfy the Stanley vengeance for the affront put upon them by Sir John. But the cradle was empty.

Here there are two versions of the legend. One tells that whilst the murderers were occupied in their bloody work upon Houlcroft and his unfortunate master, a page passed through the porter's lodge carrying a basket. The wicked porter asks—

" ' Now whither away, thou little page,
   Now whither away so fast ? '
  'They have slain Sir John,' said the little
     page,
   ' And his head in this wicker cast.'

" ' And whither goest thou with that grisly
     head ? '
   Cried the grim porter again.
 ' To Warrington Bridge they bade me run,
   And set it up amain.'

" 'There may it hang,' cried that loathly
     knave,
  ' And grin till its teeth be dry ;
While every day, with jeer and taunt,
   Will I mock it till I die !' "

It was not Sir John's head, however, that the page carried in his basket, but Sir John's child which, this version says, he conveyed " craftily " to the Priory of the Hermit Friars of St. Augustine near the bridge at Warrington, where it was recovered by the distracted mother on the following morning.

After vainly searching for the child the murderers descended the stairs, and discovered the trick played by the page upon the porter, whom they roundly accused of treachery—

"They counted down the red, red gold ;
 And the porter laughed outright :
'Now we have paid thy service well,
 For thy master's blood this night ;

'For the master's blood thou hast betrayed,
 We've paid thee thy desire ;
 But for thy treachery unto us,
 Thou hast not had thy hire.' "

its nurse in an adjoining chamber. Returning to Sir John's bedroom, the negro held the three murderers at bay in the second doorway, while the nurse effected her escape with the child. Finally he, too, was killed, but in the meantime the child was safe at the Priory by Warring-

"THE NEGRO HELD THE THREE MURDERERS AT BAY."

Taking the porter with them across the moat, they hanged him—" they payed him a greate reward, and so coming away with him, they hanged him at a tree in Bewsey Parke."

The other version of the legend is the more credible of the two. This tells that a faithful negro servant, hearing the fray in Sir John's bedroom, rushed thither, and entering by a door opposite to that forced by the murderers, snatched up the infant from its cradle, and carried it to

ton Bridge. This story has proof which the other lacks, for on the alabaster tomb of Sir John and Lady Butler, in what was formerly the Bewsey Chapel in Warrington Church, is the figure of a negro, his body having been buried with those of his master and mistress as the last earthly reward that could be paid him for preserving the life of the infant heir. In the second version of the legend the traitorous porter is also hanged, after having been paid the blood money he demanded, but this was doubtless a precautionary measure on the part of the murderers, who would naturally wish to remove so damning and treacherous a witness to their crime, and the deliberation with which it had been arranged.

Lady Butler commenced a prosecution against Sir John's murderers, but the machinery of the law in those days, especially when directed against a member of so powerful a family as the Stanleys, was not easily set in motion, and before her suit came on for hearing she had married Lord Grey, doubtless as a protection to herself and her child against her late husband's enemies. Her second husband, however, did not support her in her efforts to bring Sir John's murderers to justice, and exercising a right then existing he made her suit void. This, again, was probably due to Stanley influence. Whatever the reason, his wife did not submit tamely: " for which reason she parted from her husband and came into Lancashire, saying, ' If my lord will not let me have my will of my husband's enemies, yet shall my body be buried by him.' " Forthwith the unhappy lady began to build the elaborate alabaster monument in Warrington Church, where, in due time, she was buried beside her murdered husband and the faithful negro who had given his life in saving her child.

The descendants of Sir John continued to live at Bewsey Hall until 1603, when the estate was sold to the Irelands of Hale Hall.

THE ARVAL CAKE

THE arval cake still figures amongst the refreshments prepared for the mourners after a funeral in many parts of Lancashire, but those who eat it little think that they are following a custom of the Danes. In the far-away times when the Danes occupied England, a solemn feast was always given after the funeral of a king or a noble by his successor. This was called the " arfwol" —from *arf* meaning inheritance, and *wol* meaning ale—a word signifying that the feast was given by the heir on succeeding to an estate through a death. It is therefore from the Danes that the custom of a funeral feast, which is general throughout the country, is derived, but nowhere does the old name of the feast survive except in Lancashire, where the " arfwol " has become " *arval*," and applies only to the cakes. In some districts the ale drunk by the mourners is called arval-ale. At Dalton-in-Furness a full meal of bread and cheese and ale used to be provided at the house before the funeral ; after the burial service the parish clerk proclaimed at the grave-side that the mourners must repair to some appointed public-house. Here they sat down in companies of four, each four being served with two quarts of ale, one half of which was paid for by the conductor of the funeral and the other half by the mourners themselves. Whilst the ale was being drunk, cakes were carried round, one to each guest. The cakes were not eaten then, but carried home.

PEG O' TH' WELL

THE entertaining author of the *Pictorial History of Lancashire*, who wandered from one end of the county to the other during the early 'forties of the last century, gives an amusing description of the result of a visit he paid to Waddow Hall near Clitheroe, in order to see a wooden figure called Peg o' th' Well, which was reputed to have infinite powers for working evil.

"Its site," he says of Waddow Hall, "is transcendently beautiful, lying at the foot of an eminence covered with trees, having in front a fine sloping lawn, at the bottom of which the Ribble dashes, while on the high ground, on the Lancashire side of the river, fine, well-wooded sweeps present themselves, which are crowned by Clitheroe with its square keep and in the distance by the never-failing Pendle. The country is rich, covered with fine trees, and will in itself well repay the visitor. Something besides natural beauty, however, we confess had drawn us to the spot.

"The first question we put on entering the hall was 'Where is Peggy?' The answer was given by a neat, intelligent young woman, to whose obliging manners—as her master, Jeremiah Garnett, Esq., had gone to a hunt held in Craven that day—we were much indebted.

"'Peg o' th' Well, you mean, sir, I suppose?'

"'Yes.'

"'Oh, I've lately brought her out of those gloomy rooms at the top of the house, washed her face, and now she lives in the larder.' She uttered these words with an arch expression of look and word which told us that my informant was far beyond the weakness of ordinary superstitious fears.

"'Please let me see her,' we said. We were conducted into a large, bright-looking pantry, and there in truth was Peggy's head. It lay—bearing on the neck marks of violence—with the features upward on a long table, shining with a purity and cleanness like the atmosphere of the locality.

"'Does she ever plague you now?'

"'No, sir; there is not a better girl in the parish. I fear she was much slandered.'

"'And where is her body?'

"'By yon well i' th' field. Would you like to see what we servants call Peg's Place?'

"'Certainly.'

"We were accordingly conducted up to an attic-floor consisting of several apartments, filled with fishing tackle, rubbish, etc. This was evidently a part of the house modern improvement had spared.

"'And so, Peggy lived here?' we said, looking as directed into a small, dark room.

"'Yes, here I found her. They told me many strange tales about her, and warned me against having aught to do with her —but I ne'er heeded 'em, and took her downstairs.'"

The true story of "Peg" shows how superstitions may arise from differences of religious opinion. "Peg" had clearly been the figure of a saint occupying a niche in some neighbouring church or monastery. Carved in wood, and somewhat roughly, she was certainly not a fine specimen of the sculptor's art, doubtless being the work of some local carpenter whose religious zeal had led him to put his chisel and mallet to this service for the glory of his parish church, or in return for some kindness shown him by the monks. When all the figures of saints—"idols" they were called in the Act of Parliament—were ordered to be removed from the churches, by some unknown means this wooden image came to

Waddow Hall, where it was placed in the garden by the side of a spring, whence her name, "Peg o' th' Well." Tradition Saint Margaret, and that owing to the bitter feelings then existing between Roman Catholics and Protestants she had

"WITH ONE BLOW OF THE HATCHET SHE SEVERED PEG'S HEAD FROM HER BODY"

is silent as to the reason why the wooden figure was so christened, but it may not unreasonably be supposed that when standing in her original niche in church or monastery chapel she had represented been called Peg in derision by her Puritanical owners. Be that as it may, Peg o' th' Well she became, and a maleficent and baleful creature to boot. "The scrupulous proprietors of Waddow Hall regarded the innocuous image with distrust and aversion, nor did they think themselves otherwise than justified in ascribing to Peggy all the evils and mischances that befell the house. If a storm struck and damaged the house, Peggy was the author of the damage. If the wind whistled and moaned through the ill-fitting doors and casements, it was 'Peggy at her work,' requiring to be appeased, else some sad accident was sure to come. On one occasion Master Starkie, so the host was named—returned home very late with a broken leg. He had been hunting that day, and report said made too free with the ale afterwards. But, as usual, Peggy bore the blame; from some dissatisfaction she had waylaid the master of the house, so it was firmly believed, 'and caused his horse to fall.'" A short time after, a Puritan preacher was overtaken by a freshet in the river in attempting to cross over the stepping-stones, "the Bungerley Hippin Stones"—the very stones on which poor Henry VI. was captured. "Now Mistress Starkie had a great attachment to those preachers, and had indeed sent for the one in question to exorcise and dispossess her youngest son, a boy of ten years of age, who was grievously afflicted with a demon." The author adds that it was suspected he was being tormented by Peggy, but there is no mention of the hapless figure's name in the many documents relating to the case; and this is clearly an author's liberty. Peggy's evil influence seemed only to extend to the lesser misfortunes of the family.

Mistress Starkie, wearing her best gown and seated near a large wood-fire with the supper-table all ready for the coming of the preacher, began to grow anxious. The preacher was late, and the windows rattled under the violence of a storm of wind and rain.

"The storm seems to get worse," she said. Then suddenly rising to her feet she called to the servants, "Hark! Heard ye no cry? Yes! There again! Oh, if the dear man is in the river! Run! Run all of ye to his rescue!"

The servants obeyed her and shortly afterwards two lusty men entered the Hall panting under the huge weight of the dripping parson. Voluble with fear and anger he told his tale, how when crossing the Hippin Stones which shone high and dry out of the water, there suddenly came a wave which swept him off his feet, and sent him rolling and tossing into the river. As suddenly as it had come, so suddenly the freshet passed, surely the work of an evil spirit, which, knowing the holy work he was come upon, had endeavoured to prevent it by drowning him in the river.

"'T is Peg!" cried Mistress Starkie, "'T is Peg, at her old tricks again. This way, all of ye!"

And despite the violence of the wind and rain, and despite the fact that she was wearing her best gown in honour of the Puritan preacher — and Mistress Starkie was a careful soul—she rushed out into the garden, seizing a heavy hatchet as she went.

Followed by the servants and the dripping preacher, Mistress Starkie sped across the wet grass, her heavy farthingale billowing about her. By the side of the spring the figure of Peggy gleamed whitely under the stormy sky, as harmless and as innocent of evil as a wooden statue well could be. But to Mistress Starkie she was the incarnation of the evil spirit who had taken bits off the roof on windy nights, who had screamed down chimneys and who had fled through window-casements and keyholes, who had caused her husband's horse to fall upon him and break his leg, and above all who had tried to drown her favourite preacher when he was on his way to exorcise the demons who had taken up their abode at Waddow. With one blow of the hatchet she severed Peg's head from her body.

From that moment, so the Starkies averred, "Peg's tricks" were at an end. Her headless body was left by the side of the spring as an example to other evil spirits, the head being hidden away in an old lumber-room where it lay for over two centuries, until the kindly maidservant "washed her face" and took her to live in the larder.

In the course of time Waddow Hall passed from the Starkie family, and in 1742 the then mistress of the house died in consequence of pricking her finger with a needle. A portrait of this unfortunate lady hung in the dining-room of the Hall showing her engaged upon the fatal sewing by which she got her death.

LANCASHIRE WEATHER RHYMES

IF red the sun begins his race
  Expect that rain will fall apace.

The evening red, the morning grey,
Are certain signs of one fair day.

If woolly fleeces spread the heavenly way,
No rain, be sure, disturbs that summer day.

In the waning of the moon,
A cloudy morn—fair afternoon.

When clouds appear like rocks and towers
The earth's refreshed by constant showers.

When Pendle wears its woolly cap
The farmers all may take a nap.

If Rivington Pike do wear a hood,
Be sure the day will ne'er be good.

If Candlemas Day be fair and clear,
There will be two winters in one year.

If on the trees the leaves still hold,
The winter coming will be cold.

When the cock moults before the hen,
We shall have weather thick and thin;

When the hen moults before the cock,
The ground will be as hard as block.

When the sloe tree is white as a sheet
Sow your barley whether it be dry or weet.

If the moon shows a silver shield,
Be not afraid to reap your field.

In many parts of Lancashire it is still customary for children to repeat the following verses after saying their prayers—

"Matthew, Mark, Luke and John,
  Bless the bed that I lie on;
There are four corners to my bed,
  And four angels overspread,
Two at the feet, two at the head.

If any ill thing me betide,
  Beneath four wings my body hide,
Matthew, Mark, Luke and John,
  Bless the bed that I lie on. Amen."

An old widow washerwoman of seventy married a man some years older than herself. A day or two afterwards she met the vicar of the parish, who expressed surprise at her having married again, and asked her if she had given up her washing.

"Eh, dear o' me, nowe," was the answer. "I've noane gi'en up mi weshin'. I fun' I couldn't wheel things out mysel', an' I'd to choose between weddin' him or buyin' a donkey!"

GALLOWS HILL, LANCASTER

NTIL the year 1800 the execution of condemned criminals at Lancaster took place at a spot known as the Gallows Hill, where a permanent gallows had stood for many centuries. It was here that the Lancashire witches met their doom, and not in was a terrible spectacle. The poor wretches—sometimes as many as eight or nine in number—being huddled together in the bottom of a springless cart, with their backs to the horses and their coffins piled up behind them. The doleful procession passed along Moor Lane and Moor

EXECUTION AT GALLOWS HILL

front of the Castle, as is stated by Harrison Ainsworth in his famous novel. Now-a-days the law ordains that three clear Sundays shall elapse between condemnation and the date of execution, but as late as 1830 the execution took place upon the following day unless a Sunday intervened. The procession of the condemned from the Castle to Gallows Hill Gate and stopped at the Golden Lion public-house at the corner of Brewery Lane, in order that the condemned might take their last drink. This last drink was allowed to criminals all over the country on their way to execution, and, as was only natural, was made to last as long as possible.

It is related that in a neighbouring

county a saddler lost his life because he refused this last drink on temperance principles. On his way to execution the cart drew up at the appointed public-house, but, on the saddler's refusing the proffered bowl of ale, it drove on and he was hanged. If he had taken the drink his life would have been spared, for his reprieve had arrived at the prison shortly after the despatch of the fatal cart, and a messenger was already hastening with it to the place of execution. If there had been the usual delay at the house of call the reprieve would have arrived in time; but, as it was, the unfortunate saddler was already hanging lifeless when the messenger reached the scaffold.

The condemned cart was accompanied in its procession from Lancaster Castle by the friends and relatives of the criminals, and all the riff-raff of the town. It was a horrible spectacle, for if any of the condemned men showed signs of fear they were made the objects of coarse jests and derision by the heartless crowd. The majority, therefore, affected a bravado which added horror to the situation, laughing and talking with their friends, and exchanging obscene jests with the crowd. Many of them carried this spirit to the very scaffold itself, and it is recorded that a man called Taylor, who, with two others was condemned to death for burglary in 1814, called out as the noose was put over his neck, " Lads, kick off your shoes ! " which the others did. It is terrible to read in the records of Lancaster Castle that, out of 265 executions, 43 only were for murder ; the other crimes being burglary, passing bad notes, forgery and robberies of various kinds. But as coining, cattle-stealing, or larceny in a dwelling-house to the extent of five pounds were all punishable by death, these numbers are easily accounted for.

The Assizes generally occupied a fort-night or three weeks, and it was not un-usual for as many as forty persons to be sentenced to death at each Assize. At the Assizes opened at Lancaster on March 21, 1818, of 121 persons who were tried, the death sentence was given against 49, but of these only 15 were hanged, the power of reprieve being then vested in the judge and not in the Home Secretary as it is to-day. The judges had the right of exercising this power immediately, but it not infrequently happened that after sentence of death had been passed the judge would respite the condemned for a day or two, or even perhaps for a week, and then he would be hanged.

The bodies of all murderers were directed by the judges to be given to the surgeons for dissection, and it would seem that the doctors in the neighbourhood where the crime was committed had the first claim, for in the case of Heaton and Thomas, who were executed in 1832, their bodies were sent to the hospitals at Warrington and Liverpool. The hang-man also had his perquisites, one of them being the clothing in which the condemned were hanged.

Many gruesome and revolting scenes must have been witnessed at the gallows on Lancaster Moor, but none more terrible than the execution of Mary Hilton, who in 1772 was condemned to death for poisoning her husband. She was drawn on a sledge to the gallows, and after hanging for fifteen minutes she was cut down, and her body burnt. An old inhabitant of Lancaster, whose recollections were taken down early in the nineteenth century, said that Mary Hilton, who lived at Four Lane Ends, was burned opposite the second window of the work-house — the second window from the north. She was first strangled by a man with one arm, and before she was dead was let down into a fire consisting of faggots and two barrels of tar. She was beginning to move before the fire reached her.

After the year 1800 the executions at Lancaster took place in an angle between a tower and a wall on the east side of the terrace steps. This was called " The Hanging Corner." On the ground-floor of the tower, and communicating immediately with the scaffold, is a room known as the " Drop-room "—a very chamber of horrors. The first thing that the criminal saw as he entered this room, to be pinioned, was his own coffin resting on the window-sill. Amongst the relics kept in this room is a curious chair with very long legs fitted with wheels. It is the record of an act of unparalleled barbarity. The chair was specially constructed for a young woman called Jane Scott, who was sentenced to death for the murder of her mother at Preston in 1828. The wretched woman was so weak and emaciated that she could neither walk nor stand. She was therefore placed in this chair and wheeled on to the scaffold, two female warders supporting her whilst the noose was placed round her neck. At a signal the two women stepped back from the drop board, the chair was withdrawn and Jane Scott was left, her feet resting on the drop-board, her body only kept from falling by the rope round her neck. The

drop was released, and the half-dead woman was slowly choked.

Another relic is a chain with a piece of rope attached to it. The chain was fastened to the gallows and the rope formed the noose, and as the drop was only two feet the unhappy wretches were strangled rather than hanged. Another barbarous custom was the hanging of those condemned at the Assizes all together at one execution. Thus in April 1817 nine men, four of whom were under twenty years of age, were all hanged together—their crimes being burglary, the uttering of false notes, and highway robbery. The struggles of these men when the two-foot drop precipitated them the short length of the chain were terrible to witness ; and they were strung up so closely as to be almost upon the top of one another.

Although the scandalous and disgusting exhibitions that accompanied the procession of the condemned to the Gallows Hill were done away with by the executions taking place in " Hanging Corner," this barbarous method of fulfilling the law was still carried out in public, the space in front of the tower being always closely packed with a morbid crowd.

This sinister corner in Lancaster Castle is now railed off, the executions taking place in an inner courtyard.

LANCASHIRE COLLIERS

T HE stranger passing through the Lancashire colliery towns is generally struck with surprise by seeing groups of colliers at the street corners squatting down on their haunches, smoking and chatting. Where men in other employment lean up against the wall, or a lamp-post, in their street corner conferences the collier squats. It is a curious sight, this "squatting round," which is actually a sitting on the heels, not unlike the posture of Kaffirs or native bearers round a camp fire. The Lancashire miner can squat for hours and yet feel rested. The reason given for this curious habit is that down in the mine where the coal-seams may be thin, the collier has to curl himself up in order to do his work; he remains in this cramped position perhaps hour after hour, and consequently gets so used to it, in the course of time, that he finds ease and rest in a position which would be torture to any ordinary person.

Another curious attribute of the colliers is that the majority of them are bow-legged, and that whether they are walking or standing their bodies have a peculiar bend which is seen in no other class of workers. This is also caused by the positions he has to assume in the seams.

Of all the workers of Lancashire the colliers are the most sociable. Unlike the weavers, the spinners, the ironworkers, and those employed in the hundred-and-one trades of Lancashire, who go off for a whole week's holiday at the "wakes," the colliers prefer to go now and then for a day's excursion to the seaside; but such is their sociability that it is no pleasure unless they all go together. For months previously the colliers, their wives and their families, will save every available penny for the annual holiday, the hoard, when the day arrives, amounting to a goodly sum. On the occasion of these day's holidays or annual excursions, whole colliery towns are deserted, for the holiday is no holiday to the collier unless he spends it with his mates. The excursion trains are packed to suffocation, and they carry their sociability to such an extent that if Jack and his family see their friends Bill and his family installed already in one compartment, they must needs join them. Other friends perhaps come along and they, too, get into the carriage, and thus—although the compartment next door may be practically empty—the one of which Bill and Jack and their families have taken possession, will be so crowded that not only are they sitting upon one another's knees, on the seats, but the floor and the luggage racks are also occupied. The discomfort, to the ordinary person, would appear to be extreme, but the more tightly packed they are, both on the outward and the homeward journey, the happier the colliers seem to be. They start out in the morning with their pockets full of money, their savings of months, and they come home penniless, leaving hundreds of pounds behind them at Blackpool, or other of the seaside towns.

There are many people who are shocked at the extravagant expenditure of the colliers and their families on these excursions, but seeing that they spend a considerable portion of their lives in the bowels of the earth, one day's wild and exhilarating amusement can scarcely be denied them.

The constant danger to which miners are exposed naturally makes them superstitious. For instance, if a collier is killed at his work, all the men in the pit go home for the remainder of the day, although they may have been in another part of the mine than that in which the accident occurred.

Sunday is the collier's great day, when thousands of them go out into the country with their dogs and their homing pigeons, and exciting races are the result. But colliers, like every other class in the country, do not possess quite the same characteristics as their forbears, and many of the old stories told of them would find no parallel to-day. Times have changed since colliers drank champagne, and the following story would be

was playing with a bull pup. The little dog mistaking play for earnest, suddenly seized its master by the nose. The collier yelled and shouted for help. His son, hastening to see what was the matter when he heard his father's shouts, saw the position in an entirely different light from his unfortunate parent.

"Dunnot tak' ony notice on him, feyther," he remarked quietly, "it'll be t' makin' o' t' pup!"

COLLIERS GOSSIPING AT A STREET CORNER

impossible in this century. A vicar upbraided a collier for keeping a race-dog when he had to feed a family of little children.

"And what do you keep the dog on?" asked the vicar.

"Beefsteaks an' mutton chops when I con afford 'um," answered the collier.

"And what when you cannot afford them?" replied the vicar.

"Well, then, it has to live t' same as us."

Another story tells of a collier who

The stories of drinking were endless, but all after the manner of Baron Münchhausen. In one colliery town there were tales of a collier whose swallowing capacity was such that once, when a litter of mice was put into a quart of ale, and he had emptied the pot, he remarked that he "noticed a two-thri hops."

Another collier who was the owner of a very large mouth was also the subject of many stories, it being remarked of him "that if he had had onny moore mouth 'ud ha' no face to wesh." One of the stories was that one day whilst drinking with a company of his mates, a man came into the bar and said: "Come, chaps, sup oop, an' ha' one wi' me." In response to this generous invitation everybody called for a pint of ale, but when the large-mouthed one was asked what he would take, he replied—

"Aah, an' I think I'll have a mouthful of ale, too."

"Nay, by gum! tha 'll not," said the giver of the drinks, "tha 'll nobbut have a pint, same as t'other; I've noane comed in for a fortin."

Sir William Bailey tells a story of the opening of the public baths in Wigan, in which one of the speakers dilating upon the advantage of the baths to the colliers, humorously remarked: "Friends met face to face who had never so met before."

With regard to colliers and washing, an amusing story is told of a collier who, being summoned to give evidence in a law-suit in London, stayed at an hotel for the first time in his life. The following morning, to the amazement of the manageress, sitting in the office in the hall, he appeared at the window wearing only his trousers and a vest.

"Wheer dun yo' wesh i' this hole?" he asked indignantly.

"You will find water, basin and everything you require in your bedroom," answered the amazed woman.

A TYPICAL LANCASHIRE COLLIER

"Wayther did yo' say?"

"Yes, you will find water on your wash-hand stand."

"Dun yo' myen i' that big krem jug like?"

"Certainly."

"Whaw, I supped that i' t' neet."

At a time when work was scarce and there was much distress in the South Lancashire coalfields, a parson met a collier who was taking his dog for a walk.

"Come, come, my man!" he said. "Do you think it is right to keep that dog when your wife and children are half starving? It would be a great deal better for them and for you if you sold the dog and bought a pig."

"An' a bonny foo' I should look gooin' rattin' wi' a pig," answered the indignant collier.

One Sunday morning, in a colliery district, a collier, dressed in his "Sunday best," with fancy painted clogs and a knotted silk scarf, was seen going jauntily along, pushing a wheel-barrow.

"Where arti' gooin', Bill?" a man shouted to him from the other side of the road.

"I'm gooin' a-walkin'," was the answer.

"Gooin' a-walkin'!" called out the other. "But what arti' doin' wi' t' barrow?"

"Well, tha sees, I've lost mi dog, an' a felly looks sich a foo' goin' a-walkin' bi hisself!"

THE ROCHDALE VOLUNTEERS

WHEN France declared war against England after the execution of King Louis XVI. and his Queen Marie Antoinette, a general call was made for volunteers to defend the country in the event of an invasion. A Volunteer Corps was raised at Rochdale in 1794 of which there is a brief account in the diary of a bookseller, called Josiah Lancashire, who had a shop near the Butts.

"28 May—Found shop just opened, the cows gone. The volunteers returned through the Butts ; some had great coats ; saw them dismissed at the Cross.

"30 May. The Corps of the Royal Rochdale Volunteers is complete. It consists of 4 Companys, 50 rank and file each. The following gentlemen have commissions—John Entwistle, Esq, Col.-Commandant ; John Walmsley, junr. of Castle Hill ; James Hamer of Hamer . . . Royds, of nr. Rochdale, captains . . . Lodge of Oakenrod, Esq., lieutenant ; Thomas Drake, D.D., chaplain. One half of the corps equip themselves, at their own cost."

But Mr. Lancashire was mistaken in saying that the corps was complete, as is shown by the following placard which was posted up in the town in the month of June :—

' Not to be removed more than five miles from home, unless ordered by His Majesty on the appearance of an invasion, when they are to be called out and paid like other militia, but not to be removed out

BARBAROUS PUNISHMENTS

THERE are still many who deplore the "good old times," and who are firmly convinced that life was easier and more pleasant in the days of Queen Elizabeth, Queen Anne, or the three Georges than it is in our own more strenuous and active generation. But their belief is based upon the picturesqueness of the dress of those periods. Who that has looked at a drawing by the late Randolph Caldecott representing a street in an eighteenth-century town, has not wished that our own streets of to-day showed half so picturesque an appearance? The red brick Georgian houses are models of neatness, the men in their long coats of velvet or brocade, their knee-breeches, silk stockings and buckled shoes, with three-cornered hats worn over a white wig, are models of manly dignity and elegance; the women with their powdered hair, their hooped skirts and high-heeled shoes are miracles of fascination; the footpaths are scrupulously clean, the cobble-stoned roadways look as if they had been freshly brushed. Such is the picture. But what was the reality? Those beautiful coats and dresses were all smothered with powder which fell from their wearers' wigs every time they moved their heads; the majority of those elegant men showed evident signs of heavy drinking; scarcely one of those fascinating ladies had good teeth; many of them were disfigured by small-pox; the footpaths were full of holes and strewn with dirt, whilst by the side of the cobble-stoned roadways ran an open sewer, called the "kennel," into which every kind of garbage was flung from the houses. It was because of the dirt and filth in the streets that sedan chairs were invented.

And what were the conditions under which these picturesquely clad folk lived? There was no sanitation in those red-brick houses, there was no light save that of candles and rush-tapers. Their water was fetched from the nearest pump, unless they were lucky and possessed a well of their own. When they travelled they went armed against foot-pads and highwaymen; if they lost their reason they were chained like wild animals in a place called Bedlam; if they got into debt they were thrust into prison until they could pay; if they were obliged to undergo an operation they had to endure all the agony caused by the surgeon's knife, for anæsthetics were unknown. In London, and all the county towns throughout England, they could see scores of poor wretches hanged after every assizes for offences that are now treated under the First Offenders Act or are met with short terms of imprisonment—boys and girls of fifteen and sixteen for picking pockets, a labourer who had stolen a sheep because his wife and family were starving. In the eighteenth century they congratulated themselves upon the blessings of civilization, but their treatment of prisoners and criminals was as barbarous as it had been in the "good old days" of Queen Elizabeth or Queen Anne. The gaols were a disgrace to any civilized country, those accused of crime, no matter of what nature except murder, being herded together like animals, and if they could not afford to buy their own food at extortionate prices from the gaoler, they were half starved on the prison rations. And in every gaol was a horrible enclosure known as the "pressing yard."

An ancient law decreed that if accused persons would not plead in answer to a charge of crime their property could not be confiscated to the Crown, but all those who refused to plead were slowly tortured to death by being "pressed."

It was immaterial whether they were men or women, they were taken from the court to the "pressing yard," stripped naked and laid upon their backs upon the ground. Their arms were fastened above their heads by ropes to a staple in the wall; their legs were likewise held out straight by means of ropes. Then a board was placed upon their chest, and upon this board were laid stones of the weight prescribed by the law. If the agonized wretches still refused to plead after a certain number of hours of being "pressed," more stones were added, and more and more, until death or failure of their endurance put an end to their sufferings. To add to the torture a stone with a sharp edge was placed beneath the small of the back, and this, by the increasing weight put upon the board, was slowly pressed into the victim's body.

It is inconceivable to think of women being subjected to such barbarous torture, but no more regard was shown towards them than to the men who refused to plead.

Our ancestors held very different views as to the treatment of criminals from ourselves. The possible regeneration of a criminal never seems to have occurred to them, and the ferocity and bloodthirsty cruelty of many of the punishments in the statute book were quietly accepted by men and women who gladly subscribed to send the early missionaries into heathen lands to convert the natives. An example of the pitilessness with which the law then punished crime, not with imprisonment alone, but with the brand of a criminal for a whole lifetime, still exists in the Crown Court at Lancaster Castle. Fixed to the back of the dock is an iron rod with a wooden handle at one end, and at the other a small iron plate with the letter "M" raised upon it. Besides the rod there are two iron loops fixed upon a piece of wood to the panelling of the dock. The rod and the loops are the relics of a barbarous punishment.

When a prisoner had been found guilty of crime, and sentence had been passed, it was within the discretion of the judge that he should be branded, but such branding must take place in the judge's presence and that of the jury which had found the man guilty. When the judge gave the order the larger of the two loops was unfastened, the prisoner was forced to place the fingers of one hand under the first loop; the large loop was then fastened over his wrist, holding it in so tight a grip that he could not move his hand. Whilst this was being done the lettered plate at the end of the rod was being made red-hot in a brazier. Taking the rod by the handle the brander pressed the red-hot end upon the thick part of the prisoner's hand, near the thumb, burning an impression of the letter "M" upon the flesh, and having achieved the horrible task would examine the hand closely. If the brand had come out clearly and distinctly it was the custom for him to bow to the judge and say, "A fair mark, my lord!"

With this indelible mark upon his hand the prisoner faced the world after his term of imprisonment was over: the "M" stamped him for all his life as a malefactor. When men were charged with crimes they were ordered to hold up their left hands, so that the magistrate or judge might see whether they had ever been convicted before; the branded "M" told its own story, and if they bore it punishment was more severe.

There are stories told of men cutting off the branded hand and plunging the bleeding stump in boiling pitch to stop the bleeding, rather than face the Ishmael-like existence to which that fatal letter

"M" condemned them. In our own time we hear much of the difficulty experienced in gaining an honest employment by those who have once been sent to prison, but to bear the evidence of having once committed a crime or a punishable offence burnt into the flesh, must have closed every door upon the freed prisoner.

of the brand, and its hard application to the palm of the prisoner; they heard his piercing cries of agony as vainly he struggled to withdraw his hand, his other arm being securely held by a warder. They saw the faint blue smoke rise above the wall of the dock and float over the heads of those in the public

"'A FAIR MARK, MY LORD!'"

And it was only in 1803 that the hoops and branding-iron were used in the Court Room at Lancaster Castle for the last time! Only sixteen years before the birth of Queen Victoria a judge ordered the branding of a convicted prisoner, and with the jury, the sheriff, and the county officials watched the horrible execution of his order—the hand of the struggling man forced into the iron loops and securely fastened, the heating

gallery; and to every one in the Court Room—to the judge on his exalted seat, to the county dignitaries, to the jury, to the public behind the dock, to the barristers on their benches—there came the smell of burning human flesh.

"A fair mark, my lord," said the brander, and the branded man, moaning and gibbering with pain, was taken down the staircase to the cells. Justice had been done.

KILLING A WIZARD IN ROSSENDALE

THE following is taken from the *Transactions of the Lancashire and Cheshire Historical Society*. The proceedings it describes took place in the eighteenth century—

"Some years ago I formed the acquaintance of an elderly gentleman, who had retired from business after amassing an ample fortune by the manufacture of cotton. He was possessed of a considerable amount of general information—had studied the world by which he was surrounded—and was a leading member of the Wesleyan Connexion. The faith element, however, predominated amongst his religious principles, and hence both he and his family were firm believers in witchcraft. On one occasion, according to my informant, both he and the neighbouring farmers suffered much from loss of cattle, and from the unproductiveness of their sheep. The cream was *bynged* (soured) in the churn, and would bring forth no butter. The cows died mad in the shippons, and no farrier could be found who was able to fix upon the diseases which afflicted them. Horses were bewitched out of the stables through the loopholes, after the doors had been safely locked, and were frequently found strayed to a considerable distance when they ought to have been safe in their stalls. Lucky stones had lost their virtues; horseshoes nailed behind the doors were of little use; and sickles hung across the beams had no effect in averting the malevolence of the evil-doer. At length suspicion rested on an old man, a noted astrologer and fortune-teller, who resided near New Church, in Rossendale, and it was determined to put an end both to their ill fortune and his career by performing the requisite ceremonials for 'killing a witch.' It was a cold November evening when the process commenced. A thick fog covered the valleys, and the wind whistled across the dreary moors. The farmers, however, were not deterred. They met at the house of one of their number, whose cattle were then supposed to be under the influence of the wizard; and having procured a live cock-chicken, they stuck him full of pins and burnt him alive, whilst repeating some magical incantations. A cake was also made of oatmeal, and after having been marked with the name of the person suspected, was then burnt in a similar manner.

"The wind suddenly rose to a tempest and threatened the destruction of the house. Dreadful moanings, as of some one in intense agony, were heard without, whilst a sense of horror seized upon all within. At the moment when the storm was at the wildest, the wizard knocked at the door, and in piteous tones desired admittance. They had been previously warned by the 'wise man,' whom they had consulted, that such would be the case, and had been charged not to yield to their feelings of humanity by allowing him to enter. Had they done so he would have regained all his influence, for the virtue of the spell would have been dissolved. Again and again did he implore them to open the door, and pleaded the bitterness of the wintry blast, but no one answered from within. They were deaf to all his entreaties, and at last the wizard wended his way across the moor as best he could. The spell, therefore, was enabled to have its full effect, and within a week the Rossendale wizard was locked in the cold embrace of death."

THE LANCASHIRE CLOG

THE clog is as characteristic of Lancashire as their gay costumes are characteristic of the Neapolitan peasantry.

The Lancashire clog is actually an adaptation of the *sabot* worn by the French and Dutch peasantry, and was

DANCING CLOGS

first introduced into the county nearly six hundred years ago, when some Flemish weavers settled at Bolton, " wearing wode shoon all of a peece." At this time the Lancashire weavers and country-folk either went barefoot or wore shoes of untanned leather—not unlike the Indian mocassin. The superiority of the foot-gear of the new-comers, which kept them dry-shod in rain or snow, must at once have been evident, and they were speedily

DUCK-BILLS

adopted by the Bolton people. But the rough and stony paths and roads of Lancashire must have given more wear and tear to the stout *sabots* of the Flemings than the flat, sandy tracts of their native land, and hence came the addition of irons to the soles.

When leather uppers took the place of wood is not definitely known, but it was apparently some time early in the nineteenth century, for in *Walker's Book of Costume in Yorkshire*, published in

1814, a boy is shown wearing all-wood clogs, evidently cut from the block after the manner of the French *sabot*. It is, therefore, not improbable that the prosperity arising from the sudden growth of the cotton trade, enabled the mill-hands in the neighbouring county of Lancaster to indulge in leather uppers, whilst wooden ones were still in vogue in Yorkshire.

In the bleach-crofts and dye-works it is not unusual to find masters as well as men wearing clogs. There are thousands of Lancashire workers who have never worn a pair of boots in their lives. The wearing of clogs by children is said to

PIT CLOGS

give them strong ankles and straight legs ; and it certainly is a remarkable fact that one very rarely sees a bow-legged child in what may be called industrial Lancashire ; and there is likewise an absence of colds and kindred ailments, contracted by wearing worn or broken boots, amongst Lancashire school-children, which is in strong contrast with the south of England.

Clogs without the irons are known as " barfoot clogs." The word " barfoot "

WOMEN'S CLOGS

would suggest " barefoot," but in Lancashire it denotes the lack of iron upon shoes ; for instance, in the north of the county an unshod colt is called " a barfoot stag."

"Barfoot" and "cawked" (caulked) clogs are worn only by women and girls. If a man or boy appeared in the street

BABY'S CLOGS

wearing them, he would meet the same contempt that would be showered by boot-wearing men and women upon a man who wore ladies' shoes with high Louis XV. heels. And as "barfoot" clogs are the cheapest and most simple kind, the expression has passed into general use to describe poverty.

Besides the "barfoot" there are three other kinds of clogs—the pit-clog, dancing clogs, and "duck-bills." The pit-clog, worn by the colliers, has very stout irons, and a sole two inches in thickness, generally edged all round with small brass-headed nails. The dancing clogs are thin and light, with only a slight curve from heel to toe, but the leather uppers are things of wonder, being stamped and embossed in every conceivable pattern, with fancy tabs, and decorations along the edge of the sole of bright nails. Clog-dancing is really an art, only seen in its perfection in Lancashire. The lightness with which a really good dancer strikes the ground is shown by the story of an over-merry slater doing a quick-step in heavily ironed clogs upon a slate roof, without doing any damage.

"Duck-bills" are those most generally in use; and when they have elaborately decorated tops, like dancing clogs, they are known as "coorting clogs." Although the custom is happily dying out, there

are still many wearers of clogs in Lancashire who are as handy with their feet as with their fists in a fight. A skilfully planned kick from a pit-clog can do a considerable amount of damage, but a kick from a "duck-bill," with its sharp-pointed toe, often covered with tin, in nine cases out of ten "lays out" an opponent. In these fights victory generally lies with the men who get in the first kick. Ancoats, not so very long ago, had an unhappy reputation for the skill with which its roughs used their "purring-irons" and their adeptness in giving a victim or an opponent "a taste of clog-toe pie."

CLOGGER WITH CLOG-KNIFE

A clog is the last thing one would think could be turned inside out, yet this feat was achieved by John Collier, the son of the famous Tim Bobbin. He was very eccentric, one of his manias being to wear all his clothes inside out. For some time his clogs baffled him, since a solid piece of wood puzzled even his ingenuity. However, at length he lighted upon this plan : he took off the leather uppers, turned them, and then nailed them upon the under side of the sole; the outer curve of the sole was now inside, and although he could only hobble in this painful foot-gear, and lamed himself in consequence, Collier wore them with the greatest satisfaction for some years.

"Take the clog to the clogger and the clogger will clog it," runs a Lancashire saying that is the equivalent of "Let the cobbler stick to his last." The clogger plays an important part in Lancashire with his curiously shaped clog-knife, which serves not only to cut the clog in the rough from the solid wood, but also as a spokeshave to give it the first trimmings into shape. It is the clogger who is responsible for the varied designs upon the uppers of the dancing and "coorting" clogs.

OLD FUNERAL CUSTOMS IN THE FYLDE

WHEN a death occurred in the Fylde, a whole district, called "their side" of the country, were invited to attend the funeral and assist in carrying the coffin to the grave. At a stated hour the crowd assembled, not to mourn with the widow or the orphan, but to drink beer and to smoke, and to talk of their crops and their dairies until the funeral was ready to start. From the door of his former home, and into and out of the church the corpse was carried on the shoulders of four of his relations, his nearest kinsman, who acted as chief mourner, walking in front with the clergyman. When the funeral service was ended, sprigs of rosemary and box were thrown upon the coffin, each person also adding a sprinkling of dust. The whole company were then bidden by the parish clerk to show their further respect for the dead by attending a dinner at the village inn.

The "dinner of respect" so frequently developed into a drunken orgy that a Fylde funeral became at one time a matter of sad notoriety. One pleasing feature of these old-time funerals was the distribution of doles of money to the poor, who were sometimes fed in addition. In the case of the more well-to-do families, cloaks and other useful garments would be given to the poor to be worn in memory of the departed. Fifty-five years ago, says Mr. Thornber, writing in 1837, the more respectable portion of the inhabitants of Poulton were buried by candlelight—a custom long observed by some of the oldest families in the town. It was regarded as a sacred duty to expose a lighted candle in the window of every house as the corpse passed through the streets towards the church for interment ; and he was poor indeed who did not pay this tribute of respect to the dead.

OLD SYKES'S WIFE

NEAR Samlesbury Hall there used to stand a lonely farmhouse, which up to the reign of Henry VII. had been occupied by many generations of a yeoman family named Sykes. It stood in a dell on the banks of Mellor Brook, and was called Sykes Lumb Farm, because of its meadows and pastures, which lay close to the broad and deep portion of the brook. The Sykes family became extinct in the reign of the first Tudor king, the last Sykes and his wife having no children. Sykes was reputed to have become very rich, partly by the discovery of some treasure hidden by an ancestor, partly through the constant hoarding of his forbears, but more particularly by the miserly and covetous character of his wife.

The Wars of the Roses broke out, and Lancashire was not only denuded of its wealth, but also of its population. There was no authority to enforce the law, and no protection for an aged couple like Sykes and his wife, whose reputation for riches made them likely victims of robbery. Dame Sykes was possessed by one thought, to the exclusion of all else, the safeguarding of their money. To this end the treasure was placed in earthenware jars, the mouths of which were carefully sealed, and the jars then buried deep beneath the roots of an apple tree in the orchard. There it remained, securely hidden, during the convulsions that distracted the kingdom; but before Henry VII. wrested the crown from Richard III., and so brought peace, Old Sykes died, leaving his miserly wife possessor of their hidden money. According to tradition Old Sykes's wife did not long survive her husband, dying so suddenly that she had no opportunity of telling her relatives of the hiding-place beneath the apple tree. The most diligent search failed to bring the hidden treasure to light, and the memory of Sykes, his wife, and their rumoured riches would have speedily been forgotten if the miserly woman's ghost had not haunted the spot. It always appeared in the dusk of the evening. Sometimes it was seen on a road which crossed the Lumb, at others in an old barn, and sometimes in the farmhouse itself, but more frequently in the orchard standing by an apple tree. The ghost had the appearance of an " old wrinkled woman dressed in ancient garb," who " never lifted her . head, but helped herself noiselessly along by means of a crooked stick, which bore no resemblance to those then in use." Those who met her were too terrified to speak ; one man saw her in the orchard, and described her gown and her striped petticoat. " She was not there," he said, " when I went to pluck an apple, but no sooner did I raise my hand towards the fruit, than she made her appearance just before me." He was so frightened that he ran away from the farm.

For generations " Old Sykes's Wife " continued to haunt the house and its immediate neighbourhood, until being seen by one of its tenants he boldly asked the spirit the reason of its visits. The ghost made no answer, but gliding towards the stump of an old apple tree she pointed to its roots. Remembering the tradition of the hidden treasure, the farmer, it is said, dug beneath the roots of the apple tree and discovered the jars, the ghost meanwhile standing at the edge of the trench. As the last jar was lifted out, the story goes that " an unearthly smile passed over her withered features, her bodily form became less and less distinct, until at last it disappeared altogether." From that time the ghost was never seen again.

THE BLOODY FOOTMARK

THE old house near Bolton called Smithell's Hall is for ever associated with the name of George Marsh. He was one of the first ministers of the Reformed Church to suffer martyrdom for his faith in the reign of Queen Mary. At that time, Smithell's Hall was occupied by Sir Roger Barton, a justice of the peace, who was either the son or the nephew of Sir Andrew Barton, a noted pirate, who had built the house some fifty years previously.

Sir Andrew Barton had been knighted by James III., of Scotland, for the injuries he had inflicted upon English shipping in the early days of Henry VIII. With his two vessels, the "Lion" and the "Jenny Perwin," Andrew Barton swept up and down the North Sea, and even ventured so far as the English Channel, taking ships of all nations, but more especially those flying the English flag. His authority for these piracies was letters of reprisal, which he declared had been granted to him by James III., against the Portuguese. Armed with these letters he seized the ships, declaring that they were carrying Portuguese goods. Barton's piracy became so unrestrained and so serious a menace to English shipping that a complaint was made to the Privy Council. A meeting was hastily summoned at which the Earl of Surrey said " the narrow sea should not be infested while he had estate enough to furnish a ship or a son capable of commanding it." Two of his sons, Sir Thomas and Sir Edward Howard, immediately fitted out two ships at their own expense and put to sea ; each brother commanding his own vessel. After some days they were separated by a storm. Sir Thomas Howard coming up with the "Lion," a desperate conflict immediately ensued. For some time the issue was doubtful, for Barton was an experienced

seaman, and he and the desperadoes under his command knew only too well the fate that awaited them in the event of defeat. Barton was killed, cheering on his crew with the boatswain's whistle to the last. The death of their commander spread dismay amongst the men, who threw down their arms and gave themselves up as prisoners.

Sir Edward Howard, after being separated from his brother, had found the " Jenny Perwin," which he captured after a desperate fight on both sides. The two ships and the surviving members of the crews—about 150 men—were taken into the river Thames on the 2nd of August, 1511. The prisoners were sent to the Archbishop of York's palace, but after a short time were liberated and sent back to Scotland. James IV., of Scotland, who had succeeded to the Scottish crown after the murder of James III., bitterly resented the attack upon Barton's ships, and immediately sent ambassadors to the English King demanding satisfaction for the death of Barton and the loss of the two ships. To these ambassadors Henry answered, " that the punishment of pirates was never held a breach of peace among princes."

Sir Andrew was descended from a good Scotch family ; and, having been a pirate and freebooter throughout the greater part of his life, was supposed to have amassed a considerable sum of money ; and it has been suggested that he was led to build Smithell's Hall as a place of concealment both for himself and his booty. The roads were practically impassable ; the house was surrounded by woods in every direction ; it was at a considerable distance from the sea, and consequently far removed from the scenes of his piratical exploits.

George Marsh was a native of Dean,

near Bolton, and had been a farmer, but losing his wife when he was about thirty years old, he left his children with his father and went to Cambridge, where he was afterwards ordained. He was appointed curate of All Hallows Church in Bread Street, in the city of London.

After the accession of Queen Mary to the throne Roman Catholicism became because of the burnings and the executions of heretics which cast so deep a stain upon her reign ; but it is more than probable that if she had not married the fanatical Philip of Spain, England would have been spared the spectacle of men and women being burned alive and tortured because they would not subscribe to the tenets of the Roman Catholic Church.

SMITHELL'S HALL

the State religion. Mary was a bigoted woman, whose youth had been embittered by religious persecution and the anomalous position in which she had been placed by the divorce of her mother, Catherine of Aragon, from her father, Henry VIII. Unhappily for herself as well as for her people, Mary married Philip II., of Spain, whose bigotry was so intense that it verged upon mania. Queen Mary Tudor has come down to history and will always be known as " Bloody Mary,"

The year after Mary married Philip of Spain the persecution of the Protestants began. George Marsh appears to have attracted the unfavourable attention of the authorities in London by his zeal for the Reformed religion. Whether he suffered actual persecution is not known, but the fact that his rector, the Rev. Mr. Sanders, was burnt at the stake, and the increasing difficulties of his own situation, doubtless led him to contemplate leaving the country as so many Protestants were doing. Before exiling himself, however, he paid a visit to his mother and his children near Bolton.

Justices of the peace were given commissions to seek out " heretics," and if they found their answers unsatisfactory to send them before a higher authority, who, if they found them guilty, handed them over to the Ecclesiastical Court. The Earl of Derby, having had an intimation that Marsh was near Bolton, sent word of his presence to Sir Roger—or, as he is called in some chronicles, Mr.—Barton, with orders to apprehend him. At first Marsh concealed himself on Dean Moor from the justice's officers, but hearing that his mother and his younger brother had been made responsible for his appearance before the justice, and were to answer for him at their peril, rather than allow them to run so serious a risk he voluntarily gave himself up. He went to Smithell's Hall and submitted himself to the justice.

But although his apprehension had been determined upon, the law had to be observed, even if it were only a farce. Marsh was therefore questioned by the justice and his confessor. There were set questions, one of which touched upon the abiding difference between the Roman Catholic and Protestant religions —that of the Real Presence in the sacrament. As Sir Richard Baker says : " A common net at that time for catching all Protestants was the Real Presence; and this net was used to catch the Lady Elizabeth [afterwards Queen Elizabeth]. That Princess showed great prudence in concealing her sentiments on religion, in complying with the present modes of worship, and in eluding all questions with regard to a subject so momentous. Being asked at one time what she thought of the words of Christ, *This is My Body*— whether she thought it the true body of

Christ that was in the sacrament—it is said that after some pausing she thus answered—

' Christ was the Word that spake it ;
He took the bread and brake it ;
And what the Word did make it ;
That I believe and take it,'

which, though it may seem but a slight expression, yet hath in it more solidness than at first sight appears: at least, it served her turn at that time to escape the net, which by a direct answer she could not have done."

But for the sublety and ingenuity with which the Princess Elizabeth answered the many questions put to her, in the severe examinations to which she was subjected, there is little doubt that she, too, would have gone to the scaffold. The simple George Marsh, who himself said that he was " unlearned in disputed points, and unskilled and unlearned in scholastic disputes," had therefore little chance of meeting the ingenious questions of the justice and his confessor. He was declared to be a heretic and sent to Lord Derby at Lathom House. Both Marsh and two of his kinsmen who had accompanied him to Smithell's Hall, knew that there could only be one ending, and when the latter besought him to make some confession or in some manner conform to the Roman Catholic religion, so that he might escape a cruel and ignominious death, he cried out : " Between me and them let God witness "; and looking upwards cried again : " If my cause be just let this prayer of Thine unworthy servant be heard."

He was then being led out of the house and was standing in a passage near the door of the dining-room. He stamped violently with his foot and—so the story goes—instantly there appeared upon the stone the impression of a man's foot.

Little remains to be told of George

Marsh. He was taken to Lathom Hall, and, after being examined by the Earl of Derby, was imprisoned in what he himself describes as a "cold, windy, stone house, where there was very little room and where he was kept for two nights without a bed." From Lathom he was removed to Lancaster Castle, and subsequently taken to Chester, where he was brought before the Ecclesiastical Court. The accusation against him was of having preached at Dean, Eccles, Bolton, Bury, and many other places in the diocese against the Pope's authority and the Catholic Church of Rome. From this charge it would appear that Marsh had ministered to the proscribed Protestants during his hiding. He did not deny the preaching, but asserted that he had only, as occasion served, maintained the truth touching these subjects. He was called upon to recant, but on his repeated refusals the Bishop "put his spectacles on his nose and read his terrible sentence, adding : 'Now will I no more pray for thee than I will for a dog'!"

He was delivered over to the sheriffs and executed a few days later. When brought to the stake he was once more asked to recant, but firmly refused, whereupon he was chained to a post and "a thing made like a firkin, with pitch and tar in it, was put over his head, and the faggots around him were lighted."

The footmark may still be seen at Smithell's Hall. In shape the impression is exactly that of a human foot except that it is rather longer ; it is dark brown, or rather reddish, in colour, and is plainly seen in damp weather or when moistened by cleaning. Its curious colour gives it the name of the "Bloody footmark."

A story is told that the stone was once removed in a frolic by two or three young men, who, being left in the house took advantage of their parents' absence from home, to pull up the stone and throw it into a glen at the back of the Hall. That same night strange and hideous noises were heard throughout the house, and, being thoroughly alarmed, the young men confessed their folly. The stone was thereupon sought for in the glen and reverently placed in the passage. Some fragments had been broken off in its removal, and these, too, were carefully put back. Tradition has it that the noises were never afterwards heard again.

It is said that the examination of George Marsh by the justice took place in a room called the "Green Chamber," and a story, which was current in the neighbourhood some two centuries later, gave rise to a belief that the martyr still haunted the scene where his persecution began. According to the story, about the latter end of the year 1732, a stranger, sleeping alone in the Green Chamber, was much terrified by an apparition. "He stated that about ten o'clock, as he was preparing for bed, there appeared a person before him dressed like a minister, in a white robe and bands, with a book in his hand. The stranger getting into bed saw it stand by his bedside for a short time. It then slowly retired out of the door, as if going downstairs, and he saw it no more. This person invariably persisted in the same story ; and the owner of the estate immediately ordered Divine Service at the chapel on a Sunday, which had long been discontinued."

JAMIE=GO=DEEPER AND THE BARRISTER

WE have often heard of the most subtle and clever barrister being routed by the native wit of men unlettered in the law. Mr. Newbigging, in his book on Lancashire humour, gives a striking instance of this, at the same time showing how a quick intelligence can sometimes foil the ablest lawyer. He tells the story of a man called Jim Shackleton, who was better known by the nickname of "Jamie-go-deeper," who after having been a navvy in his younger days had risen to be a ganger, and was employed upon the Manchester Ship Canal when it was being constructed. He describes him as a "sturdy Lancashire ganger, honest and shrewd as they make 'em, a hard and steady worker—faithful and staunch to his employers." The Canal Company in several places were obliged to purchase property through which its course had to run, and some of the owners of these properties put absurd values upon their lands, some on the ground of the value for building sites, others because of the value of the minerals beneath. "Jamie-go-deeper" was in charge of a large gang of navvies working below Latchford Locks, and every day as he passed to and from his lodgings and the cutting, he crossed a field the purchase price of which was in dispute between the owner and the Canal Company. The owner asked a huge sum of money for the field, because, he declared, a valuable seam of coal lay beneath. The company declined to pay the amount demanded, and the matter was referred to arbitration, before an umpire, with counsel and expert valuers representing both sides.

"Jamie-go-deeper" was subpœnaed by the owner of the land in order that he might give evidence that he had seen boring for coal going on at this particular time during a certain period. Mr. Newbigging gives a full report of the honest ganger's evidence, which at once shows his Lancashire shrewdness and carefulness—

Counsel. "Your name is James Shackleton?"

Jim. "For onything I know, it is."

Counsel. "And you are employed as a ganger on this section of the Canal?".

Jim. "Aw believe aw am."

Counsel. "And you lodge over here?" (*pointing to some cottages shown on a plan of the locality*).

Jim. "Aw do."

Counsel. "And you cross this field (*again pointing to the plan*) daily—two or three times a day—going to and coming from your work?"

Jim. "Yea."

Counsel. "And in going and coming you have, of course, seen men engaged in boring for coal?"

Jim. "Noa, aw haven't."

Counsel. "You have not seen men boring for coal in this particular field?" (*again pointing to the plan*).

Jim. "Noa."

Counsel. "Yet you live here and pass and repass this field several times a day."

Jim. "Aw do."

Counsel. "Now, on your oath — be careful!—have you not seen men engaged in making borings in this field?"

Jim. "Oh, ay! Aw've seed 'em boring."

Counsel (with a triumphant smile round the court). "You *have* seen them boring for coal, then?"

Jim. "Noa."

Counsel (getting angry). "You have not seen them boring for coal?"

Jim. "Noa, not for coal. Aw *have* seen 'em boring."

Counsel (losing his temper). "Then, what the d——l were they boring for?"

Jim. "They were boring for compensation."

Amid a roar of irrepressible laughter the Counsel sat down, utterly defeated by his own witness. As Mr. Newbigging points out, a less shrewd and careful man would have taken the first opportunity that presented itself in giving his evidence, to express his belief that the borings were a pretence, and thus would have placed himself at the Counsel's mercy, whereas, by only answering the questions put to him, Jim produced his opinion with crushing effect.

WARRINGTON ALE

YOUR doctors may boast of their lotions,
   And ladies may talk of their tea;
   But I envy them none of their potions;
A glass of good stingo for me.
The doctor may sneer if he pleases,
   But my récipé never will fail;
For the physic that cures all diseases,
   Is a bumper of Warrington ale.

D'ye mind me, I once was a sailor,
   And in different countries I've been;
If I lie, may I go for a tailor,
   But a thousand fine sights have I seen.
I've been crammed with good things like a wallet,
   And I've guzzled more drink than a whale;
But the very best stuff to my palate
   Is a glass of your Warrington ale.

When my trade was upon the salt ocean,
   Why, there I got plenty of grog,
And I liked it because I'd a notion
   It set one's good spirits agog.
But since upon land I've been steering,
   Experience has alter'd my tale;
For nothing on earth is so cheering
   As a bumper of Warrington ale.

Into France I have oftentimes follow'd
   And once took a trip into Spain;
And all kinds of liquids I've swallow'd
   From spring-water up to champagne.
But the richest of wines to my thinking,
   Compared with good stingo is stale;
For there's nothing in life that's worth drinking,
   Like a bumper of Warrington ale.

SOME OLD LANCASHIRE SUPERSTITIONS

THE general spread of education has, in a very large measure, destroyed all belief in the numerous old superstitions which were rife in every part of the county. How these superstitions arose it would take many years of research to discover. Some of them can be traced back to pagan times, others have arisen from purely local circumstances. At a period when natural phenomena such as floods, thunder and lightning, or hail and snow in the late spring, were regarded as being brought about by occult means, and when the powers of evil were believed to possess unlimited influence over the destinies of mankind, the ignorant mind naturally saw signs and portents when trouble or disaster befell him after the occurrence of these phenomena. Nor did this belief apply to the elements alone, the actions of birds and animals were likewise held to have a special significance with regard to the fortunes of human beings, founded in the first instance, in all probability, upon some circumstance which followed closely upon the witnessing of the action. In no other way can the origin of these superstitions be accounted for. Each generation handed down its own store of superstition in addition to those it had inherited from its forerunner, with the natural result that superstition ultimately held as strong a hold, if not a stronger, in Lancashire as religion. The climax was reached at the end of the sixteenth and at the beginning of the seventeenth century, when courts of law gravely accepted evidence to prove that women rode on broomsticks through the sky, and had the power to change themselves into animals, to bewitch cattle, and to cause strong and hale people to perish and die by making wax figures of them, and melting the figures slowly before a fire.

Many curious superstitions have come down from those times, happily not so sinister in their effect. Thus, if a cat tore at the cushions or carpets with its claws it was considered to be a sign of wind; this was the origin of the expression: " The cat is raising the wind." If a cat in washing its face drew its paw right over its forehead it was taken as a sign of fair weather : if the paw was only drawn partially over, it was a sign of speedy rain. It was also considered very unhealthy to allow a cat to sleep with a human being. They were said to " draw the health away," and when any child or young person showed symptoms of bad health, the house cat would either be sent away until they recovered, or else destroyed. Those who played much with cats were said never to enjoy good health, and whilst some believed that to swallow a cat's hair meant death, others believed that it could be dissolved in the stomach by eating a piece of an eggshell every morning fasting. To allow a cat to die in the house was to bring ill-luck, but on the other hand if a kitten walked into the house it was considered an omen of good luck. Cats, too, were always associated with witches in the belief that their natures were much alike and that they both helped to form a portion of every " load of mischief."

Dogs were held to have communication with the spirit world, and were said to sit down and howl before the door when any one was about to be ill, or die. A death in the family was considered to be certain if a dog returned to the house as often as it was driven away, whilst the whining of a favourite dog was believed by many to betoken calamity to the family to which it belonged.

Even lambs were harbingers of good- or ill-luck. If when seen for the first time in the spring they had their faces turned towards the spectator it was a sign of good-luck, and if they were looking towards the east the sign was still more favourable.

But it is the birds that furnish the most curious superstitions. Swallows, wrens and redbreasts were always considered as fortune-bringing birds, and great was the misfortune which befell those who injured them in any way, especially the swallow. If swallows or martins began to build their nests about a house or barn it was looked upon as a sign of good luck to the occupier, "The more birds the better luck," was the saying. On the other hand, if swallows and martins forsook nests, which they had visited regularly for several summers, it was taken as a sign of coming misfortune. Farmers had the belief that if they killed a robin their cows would give blood instead of milk. An old rhyme ran thus—

" A cock robin and a jenny wren
Are God Almighty's cock and hen ;
A spink and a sparrow
Are the Devil's bow and arrow."

Birds, like dogs, were believed to have knowledge of the future, and if a jackdaw alighted on the window-sill of a sickroom it was taken as a sign of coming death. A white pigeon at a sick-window had a double significance ; it could be taken either as a sign of a recovery, or that an angel had taken this form and was waiting to carry the soul of the sick person to heaven. When a canary sang cheerfully all was supposed to be well with the family to whom it belonged ; but when it became silent and moped, calamity was in store for the household.

The magpie occupied a curious position in this world of superstitious belief. A single magpie was one of the worst of evil omens, but when accompanied by others there was a different significance attaching to each number, as set out in the rhyme—

" One for sorrow,
Two for mirth,
Three for a wedding
Four for a birth."

In some parts of Lancashire they carried on the numbers thus—

" Five for rich,
Six for poor,
Seven for a witch,
I can tell you no more."

Gentle and simple alike regarded the single magpie as the harbinger of evil, and various charms were resorted to, which were supposed to avert the evil influence, when the bird was seen. One was to raise the hat, if it was a man, or to curtsey, if it was a woman, in polite salutation ; another was to make the sign of the cross upon the breast, or make the same sign by crossing the thumbs. Amongst anglers the single " pyat " in the spring was regarded with special disfavour, but two were a favourable sign. And the explanation is simple. In cold weather only one bird leaves the nest in search of food, the other remaining to keep the eggs or the young ones warm ; but when both are out together the weather is warm and mild, and therefore good for fishing.

"THE DULE UPO' DUN"

ONCE upon a time at the entrance to a village on the highroad to Gisburne, some three miles from Clitheroe, there used to stand a public house with a curious sign, "The Dule upo' Dun" ("The Devil upon the Dun Horse"). On it was painted his Satanic Majesty seated upon a dun horse, with neither saddle nor bridle, his arms raised in fury, and his forked tail sticking out fiercely behind him. The horse was going at a mad gallop past a cottage, in the doorway of which stood a small tailor with a grin of delight upon his face, and joyfully shaking his shears and measure at the departing monarch of evil.

The old inn was said to have formerly been the abode of a tailor of whom the following story was told. The tailor's fondness for ale and the good company at the ale-house often reduced him to sore straits for money, and on these occasions both he and his wife would have starved if she had not been able to scrape together a few pence and broken victuals by selling firewood and doing odd jobs of housework for her neighbours. One night at the ale-house the little tailor had not only spent all his money but, in his craving for drink, had likewise exhausted his credit with the landlord.

"I wish I were the Squire's footman or e'en his errand-boy, and could get a soup of good liquor without rivin' and tuggin' for 't," he said bitterly.

At that moment a stranger appeared amongst the village worthies collected in the bar parlour, a stranger who afterwards proved to be none other than Satan himself. But this is how he appeared to the penniless tailor and his boon companions : "The new-comer was dressed in a respectable suit of black ; a wig of the same colour adorned his wide and ample head, which was again surmounted by a peaked hat, having a band and buckle above its brim, and a black rose in front. He looked an elderly and well-ordered gentleman, mighty spruce and full of courtesy ; his cane was black as ebony, with a yellow knob that glittered like gold. He had a huge beaked nose, and a little black ferrety eye, which almost pierced what it gazed upon." The stranger, whilst talking affably with the rest of the company, kept his eyes fixed upon the little tailor, much to the latter's discomfort—"a dark, bright burning eye, such as made the recreant tailor look aside, for he could not endure the brightness." Unable to bear this piercing glare, and his ale being finished, the tailor left the public house and wended his way homeward. But before long the stranger was beside him, and stalking through the snow, told him how he could gain incalculable wealth by the aid of the powers of darkness. The tailor's hair stood on end with terror, his knees knocked together, and giving voice to his fear he was about to call upon the powers of good for protection when the stranger, seizing him roughly by the hand, said, "Hold ! Another such outcry, and I will leave thee to thy seams and patches, to starve and linger on as best thou mayest."

Gradually the tailor's fears were appeased. There was no harm or wickedness, the stranger assured him, in seeking the aid he proposed, and in reply to his eager questions as to the secret by which he might obtain riches and ease of days, said—

"Thou mayest say two Aves, the Creed, and the Paternoster backwards thrice, and call upon the Invisible Demon to appear, when he will tell thee what thou shalt do."

The next day the tailor went to a solitary place near the river, fortifying his sinking spirits with the reflection that he only wished to know how such great wealth might be gained, and that if there were anything wicked about the proceeding, he would have nothing to do with it. Accordingly he repeated the Aves, the Creed, and the Paternoster backwards. Scarcely had he spoken the last words when a terrific clap of thunder was heard, and Satan himself stood before him demanding to know why he had been summoned. In vain the wretched tailor, prostrate with terror, vowed that he wanted nothing, but was finally obliged to confess that he wanted riches. Upon this Satan granted him three wishes, and the relieved tailor was about to depart when the Evil One told him that a contract must be made between them, by which in return for the granting of the three wishes he bound himself to bear his Satanic Majesty company at the end of seven years.

"Me!" cried the terrified wretch. "Nay, then, keep thy gifts to thyself; I'll none o' them on this condition."

But Master Snip was already in Satan's power, as that dark gentleman reminded him. All those who summoned the devil were delivered into his hands, and the tailor had to choose whether he should then and there be carried off to the infernal regions, or sign the contract which gave him a respite for seven years and left him the enjoyment of the three wishes. With the philosophic reflection that one never knows what may turn up in seven years, the tailor signed the bond, with a drop of blood squeezed from his own finger; Satan seized the bond, and with another clap of thunder disappeared.

The tailor, now a prey to the liveliest misery, made his way homewards. His wife had prepared their evening meal of oaten bread, to which she had added the unusual delicacy of a collop of bacon, given her by a kindly neighbour. But the wretched tailor could not eat; overcome with the awful prospect of his fate at the end of seven years he could only sit in brooding silence. Vainly his wife tried to cheer him, and thinking that he was plunged in remorse because his drinking habits had reduced them to such poverty, in order to distract his thoughts she urged him to eat, saying—

"Come, come, goodman, if one collop winna content thee, I wish we'd two, that's all."

At that moment a second rasher, smoking hot and savoury, appeared by the first one upon the dish. The tailor, gazing at it with terrified eyes, saw the fulfilment of the first of the three wishes.

"Woman, woman! What hast thou done?" he cried. "I wish thou wert far enough for thy pains."

Instantly his wife disappeared, and the wretched tailor knew that two of his wishes were already gone.

Now there remained but one wish, and for a long time the tailor pondered as to what he should desire. He could not decide, and so fearful was he lest he should waste so precious an opportunity that he hesitated to use it. Meanwhile he was most uncomfortable; the house grew dirty and untidy, and one day when he had to go out into the snow to get some wood for the fire, his misery got the better of his caution, and he exclaimed, "I wish Matty were here!" Scarcely had he uttered the words when his wife was standing beside him. And the third wish was gone.

Bacon collops cannot suddenly appear upon tables, wives cannot be mysteriously wafted from their homes, and as mysteriously wafted back again, without some explanation. The tailor, therefore, wisely made a full confession to the wife of his bosom, and at the same time swore that, as he had been brought to this parlous carefully that he became a man of substance.

When the seven years were nearing

"'I WISH THOU WERT RIDING BACK TO THY QUARTERS ON YONDER DUN HORSE'"

position through idleness and drink, he would never enter the ale-house again. He kept his word, and during the next seven years he worked so hard and lived so completion the poor little tailor fell into deep dejection; he knew that his days were numbered, and that Satan would seek the fulfilment of the bond. On his wife's advice he sought counsel from a hermit who dwelt in a cave near by, and this holy man, learning that no benefit had been received from the devil's three wishes, except a bacon collop, "that was cast out untouched," set forth the legal reasons upon which the bond could be set aside. As time approached for the appearance of the bond-holder, the tailor spent his days in fasting and prayer.

At noon on the day appointed, the inevitable thunder-clap announced the coming of his Satanic Majesty. Primed and fortified with the legal reasoning of the hermit, the tailor faced the Infernal One, tremblingly, but with courage. He denied the validity of the contract, arguing that it had been won from him by fraud and dishonest pretences. To this, Satan, in a voice of thunder, replied that the wishes had been fulfilled, and that he had performed his part of the contract to the letter. Whereupon the tailor boldly answered, "I fear me that thou knewest I should never be a pin the richer or better for thy gifts; and thine aim was but to flatter and cheat. It is not in thy power, I do verily believe, to grant me riches or any great thing that I might wish; so thou didst prompt, and, in a manner, force me to those vain wishes, unthinkingly, by which I have been beguiled."

This answer seems to have wounded Satan's pride, for he insisted that, had the tailor been more careful in his desires, his "most unbounded wishes would have been accomplished." But the tailor, unmoved, stoutly replied—

"I say, and will vouch for it that all thy promises are lying cheats, and that thou could'st not give me a beggarly bodle, if thou wert to lay down thy two horns for it; so I demand my bond, according to thy pledge."

This doubting of his powers was apparently more than the Evil One could bear.

"To show thee that I can keep the bond," he cried, "even conformably to the terms of my own offer just now, and thy pitiful carcass to boot, I'll e'en grant thee another wish that thou mayest be satisfied thou art past all hope of redemption. Said I not, that if I could not fulfil any wish of thine, even to the compass of all possible things, and the riches of this great globe itself, I would release thee from this bond?" The tailor agreed. "Then wish once more," continued Satan in his terrible voice, "and mind it be no beggarly desire. Wish to the very summit of wealth, or the topmost pinnacle of thy ambition, for it shall be given thee."

Glancing fearfully around, the trembling tailor saw through the window a dun horse grazing quietly in the lane.

"I wish thou wert riding back to thy quarters on yonder dun horse, and never be able to plague me again, or any other poor wretch whom thou hast gotten into thy clutches!" he cried.

With a loud roar of rage and fury Satan was whirled into the air and seated upon the back of the dun horse, which instantly set off at a mad gallop.

Such is the story of the deliverance of the tailor from the snares of the devil.

History further relates that, having lived happily to a good old age, the tailor died, and having no children, left his little fortune to be divided amongst his poorer relatives, and that one of them buying the house where the tailor had lived, and which had been the scene of Satan's final discomfiture, set up as a publican, using as his sign "The Dule upo' Dun," and so perpetuating his kinsman's victory over the King of Darkness.

THE HOLY HAND

AMIDST such prosaic surroundings as collieries and manufactories one would not expect to find a relic so venerated that each week it is the object of pilgrimage to many faithful Roman Catholics. But Lancashire is the county of surprises, and in the Church of St. Oswald, at Ashton-in-Makerfield, there is treasured, with all the reverence and belief attaching to relics that one finds in the Italian and Spanish churches, the hand of Father Arrowsmith, who suffered martyrdom for his faith in the reign of Charles I. at Lancaster. The hand is wrapped in linen and kept in a silver casket.

Father Arrowsmith was the son of a Lancashire yeoman, and was born at Haydock, between Wigan and Warrington, in 1585. His mother was a relative of the Gerard family, and both she and her husband had remained steadfast to the Roman Catholic faith, in which they had been born and bred, throughout all the persecutions of the times. From his earliest years, Father Arrowsmith had shown a disposition of great piety, and was therefore devoted to the priesthood. But in that age so closely were the Roman Catholics watched that no priest of the faith could be ordained in England; nor could a subject leave the country without the permission of the Sovereign. For these reasons Father Arrowsmith was twenty years old before he could get to Douai,

FATHER ARROWSMITH

in France, then the headquarters of the English Roman Catholic priesthood, and so prepare himself for his vocation. He was twenty-seven when he was ordained priest at Arras, and returned immediately afterwards to labour in his native county. Such a step speaks of high courage, for death was the penalty for saying the Mass; and those priests who laboured in secret amongst the faithful, literally carried their lives in their hands. Strong in his belief, however, Arrowsmith for ten years laboured in the Lancashire vineyard, saying Mass in secret places, visiting and comforting the sick and dying, each year increasing the love and reverence of his proscribed flock for their pastor. Then he was suddenly arrested and thrown into Lancaster Castle. But after a while he was released and upon regaining his liberty joined the Society of Jesus, and started his ministry again with renewed courage and vigour, Brindle being his headquarters.

Even in these days Brindle, although shut in by Preston, Blackburn and Chorley, is a pleasant spot; in Father Arrowsmith's time it was all open country, with lonely farms and halls, most of whose occupants adhered to the old faith, scattered about it. His area of work was very large, and he was consequently obliged to ride about on horseback. A man attended him in order to take his horse away when he had alighted at any place to say Mass, lest suspicion should be aroused by the sight of the waiting horses. He is reputed to have said Mass at Lower Green; Church Bottoms; Fleetwood Hall, in Salmesbury; Jack Green, Brindle; Wickenhouse Farm, Withnell; Wheelton; Denham Hall, near Clayton Green; Woodcock Hall; Cuerden, and at Livesey Hall, near Blackburn. At Denham Hall Father Arrowsmith said Mass upon a missionary altar belonging to the Burgess family, which is still carefully preserved.[1]

The house in which Father Arrowsmith is believed to have said his last Mass is still standing at Brindle, in Gregson Lane, facing the entrance to Gregson Lane Mill. Mr. George Hull in his *Historical Sketch of St Joseph's, Brindle*, gives some interesting facts about the old house. He says: " It is believed to have been erected about 1580, and is a fine example of the comfortable yeoman's dwelling of that period, an interesting feature of the building being a small room in which the ironwork round the fireplace is hammered into a representation of the wheat and vine, emblematic of the bread and wine used at the Mass. It is said that at the beginning of the eighteenth century this house was the residence of the Gregsons of Gregson Lane, one of whom placed his initails ' G. G.' with a cross and the date 1700 on the lintel of the porch, thus giving later generations the erroneous impression that the building was erected in 1700. Near this house was dug up, in 1899, a very ancient font, possibly of the ninth century, and in a garden of a cottage close by stands a beautiful old wayside cross. Local tradition asserts that at this same old house the venerable Edmund Arrowsmith, the Jesuit martyr, said his last Mass."

Under the roof of one of the gables in

this house in Gregson Lane there still exists a dark attic, reached by a ladder and a trap-door from one of the bedrooms. In all probability this was a priest's hiding place, which were so common in all the Roman Catholic houses of the time.

During four years after his liberation from Lancaster Castle, Father Arrowsmith continued his ministrations in Brindle and the district, and was then betrayed to the authorities by members of his own faith. On the left-hand side of the road leading from Hoghton Station to Walton-le-Dale there is a portion called the Straits, and here until within a fews years ago there stood the Blue Anchor Inn, an old house, half-timbered and with a thatched roof. The innkeeper was named Holden, a devout Catholic, who gladly allowed Father Arrowsmith to make his house his headquarters as a place of refuge. There was also a priest's hiding-place at the Blue Anchor, concealed in the roof, and doubtless used by Arrowsmith in times of danger.

His betrayal was brought about by feminine spite and annoyance. One of his landlord's sons, a Roman Catholic like his father, had married a first cousin who was a Protestant, the marriage ceremony having been performed according to the Protestant rite and by a Protestant minister. The young couple went to live at the Blue Anchor Inn with the elder Holden. Now, the marriage of first cousins is not permitted by the Church of Rome without a dispensation from the Pope. A Roman Catholic priest, therefore, could have only one opinion; so far as his religion was concerned the marriage was no marriage, and therefore the young bridegroom, being Catholic, was living in sin. But Father Arrowsmith in place of denouncing the marriage and using his priestly authority over the husband—as, according to the Roman Catholic point of

[1] Story of the Martyr's Altar.

view, he had every priestly right—remembered the many benefits conferred upon him by the elder Holden, and the shelter he had so generously given him, even at the risk of his own liberty. Remembering all these things, and anxious to remove what he believed to be the immortal peril of the young husband, he applied directly to Rome for a dispensation sanctioning the marriage of the young man with his first cousin. When the dispensation arrived the wife had become a Roman Catholic, which again altered the situation so far as Father Arrowsmith was concerned. As a priest he was now answerable for both the husband and wife, and he insisted that he would not make use of the dispensation unless they separated for fourteen days. This they declined to do, and Father Arrowsmith remaining firm in his demand, they determined to betray him to the authorities. The wife, it is said, was the prime instigator—Father Arrowsmith's declaration that she was not religiously married to her husband having incensed her whilst he was still a Protestant.

When he insisted upon her husband separating from her, although only for a fortnight, she could only see personal spite in his action, and working upon her husband's feelings, she persuaded him to send word to Captain Rawsthorn, a justice of the peace, that Arrowsmith was a priest, that he said Mass, and that he was in hiding at the Blue Anchor Inn. With diabolical ingenuity the notice was sent to Captain Rawsthorn at a time when young Holden and his wife knew that Arrowsmith would be returning to the inn.

THE HOUSE WHERE FATHER ARROWSMITH SAID HIS LAST MASS

Captain Rawsthorn, however, was very anxious not to bring any trouble upon the elder Holden, who was a neighbour of his; therefore he sent word warning him to get rid of the priest before he came to search the house. Father Arrowsmith hastily collected all his possessions lest any sign should be left of his sojourn at the inn and so bring his protector before the authorities, and set out on horseback with the intention of seeking a refuge in a lonely farmhouse at Withnell. The justice and his servants went along the Blackburn Road in pursuit, but the priest had gone the opposite direction. Unluckily, however, in doubling back upon his track he ran into one of Captain Rawsthorn's servants and his son, a boy of twelve, and was promptly taken.

At the trial both the servant and the boy swore that Father Arrowsmith had tried to entice them from the Protestant religion. This is Father Arrowsmith's own account at his trial of the arrest: "The servant of God upon this humbly begged leave to speak, which being granted, he spoke to this effect: 'My Lord, as I was upon the road that very design was to take my purse and my life. He answered that perhaps it was, and then I fled again from him, but was soon overtaken. Then came up this youth [the justice's son] who has given evidence against me, with others to assist him. They used me with much indignity,

THE ROOM WHERE THE LAST MASS WAS SAID

man, as I take it [the justice's servant], rushed out upon me with a drawn sword. He was meanly dressed and upon horseback. I made what haste I could from him, but being weak and sickly was forced by him at last to the Moss, where I alighted, and fled with all the speed I was able—which yet could not be very great, seeing I was loaded with heavy clothes, boots, and other things. At length he came up to me at the Moss Ditch, and struck at me, though I had nothing to defend myself with but a little walking-stick, and a sword which I did not draw; with the blow he cut the stick close to my hand and did me some little hurt. I then asked him if his and took me to an alehouse, and searched me to the skin, offering insults which modesty forbids me to relate, and which I resisted as far as I was able. That done, they fell to drinking, and spent nine shillings of my money in an hour. They told me that the justice of the peace, by whose warrant I was apprehended, was there in person, but that I would not believe. Upon this occasion, my Lord, I began to find fault with the man's wicked and rude behaviour who seemed to be the ringleader; and I besought him, for Jesus' sake, to give up his disordered life, drinking and foolish talk, and whatever might offend Almighty God. Upon my word and my life, this, or to this effect, is all I said to him. Let him look on me, and gainsay it, if he can. As for that youth, I deny not to have told him that I hoped when he came to riper years, he would look better into himself, and become a true Catholic, for that, and that alone, would be the means to save his soul, to which he made no answer at all. And I hope, my Lord, that neither they nor any other can prove ill against me.'"

Nook'), and then turned to the left towards Marsh Lane Head. They turned again to the left at the Well, where there is a farm-house, then occupied by a family called Crook, past Windmill Hill, on to Brindle Moss. Meanwhile the pursuer had got on the scent, and inquired at the farm at the Well which way the two horsemen had gone. Crook, the farmer, directed him, as he had observed the

THE OLD BLUE ANCHOR INN, HOGHTON, from which the
Ven. Edmund Arrowsmith, S.J. escaped.
The + show position of hiding place.

A previous occupier of the house in Gregson Lane where Father Arrowsmith said his last Mass, a Mr. Worden, gives a fuller account of the priest's flight and apprehension. "It is thought," he says, "that he intended to go to Wickenhouse Farm, Withnell, an isolated place where he sometimes said Mass. A man accompanied him on horseback. They set off in a contrary direction to Withnell, going on the road towards Preston, but turned to the left past the Oak Tree Inn, and went up Gregson Lane. They passed over Jack Green by the Town House (a gentleman's house now known as 'The

fugitives pass his house. The pursuer overtook them at the Moss (which abuts on Duxon Hill) and ran on our martyr with his drawn sword. Finding that his horse refused to jump the Moss Ditch, the Father dismounted and ran along by its side, hoping to reach the place higher up where the ditch is much narrower. The ditch still exists, but is roughly bridged over with thick stones or flags. He ran on for some little time till he came to the narrower part, but here, as he tells us, the pursuer overtook him. Meanwhile the man who should have been his protector deserted him. The martyr was apprehended with the help of the rest of the party, who soon came up, and was carried by them, first to the toll-house at Marsh Lane End, and thence to the Boar's Head Inn in Hoghton Lane, not far from the present railway station. Here he was subjected to the infamies of which he complained at his trial. He was then carried off to the dungeons at Lancaster Castle."

But for his horse refusing to jump the Moss Ditch, Father Arrowsmith would have got safely away. As Mr. Worden points out, once on the other side of the ditch "he would soon have been on the Blackburn Road. By turning to the right at Riley Green, he could have got to Billy Street on the Chorley Road. Then to the right, they would soon have reached the occupation road leading to Wickenhouse Farm. Father Arrowsmith could then have dismounted and walked by this secluded road to the farm unobserved. The man would have gone on with both horses to Wheelton, then by Copthurst, Waterhouse Green, and through Brindle Lane. That is supposed to have been the plan." Mr. Worden also says that he was told by a very old man living in Brindle, whose mother had been a Livesey, that the Livesey family had lived at Wickenhouse Farm ever since the reign of Henry VIII., and, so late as 1899, the room in the farm in which Father Arrowsmith and other priests had said Mass was still shown. In that year it began to fall into ruin, and was eventually demolished to provide material for the repair of another farm near by, to which the Liveseys had removed, the former name of which—Taylor's Farm—was changed to New Wickenhouse Farm.

Many curious stories are told of the evil that befell those who aided in the capture of Father Arrowsmith. Misfortune, according to Mr. Worden, dogged the family of the farmer, Crook, who directed the pursuers as to the way the Father and his servant had gone, for many generations. He says: "My uncle, William Walmsley, told me that Crook the farmer went after the pursuer of Father Arrowsmith, and was given his cloak as a reward for the information he had given. He had a fine boy about eleven years of age, and he got a tailor to come to the house to make the child a suit out of the martyr's cloak. When he put it on the family was much pleased with his appearance, and to celebrate the event he was put on the back of a horse, to take a triumphant ride. But though the child had previously ridden this horse, which was a quiet one, it at once, on feeling his weight, set off at a gallop and threw him. His head struck a stone on the road-side, and the poor boy was killed on the spot. The stone was visible for a long distance when I was a boy, but the road has been raised at that part and the stone covered. The family were so frightened that they returned to the Catholic faith. They were up to that time noted for their good looks, but the children of their descendants were for long afterwards in some way deformed or dwarfs. My uncle said that God had punished them severely, though they afterwards kept the faith and were very striving. One of the last I remember was James, alias 'Turk,' a dwarf. They lived at a place called Bullocks, on the river Darwen side, above Salmesbury Mill. He was drowned in the river Darwen in 1862."

Father Arrowsmith's trial at Lancaster, as the law then stood, could have only one outcome. The saying of the Mass was an offence punishable by death. And Father Arrowsmith was condemned to die the death of a traitor—to be hanged, drawn and quartered. The gallows was set on Lancaster Moor, a quarter of a mile from the Castle. Thither he was dragged on a hurdle. But the fire in which his heart and entrails were to be cast, the cauldron of bubbling pitch into which the quarters of his body would be thrown before they were exposed on John of Gaunt's Tower, the great butcher's knife which was to do its hideous work when, half strangled, he was cut down from the gibbet, left his exalted spirit unmoved. "Nothing grieves me," he cried from the steps of the fatal ladder, "so much as this England which I pray God soon to convert." Then bidding the concourse of people bear witness that he died a steadfast Roman Catholic, he was thrown from the ladder, crying, *Bone Jesu* ("O Good Jesus"), and after a few minutes was cut down for the further butchery.

P Edmundus A rou/mith æus Angl, Soc IESV pro Fide Ca tholica su/pen/us, et dissectus Lanca/trïæ in Anglia 7 Sept.1.6z.

THE EXECUTION OF FATHER ARROWSMITH

Father Arrowsmith excited the veneration of the Lancashire people to a greater degree than any of his fellow-martyrs—a veneration that was shared by Protestants. In Lancaster itself so strong was the sympathy, says one of Arrowsmith's biographers, that "in proof of their detestation of this judicial murder, no man could be prevailed upon to undertake the execution except a butcher, who though ashamed to become the hangman

himself, engaged for five pounds that his servant should despatch the martyr. This the servant, out of a feeling of humanity and respect for that good man, refused, and when informed of his master's shameful contract, he fled from his service, and was never seen by him again. Within the gaol itself the same spirit was displayed. Felons and malefactors, though offered their own lives, would lend no hand to injustice; till a deserter, under sentence of death for leaving his regiment, offered for the sum of forty shillings, the prisoner's clothes, and his own liberty, to be the vile instrument of the murder. But this made him so detested by the good people of Lancaster, that none would lend him an axe wherewith to slay the servant of God." Even the warders in the Castle helped the martyr's friends in procuring relics, and one of them, Henry Holme, wrote a letter testifying to the authenticity of certain relics he himself had given to a Roman Catholic priest called Metcalfe, who seems to have been a prisoner in Lancaster Castle, but was discharged before the martyrdom. "The certainty of those things which I did deliver you at your being at Lancaster," he says, "I will affirm to be true, for the hair and the pieces of the ribs I did take myself at the going up of the plumbers to see the leads, when they were to mend them. [These would be the leads upon John of Gaunt's Tower where Arrowsmith's head and quarters were exposed.] And the handkerchief was dipped in his blood at the time of his quarters coming back from the execution to the Castle by

THE HOLY HAND

me, likewise with my own hands. You know the handkerchief was your own which you gave me at your departure, and for the piece of the quarter, both I and some others had taken part of it for our friends, which Mr. Southworth can witness; and that which I gave you, John Rigmaden, our keeper, gave me the leave to take." In further proof of the authenticity of the relics, John Rigmaden, the keeper of Lancaster Castle, endorsed this letter. Since Roman Catholics were debarred from occupying such positions, this letter from the warder and its endorsement by the keeper, are eloquent

testimony of the respect in which Father Arrowsmith was held by those not of his own faith.

Every relic that could be obtained was most reverently sought by the faithful, and as reverently treasured. His clothes, and the knife with which his body was cut up, were secured by Sir Cuthbert Clifton. His relatives, the Gerards, obtained his right hand, which they kept for many generations at Garswood, a member of the family later giving it into the keeping of St. Oswald's Church at Ashton-in-Makerfield. Many are the miracles declared to have been wrought by the martyr's hand, known far and near as "The Holy Hand." In 1737 it was recorded that a boy at Appleton-within-Widnes had been healed of a sickness by being touched by the hand, nineteen witnesses, some of whom were Protestants, signing the paper of attestation; and miracles are still recorded to-day when as many as sixty people visit the shrine of the Holy Hand in pilgrimage each week.

In his hurried flight from the Blue Anchor Inn, with all his possessions, Father Arrowsmith dropped a small ivory statue of the Virgin Mary, holding the infant Saviour in her arms, enclosed in an ivory niche. This has been carefully preserved, and is now in the possession of Mr. George Hull. Other relics of the martyr were discovered in 1841, when part of a wall in the attic of the house in Gregson Lane, where he said his last Mass, was blown down, disclosing a hiding-place behind it. Here was found a box containing two priest's vestments, a chalice and two altar-stones, one of which was broken; miracles are also attributed to one of these vestments. And in this room of Father Arrowsmith's last Mass, a curious phenomenon is observed from time to time. High up on the wall there appears a cross of light.

Dom Bede Camm, O.S.B., in his *Forgotten Shrines* says that a doctor in the neighbourhood has told him, " there is no possible natural explanation of this phenomenon," and that both the present and the previous occupiers of the house have frequently seen it.

Amongst the Roman Catholics of Lancashire the memory of Father Arrowsmith is venerated as that of a saint.

IVORY SHRINE SAID TO HAVE BELONGED TO THE VENERABLE EDMUND ARROWSMITH

CHARMS and spells to cure or prevent sickness were very common in Lancashire, and are still believed in, in some country districts. Thus, a string with nine knots tied in it and placed round the neck of a child suffering from whooping cough was believed to be an infallible remedy; another remedy for the same complaint was to pass a child nine times round the neck of a she-ass.

Three spiders hung round the neck in a bag were said to prevent ague, and in old days silver rings made from the hinges of a coffin were worn to cure fits, and also to prevent cramp and rheumatism. Of all the Lancashire charms this has had the longest life. Coffins rarely have hinges of silver in these days, but the " galvanized" rings, made of a ring of zinc and a ring of copper soldered together, which so many of the poorer Lancashire folk wear to-day, are worn for the same purpose as the old gruesome rings made from coffin hinges, and are believed to be equally efficacious in preventing rheumatism. Moisture from the finger undoubtedly set up a slight action between the two metals, and it is this action which is supposed to draw the rheumatism from the body.

Some people wear a belt round the waist to ward off rheumatism, whilst others are firmly convinced that if they carry a piece of brimstone in their pocket they will never have cramp. Another charm against cramp is to place the shoes under the bed at night with their toes peeping outwards.

LANCASHIRE AND TEETOTALISM

ALTHOUGH the first Temperance Society was founded in America in 1789 and its tenets gradually spread through Ireland to various parts of England and Scotland, modern teetotalism had its birth in Preston, where on the first of September, 1832, Joseph Livesay and six others signed a pledge " to abstain from all liquors of an intoxicating quality, whether ale, porter, wine or ardent spirits, except as medicine." And of these " Seven Men of Preston " as they were called, only two broke their pledge. At that time there were some thirty temperance societies in existence, but their members were pledged to " moderation" in the use of intoxicants, or, at the utmost, abstinence from spirits, it being believed that malt liquors were harmless. It was after a discussion on the rules of the existing temperance societies that Livesay and his companions came to the conclusion that total abstinence was the only remedy against the drunkenness which then prevailed in every class, and which was unhappily a characteristic of the whole nation.

" The Seven Men of Preston " were not content with forming their new society and drawing up rules. They started an energetic propaganda, hiring a cart and visiting Blackburn, Haslingden, Bury, Heywood, Ashton, Oldham, Rochdale, Stockport, Manchester, and Bolton, stopping at all the villages on the road. On this tour they distributed over 9000 temperance tracts.

Many were the devices to which they were compelled to resort to attract the attention of the townsfolk and villagers. Their usual custom was to borrow the bell from the town or village bellman, and whilst one of the party rang it vigorously another would wave a silken banner bearing a temperance motto ; having thus gained the notice of the passers-by, a third member of the party, who possessed a loud voice, would announce the time and place at which the meeting was to be held.

One of the earliest of their converts was a drunkard called Richard Turner, a Preston man, and it was he who invented the word " teetotal," the name by which total abstinence is now known all the world over. It is generally supposed that the word owed its origin to a stammerer trying to say " total," but Mr. Winshill in his *History of the Temperance Movement* gives the actual story of how it came to be invented. Richard Turner, who was locally known as " Dicky " Turner, after his conversion from drunkenness became one of the most zealous advocates of the cause. " In the month of September, 1833, ' Dicky ' Turner was speaking at a meeting in the cockpit at Preston, when, in his own peculiar way, he used these words, ' I'll have nowt to do wi' this moderation botheration pledge. I'll be reet down out-an'-out tee-tee total for ever and ever!' ' Well done!' exclaimed the audience. ' Well done, Dicky!' exclaimed Mr. Livesay, ' that shall be the name of our new pledge.'" Mr. Livesay, who was present, bore out this statement, saying that it was a mistake to suppose that the word arose from the mispronunciation of a stammerer. " The truth is," he added, " that Dicky was never at a loss for a word—if a suitable one was not at his tongue end he coined one."

There is another authority, however, who proves that Dicky Turner did not invent the word " teetotal," as Mr. Livesay supposed. This is Dr. F. R. Lees, who says, " It is a vulgar error to suppose that he either invented the word or stuttered it forth. The term has been in common use in Ireland and in Lancashire these hundred years, and was familiar to the writer [Doctor Lees] when a lad in that country about forty years ago. It can be found in the literature of England long prior to the Preston movement, in application to various things. Banim, the Irish novelist, employed it. Maginn in *Maga* uses it, and De Quincey, also a master of English, who probably acquired it in Lancashire, amidst the idioms of which county he spent his early years. Richard Turner used the word because it had an established meaning. It was one of those designations to which children and uneducated persons were apt to give spontaneous expression; and because it fell in with popular usage and feeling, Mr. Livesay, wisely or unwisely, adopted it as the name of the new society.

Dicky Turner was buried in the churchyard of St. Peter's Church at Preston, and his epitaph, which may still be seen, runs—

" Beneath this stone are deposited the remains of Richard Turner, author of the word Teetotal as applied to abstinence from all intoxicating liquors, who departed this life on the 27th day of October 1846, aged 56 years."

Although there is no doubt that Dicky Turner used an old Lancashire expression when he said he was " out an' out tee-tee total for ever and ever," he had actually been anticipated in America. There, in the State of New York, a Temperance Society had been formed in 1819, the members of which promised to abstain from all intoxicating drink. So absolute a rule was held by many to be too narrow, therefore another society— the Lancing Temperance Society—was formed, which allowed two pledges: one against distilled spirits, the other against all alcoholic liquors. The first pledge was marked " O. P. " (Old Pledge); and the second " T," meaning (Total). A large number of the members signed the second pledge, and they were spoken of as " T—totallers "—the initial letter " T " and its explanation " Total," being spoken as one word.

It is generally believed that total abstinence was unknown before " The Seven Men of Preston," headed by Joseph Livesay, created the modern movement, but it dates from very ancient days. Mahomet forbade wine (the only intoxicating drink then known in the East) to his followers; one of the five commandments of Buddha is directed against strong drink; amongst the Jews, the sects of the Rechabites, Essenes and Nazarites were compelled to take vows of total abstinence. The famous Dr. Johnson was a total abstainer, as were also many statesmen, prelates and soldiers distinguished in the roll of English history. But total abstinence was not regarded sympathetically in ages when drunkenness was taken as a matter of course; and even amongst moderate drinkers wine and spirits were believed necessary to the human body, not as stimulants, but as giving strength to brain and body alike. This opinion was expressed, in some lines written upon a total abstainer, Andrew Tiraqueau, an author, who wrote twenty books and who was also the father of twenty children—

" Here lies a man who drinking only water,
   Wrote twenty books, with each had son
      or daughter;
   Had he but used the juice of generous
      vats,
   The world would scarce have held his
      books and brats."

UNDERGROUND LANCASHIRE

IT is estimated that more than one-half of Lancashire is undermined by coal-pits, many of which are disused. In some of the colliery districts, notably at Wigan, nearly all the coal has been extracted to a considerable depth, and it is said that under the town itself little or no mining now goes on. In one colliery near Wigan the miners, when they reach the bottom of the shaft, have to walk for nearly half-an-hour through exhausted galleries before they come to the "face." Around Clifton there is a large number of disused workings, whilst the Duke of Bridgewater's famous underground canal exhausted many of the mines round about Bolton. The main portion of this canal ran for about six miles from Worsley in the direction of Bolton, but it had innumerable branches, which brought its total length to about forty-five miles. It was eighty feet below the level of the ground, and although only seven or eight feet wide, as much as a thousand tons of coal passed along at a time. The method of its working was most ingenious. A slight fall from the top to Worsley, where it joins the Bridgewater Canal, causes a continuous flow of water throughout the whole length of the subterranean channels. The branches were cut upon the same principle, descending from their starting-point to the main stream. As the water is the drainage from the mines, Brindley's genius had a twofold effect. He used an ever-present danger in coal-mines before the days of scientific pumping, to carry coals from the bowels of the earth to the barges on the Bridgewater Canal. At intervals there are gates, which, on the principle of lock-gates, keep the water in the upper parts of the canal at a higher level than in the

lower parts. When the gates were opened the water behind them of course flowed onward to find its level, and the impetus, frequently repeated from level to level, combined with the slope of the canal, gave the boats laden with coal a considerable speed. As many as a hundred of these boats, all fastened together, and carrying in all a thousand tons of coal, were sent through the canal at a time—a revelation in those days of slow transit and hand labour.

The return journey of the empty boats, however, was not so easy a matter. Light as they were, they were going against stream. It was, therefore, necessary to push them forward with poles, but more frequently the men in charge of them used to lie upon their backs and push with their feet against the roof. It was a method they discovered for themselves, as being easier than poling, and to give their pushes greater impetus staples were fixed in the walls and roof which gave them a firmer "take off" than the rock. Other times, other methods! The underground canal is still in working order, but it is rarely ever used except to get rid of rubbish from the mines. When it was made by the Duke of Bridgewater under the plans of Brindley, it was considered the most remarkable waterway in the world. Now it serves as little more than a drain.

Thousands of pounds' worth of material lie buried in the disused collieries of Lancashire. Tons of timber, of bricks, and of machinery lie buried beneath the water that has accumulated, or under the roofs and sides of galleries that have fallen in. When a mine is exhausted, little or nothing can be taken out of it; and in the course of time the roads get choked up and everything is destroyed by the ever-reaching water. Sometimes, however, a disused pit will remain for years exactly as it was left, as is shown in the following story.

A collier had committed some offence, and being closely pursued by a policeman succeeded in getting into a cage that was about to descend into a pit, leaving the constable " lamenting " upon the bank. When he reached the bottom he took a road which he knew led into an old pit, through an opening made for ventilation. Passing through the disused pit—which must, therefore, have been free of water and poisonous gases—he got into another colliery where work was in full swing, and taking the cage returned to earth again, some two miles distant from the spot where he had disappeared. The policeman, determined to capture his man, followed him into Mine No. 1 by the next cage, but he was not a collier, and after following a multitude of directions, each of which brought him into a blind alley, he was obliged to give up a search in what he afterwards described as a " pocket hell," and return, grimy and discomfited, to the pit mouth. But he had his reward six months later, for the fox-like collier who had " run to earth," unwisely appeared in the neighbourhood where he had committed his delinquency, and was promptly haled before the magistrate by the constable he had so cleverly outwitted.

The falling-in of the roofs and sides of the galleries of disused coal-mines some-times causes serious subsidence in the ground above; but owing to the depth of the pits this is not of frequent occurrence in Lancashire. At Wigan, however, some years ago, a stable in which there were two horses disappeared entirely one night, leaving a yawning chasm where it had stood. Tons of rubbish were required to fill the great hole.

A touching instance of wifely devotion once gave a disused pit in South Lancashire the reputation of being haunted. A white figure, it was rumoured, had been seen " flitting " about the pit-head. The mine was watched, and sure enough night after night the figure was seen, gliding around the shaft. It was firmly believed to be a ghost, and the pit-head was, therefore, given a wide berth. But one collier, bolder than his fellows, and disbelieving all their stories of ghosts and boggarts, one night lay in wait for the ghostly visitor. By and by the figure appeared, wandering round the top of the shaft. Rushing forward, he clasped his arms around it and found—not a ghost or a practical joker, but a poor old woman with a grey shawl over her head ! Years and years before, the old woman's husband had lost his life in the now disused pit. Fallen into dotage, the poor soul's thoughts had turned to the place where all her hopes had been shattered, and night after night she wandered round the pit-head to which her dead husband's body had been brought, her clouded brain finding comfort and solace in " being near him."

"THE CHEERYBLE BROTHERS"

THE name of Grant will be for ever associated with the village of Ramsbottom, near Bury. They were the first manufacturers in the district. Two members of the family—William and Charles—Dickens has made known to all the world as the Cheeryble Brothers in *Nicholas Nickleby*. Their father was a farmer in Inverness, and a disastrous flood having swept away not only all his stock but the very soil of the farm itself, he and his sons were compelled to go elsewhere to gain a living. They made their way southwards and found work in some print-works near Bury, where the elder served his apprenticeship. It is said that when they wished to set up in business for themselves they were at some loss to know where to settle, and going to the top of a hill near Ramsbottom they surveyed the whole country round. They saw the advantage which that particular spot offered, but other localities also had their recommendation. In order to settle the difficulty a stick was put into the ground, and they decided where it fell in that direction would they betake themselves for a home. The stick fell pointing towards Ramsbottom, and there the Grants settled, in after years erecting the monument which may still be seen in commemoration of this event.

In the course of years of ceaseless and untiring industry the brothers accumulated a fortune of one million sterling. The greatest affection united them, and for fifteen years they might have been seen driving into Manchester on market days seated side by side in their carriage, "looking of all things like a pair of brothers happy in themselves and happy in each other." Their benevolence and kindness were proverbial, and many stories were told of the assistance which they had given to those in misfortune. The following stories are characteristic of the large-minded charity of the brothers.

A warehouseman published a scurrilous pamphlet, in which he endeavoured, but without success, to hold up the house of Grant Brothers to public ridicule. William, the elder, remarked that the man would live to repent what he had done. This remark was repeated to the writer of the pamphlet, who said: " Oh, I suppose he thinks I shall some time or other be in his debt, but I will take good care of that." But it chanced that many years afterwards the pamphleteer became

THE GRANT MEMORIAL

a bankrupt, and that the Brothers Grant held an acceptance of his which had been endorsed to them by the drawer, who had also become a bankrupt. The libelled firm thus held their traducer completely in their power. He had obtained all the signatures required by the bankrupt law except one, without this one signature he could not obtain the certificate for his discharge, and without that discharge he could not enter into business again.

The Brothers Grant were the only people who could give him this signature, and in his despair the bankrupt went to their office. William Grant was there alone : " Shut the door, sir," he said sternly. The bankrupt told his tale with much trembling and many fears, and produced his certificate.

" You wrote a pamphlet against us once," said William Grant, looking at the certificate. The suppliant was obliged to confess that he had, at the same time expecting to see his parchment thrown on to the fire, but Mr. Grant took a pen, and writing something upon the document, handed it back to the bankrupt who, instead of " rogue, scoundrel, libeller," which he fully expected to see, read the signature of the firm. " We make it a rule," said Mr. Grant, " never to refuse signing the certificate of an honest tradesman, and we have never heard that you were anything else." The tears started into the bankrupt's eyes.

" Ah ! " said Mr. Grant, " my saying was true. I said you would live to repent writing that pamphlet. I did not mean it as a threat, I only meant that some day you would know us better and repent you had tried to injure us. I see you have repented it now."

" I do. I do," said the grateful man. " I bitterly repent it."

" Well, my dear fellow," said Mr. Grant, " you know us now. How do you get on ? What are you going to do ? " The poor man stated that he had friends who would assist him when he had obtained his certificate of discharge. " But how are you off in the meantime ? " asked the kindly man. The bankrupt was obliged to confess that, having given up every farthing to his creditors, he had been obliged to deprive his family of even common necessaries that he might be able to afford the cost of the certificate.

" My dear fellow, this will not do ; your family must not suffer," exclaimed Mr. Grant. " Be kind enough to take this ten pounds in to your wife from me—there, there, my dear fellow—no, don't cry—it will be all well with you yet ; keep up your spirits, set to work like a man, and you will raise your head amongst us yet." Vainly the poor bankrupt endeavoured to express his thanks, but he could not speak, and putting his handkerchief to his face, went out of the door crying like a child.

Meeting a gentleman who devoted his time and energies to writing and lecturing on the necessity of children being given an early moral, religious and secular education—at that time practically unknown, Mr. Grant asked—

" Well, how do you go on in establishing schools for infants ? "

" Very encouragingly indeed," was the answer. " Wherever I have gone, I have succeeded either in inducing good people to establish them, or in procuring better support to those that are already established. But I must give over my labours ; for what with printing bills, coach fare, and other expenses, every lecture I deliver in any neighbouring town costs me a sovereign, and I cannot afford to ride my hobby at such a cost."

Whereupon Mr. Grant said : " You must not give over your labours. God has blessed them with success. He has blessed you with talents, and He has blessed me with wealth. If you give your time I ought to give my money. You must oblige me by taking this twenty-pound note and spending it in promoting the education of the poor."

A young student, who was very poor, was stricken down with consumption. His only chance of life was to go to a warm climate. The young man was very proud, and in order to help him in spite of himself, Mr. Grant planned an elaborate, albeit a pious and justifiable fraud. He said to him—

"We have a vessel which is to touch at M—— The Captain will be glad to have your company so far, and our correspondent will find you lodgings for the winter at a cheap rate."

Believing he was going as companion to the Captain, and that the voyage was the payment for his services, the young man joyfully accepted. A few days before the ship sailed, Mr. Grant sent for him and said—

"We are sending a young man to our agent by the vessel you sail in. Will you be kind enough to pay him some attention on the voyage?"

This young man was really a nurse, engaged by Mr. Grant to look after the student.

On their arrival at M—— Mr. Grant's agent, acting on instruction from home, invited the student to stay in his house until he could find lodgings for him. But day after day he invented excuses for not being able to do so. Finally, when the student began to get impatient, the agent said: "It is such a comfort to me to have an Englishman to talk to, that you could do me a great favour if you would take up your abode with me."

All this had been arranged by Mr. Grant, and when, despite the warmer climate, the student died, his benefactor said—

"Poor fellow, but I have the consolation of thinking that he never found out how we had managed for him."

Mr. Grant was once asked for a subscription by two gentlemen who were raising a fund to help a widow whose husband shortly before he died had had serious business troubles, and had left her unprovided for.

"We lost two hundred pounds by him," said Mr. Grant, "and how do you expect that I should subscribe for his widow?"

"Because," was the answer, "what you lost by the husband does not alter the widow's claim on your benevolence."

"Neither shall it," Mr. Grant replied. "Here are five pounds. If you cannot make up the sum you want for her, come back to me, and I'll give you five more."

~~~~~~~~~~~~~~~~~

SOME OLD LANCASHIRE RHYMES

"God made man, man made money,
God made bees, bees made honey;
God made the devil, the devil made sin,
God made a hole to put the devil in."

An old Furness farmer, whose goods had been distrained upon, added the following two lines—

"But the devil hisself made lawyers and 'turnies,
And placed 'em at U'ston[1] and Dawton[2] in Furness."

[1] Ulverston.   [2] Dalton.

"Them that buys beef buys bones;
Them that buys land buys stones;
Them that buys eggs buys shells;
Them that buys ale buys nought else."

"Many men has many minds,
But women has but two;
Everything is what they'd have
And nothing would they do."

"Prescot, Huyton and merry Childow,
Three parish churches all in a row:
Prescot for mugs; Huyton for ploydes;[3]
Childow for ringing and singing besides."

[3] Ploydes are ploys or merry-makings, but me think the word "ploughs" is meant.

PIT-BROW LASSES

THE pit-brow lass is one of the features of Wigan, and although there has been more than one attempt to prohibit the work by the authorities, the opposition of the "Lasses" themselves has so far been triumphant. The girls declare that the stacking of coal, pushing wagons from the shaft to a stock heap; or raking stones and rubbish from the coal as it passes on an endless iron belt in a large sieve; or keeping the shoots, down which coal is tipped into the canal boats, clear with a small rake, is not hard work. Most of the lasses are single, generally the daughters of colliers, but there are a number of married women amongst them and widows. In most collieries where the pit-brow lasses are employed, if a collier is killed and his widow applies for work at the pit-brow, she is invariably given a place.

A girl must be fif-

PIT-BROW LASSES

teen before she can be employed, and as a rule they give up the work at about twenty or twenty-four when they get married. But there are cases in which they still go on working, even after marriage, and some years ago, on one of the mines at Wigan, there was a woman of over sixty who had been at the pit-brow all her life.

The dress of the 'pit-brow lass' is distinctive of her calling, but it is not quite so mannish as it used to be. She wears a pair of trousers which formerly were scarcely hidden at all, but are now covered with a skirt reaching just below the knees. Her head is cunningly bandaged with a red handkerchief, which entirely protects the hair from coal-dust; across this is wrapped a piece of cloth which comes under her chin, with the result that only the face is exposed. A flannel jacket completes the costume. When she is at work the pit-brow lass tucks the skirt round her waist, but when she is walking to and from her home it is let down, and there is nothing to distinguish her from any ordinary working woman.

The healthiness of the pit-brow lass is proverbial, and a manager of one of the large coal-mines near Wigan said: "We frequently get a lass who has been in a cotton mill, and on whom the hard life and vitiated air have wrought havoc. She sets to work on the pit-brow, and in a month or two she is another girl altogether and as healthy as her companions, which is saying a lot. I hardly think we get such strong and hearty girls as we did in bygone years, for I can remember many a one who could beat the men with the shovel, but our pit-brow lasses are still very strong; it would amuse you to see them cleaning the engine-room and places, they get over the floor in no time, and handle a big scrubbing-brush as if it were a toothbrush. It is mere play to them, I assure you." The same manager said that for as long as he could remember, which was a great many years, the pit-brow lasses had been noted for their fresh complexions, and that when they were dressed after their working hours, their own foreman often passed them without recognizing them.

On two occasions when suggestions have been made of clauses being inserted in Acts of Parliament, dealing with coal mines, that the pit-brow lasses should be abolished, such was the indignation amongst the lasses themselves that they sent deputations to the Home Secretary; and the Palace of Westminster saw the unusual spectacle of these Lancashire girls in their working clothes, donned for the occasion to prove to the authorities that their garb was not unfeminine. And they themselves were living evidence of the incorrectness of statements put forward as to the unhealthiness of their occupation.

OLD WORLD CHARMS TO STOP BLEEDING

IN an ancient book, giving a description of the Abbey of Whalley and its history, there are two charms against bleeding, which clearly show that the monks, like our modern doctors, were fully alive to the effect of the patient's mind upon his physical condition.

"*For Staunching Bleeding from the Nostrils, or from Wounds, an Approved Remedy.*—O God, be Thou merciful to this Thy servant, nor allow to flow from his body more than one drop of blood, so may it please Thee, Son of God. So his mother Mary. In the name of the Father, stop, O blood! In the name of the Son, stop O blood! In the name of the Holy Ghost, stop, O blood! In the name of the Holy Trinity!

"*To Staunch Bleeding.*—A soldier of old thrust a lance into the side of the Saviour; immediately there flowed thence blood and water—the Blood of Redemption and the water of Baptism. In the name of the Father ✠ may the blood cease. In the name of the Son ✠ may the blood remain. In the name of the Holy Ghost ✠ may no more blood flow from the mouth, the vein, or the nose."

At a time when the priests were believed to hold the powers of life and death in their hand, it is easy to understand the effect of so solemn an adjuration as either of these "approved" remedies upon the mind; and such being the mysterious sympathy between the mind and the body, it is not improbable that the implicit belief inspired in the one, would affect the physical condition of the other. An hypnotic power was undoubtedly possessed in this direction by some people. A woman called Bamber, who lived at Marton, near Blackpool, was able to stop bleeding "by a word," and so great was her success that for twenty miles round her services were in continual request.

LANCASHIRE PRISONS IN THE EIGHTEENTH CENTURY

THE state of prisons in the eighteenth century was a terrible indictment against the age; but it must be admitted that when John Howard the philanthropist, after travelling all over the country and inspecting the gaols, laid the result of his inquiries before the House of Commons, instant steps were taken to remedy matters by the passing of two Acts of Parliament. This was in 1774; but although copies of these acts were printed at Howard's expense and sent by him to the gaoler of every county gaol in England, the new laws were, for the most part, cleverly evaded.

John Howard was the son of an upholsterer, who, when he died, left him comfortably off, and with a small property in Bedfordshire, of which county Howard became High Sheriff. It was whilst occupying this position that he made the discoveries which resulted in his becoming a prison reformer. In his famous book, *The State of Prisons in England and Wales*, which was printed at the Eyre Press in Warrington, he told the world that he found amongst the Bedfordshire prisoners "some who by the verdict of juries were declared not guilty, some on whom the grand jury did not find such an appearance of guilt as subjected them to trial; and some whose prosecutors did not appear against them; after having been confined for months, dragged back to gaol, and locked up again till they should pay sundry fees to the gaoler, the clerk of assize, etc."

Profoundly shocked by this shameful practice, which arose from the gaoler having no salary, Howard applied to the justices of the county to pay a salary and abolish fees. The justices were quite willing to remove the grievance, but could not charge the county with the expense without a precedent. "I therefore rode into several neighbouring counties in search of a precedent," says Howard, "but I soon learned that the same injustice was practised in them, and looking into the prisons I beheld scenes of calamity which I grew daily more and more anxious to alleviate." He then visited nearly all the county gaols in England, and in the following year he inspected the bridewells, or houses of correction, and the town and city gaols. As said above, he laid the information so gained before the House of Commons, and was afterwards called to the Bar of the House to receive its thanks for "the humanity and zeal which have led him to visit the several gaols of this kingdom, and to communicate to the House the interesting observations he has made on the subject." The publication of his book in 1777, in Warrington, where he had retired to write it, brought home to the whole nation the terrible conditions of the prisons and their unfortunate occupants.

Lancashire, with the exception of Manchester, does not receive favourable reports. Howard begins with the County Gaol at Lancaster Castle. Here, the gaoler, John Dane, had no salary, but received eight shillings from every debtor and thirteen and fourpence from every felon, on their discharge. The prisoners, both felons and debtors, had an allowance of one shilling each on Saturday morning. These are Howard's remarks on the Lancaster Gaol of his time:—" The Castle yard is spacious. Master's side Debtors have many apartments. One of them which they call the *Oven* is said to have been used as such in the time of John of Gaunt, Duke of Lancaster; the diameter twenty-four feet, the height, now, that of an ordinary room. The Free Ward for

Debtors is large but dark. These, as well as those on the Master's side are allowed to walk, and work (spin, knit, etc.) in the Crown and Shire hall.

" Men and women felons have their Day-rooms apart, at the upper end of the Yard. Women sleep in their Day-rooms —Men have for their Night-rooms two vaulted Cells. One of these, the Low Dungeon, is ten steps under ground, twenty-one feet by nine, extremely close, dark, and unwholesome ; so very hot even in Winter that coming from it in the morning into the cold air must be pernicious. Their other Cell, the High Dungeon, is larger but close and offensive, though not under ground."

There was no infirmary in the prison. When prisoners were convicted at Preston or Manchester and sent to Lancaster to serve their sentences, the gaoler was given a shilling a mile " Conduct Money " for each.

" One of the rooms for debtors," Howard continues, " is called the Quaker's Room ; because it is said when these people were so cruelly persecuted in the last century, vast numbers of them were confined in it."

The misery and wretchedness of prisoners, especially of the debtors, was so well known, that charitable folk left legacies in their wills for the amelioration of their hardships. In 1770 the debtors in Lancaster Gaol benefited by six of these legacies to the amount of twenty-two pounds fifteen shillings a year.

At Preston, Howard found the Bridewell with no water accessible to the prisoners, and no allowance made to them. " This prison," he says, " a little distant from the Town was a Friary. On the ground floor is a large Room, in which are eleven Closets, called Boxes, to sleep in, and in another Room, the Dungeon. Over these are a large Working-room for Men, and a less for Women. All the rooms are dirty, and the Prison out of repair— A Courtyard in front (the Prisoners have no use of it) and a spacious garden backwards for the Keeper."

The Liverpool Borough Gaol was " out of repair. Apartments close and dirty. Seven close Dungeons ten steps under ground, each six feet and a half by five feet nine inches, and six feet high. Three prisoners are locked up in each of them at night. There is another Dungeon larger, but not secure. No Infirmary. The Keeper told me in November 1775, that after I was there last year and said his Prisoners were in danger of Gaol-Fever, twenty-eight of them had been ill of it at one time. What led me to think so was the offensiveness of the Dungeons, and the number of Prisoners. The Prison is surrounded with other buildings and cannot be made healthy or convenient— Allowance in common on Sunday, bread 4s., beef and broth about 6s. Firing from October to May." The gaoler paid the widow of the late gaoler twenty pounds a year, and put in a deputy who paid him sixty-five pounds. The prisoners were for the most part debtors, there being no less than 60 in 1775, and it was from these unfortunate people that the deputy gaoler made his income in fees. Those who could not pay were obliged to stay until they found the money for the discharge fees.

At Warrington the Town Bridewell consisted of ten rooms in the Workhouse yard, " One about nine feet square, with bedstead and straw; no window; the other about nine feet by five, with an aperture for air eighteen inches by four."

Gaol-fever and small-pox were rife in all prisons throughout the country, and those of Lancashire, as we see in the reference to the Liverpool Borough Gaol, were no exception.

" My attention," Howard says upon

this matter, " was principally fixed by the gaol-fever and the small-pox, which I saw prevailing to the destruction of multitudes, not only of felons in their dungeons, but of debtors also." So poisonous was the air of the prisons that visitors frequently contracted gaol-fever, and on more of prisoners, two judges, the Lord Mayor, one alderman, and many others, fell victims to this prison scourge in London in one year.

In many gaols no straw was given for the prisoners to sleep upon, and where it was given it remained unchanged for

JOHN HOWARD

than one occasion prisoners whilst being tried infected a whole court. At Oxford Assizes in 1577, " all who were present died within forty hours: the Lord Chief Baron, the Sheriff, and about three hundred more." Judges and counsel frequently died of gaol-fever, and only twenty years before Howard began his agitation for the more humane treatment months together. Both debtors and felons were condemned to live in a state of indescribable filth, herded together. " Some lie upon rags," says Howard, " others upon the bare floor. When I have complained of this to the keepers, their justification has been ' The county allows no straw ; the prisoners have none but at my cost.' "

The atmosphere of a prison, and they were the same all over the country when George III. was king, can be imagined from Howard's description: "My reader will judge of its malignity, when I assure him, that my cloaths were in my first journeys so offensive, that in a post-chaise I could not bear the windows drawn up: and was therefore often obliged to travel on horse-back. The leaves of my memorandom book were often so tainted, that I could not use it till after spreading it an hour or so before the fire: and even my antidote, a vial of vinegar, has often, after using it in a few prisons, become intolerably disagreeable. I did not wonder that in those journeys many gaolers made excuses; and did not go with me into the felons' wards."

From his observations during 1773 and 1774, Howard was convinced that many more were destroyed by gaol-fever in the prisons than were put to death by all the public executions in the country.

His choice of the Eyre Press for printing his book led him to take up his residence for some time in Warrington. In addition to inspecting prisons all over England he travelled from one end of the Continent to the other for the same purpose, publishing all his investigations in various volumes through the Eyre Press. During a journey in 1790, in Southern Russia to inspect the hospitals of the Russian Army, then on the confines of Turkey, he caught camp-fever, a disease analogous to gaol-fever, and died. It is said that he travelled upwards of fifty thousand miles in his self-imposed mission of inspecting prisons, hospitals, etc. He refused all offers of assistance from the Government, and spent thirty thousand pounds of his own money on a mission which ultimately proved to be a mission of mercy to prisoners. Howard's representations entirely changed the prison conditions of England. Dr. Aiken, the Lancashire writer, assisted him in the preparation of his books.

A statue of Howard was placed in St. Paul's Cathedral, the first ever admitted there. In Lancashire, where he did so much to reform the prisons, he had many friends and was greatly revered.

Howard's book shows us that the lot of the debtor was even harder than that of the convicted felon. In half of the county gaols debtors had not even bread, "although it is granted to the highwayman, the housebreaker and the murderer; and medical assistance, which is provided for the latter is withheld from the former. In many of these Gaols debtors who would work are not permitted to have any tools, lest they should furnish felons with them for escape or other mischief. I have often seen these prisoners eating their water-soup (bread boiled in mere water) and heard them say, 'We are locked up and almost starved to death.'" By a law passed in the reign of George II. a debtor thrust into prison by his creditors was entitled to fourpence a day from them. Yet fifteen years after the passing of this Act, with the exception of Middlesex and Surrey, Howard did not find "in all England and Wales twelve debtors who had obtained from their creditors the fourpence a day, to which they had a right by that Act; the means of procuring it were out of their reach. In one of my journeys I found near six hundred prisoners, whose debts were under twenty pounds each: some of them did not owe above three or four pounds: and the expence of sueing for the aliment is in many places equal to those smaller debts; for which some of these prisoners had been confined several months. . . . The truth is some debtors are the most pitiable objects in our gaols."

In the eighteenth century the threat

of any creditor that he would send a debtor "to rot in gaol" had a horrible significance.

For a debt of a few pounds hundreds fell victims to gaol-fever. As we have seen, in 1775 twenty-eight out of the sixty debtors in Liverpool Gaol were attacked by this scourge at one time.

THE FIRST CHURCH IN LANCASHIRE

VERY early in the days of the Saxon domination of England, a small chapel, or oratory, was built upon a projecting point of rock at Heysham, and dedicated to St. Patrick. It was only twenty-four feet in length, and seven and a half in width, with one narrow window, and a doorway through which a bulky man could not possibly pass. It is supposed to have been founded by a colony of Irish Christians in the sixth or seventh century. As there was no earth, excavations were made in the rock, exactly in the shape of coffins, with grooves for the covers, and sockets at the head in which crosses could be placed. Eight of these rock-tombs have been found, one of them being that of a child. Further down, the rock has been quarried out to a depth of several feet to allow of other burials. These curious coffins—shown in the illustration —together with the Saxon part of the church and the Runic cross, lead those who are learned in such signs to believe that this was the site of the first church in Lancashire.

ANCIENT STONE COFFINS AT HEYSHAM

UNCLE TOM'S CABIN

SOME thirty or forty years ago "Uncle Tom's Cabin" was one of the chief attractions and places of amusement at Blackpool; now it is only a memory. Originally it was a little wooden hut, built by a man called Thomas Parkinson, but who always went by the name of Uncle Tom. Thus the hut became known as Uncle Tom's Cabin. Here, in the summer-time he sold sweetmeats and ginger-beer to the visitors who had climbed to the top of the promontory, some hundred feet above the sea, upon which it stood. Then, there were nearly a hundred yards of sward between the hut and the edge of the cliffs, and as time went on, it became more and more popular as a resort for Blackpool visitors. They were not so numerous nor so exacting in their requirements in those days.

After a while there was a change of ownership, a man called Taylor buying Uncle Tom out for £5. Mr. Taylor was an enterprising person who saw the possibility of increasing the popularity of the little place. He therefore took in a partner, but although the field in which the hut stood, together with an adjoining one, were offered to them for £15 they

declined because of the high price ! That was fifty years ago , one wonders what the value of the land is to-day. By a curious coincidence, very shortly after the two partners commenced business the bust of a negro was washed upon the sea-shore, probably the figure-head of a ship, and seeing its appropriateness to the name of their hut, they stuck it up on the roof and added rudely-carved figures of characters in Mrs. Beecher Stowe's novel, *Uncle Tom's Cabin*, which was then being sold by the thousand. Thus, they very cleverly seized upon the popularity of the book by giving the impression that their humble place of refreshment was named after its principal hero.

Each year saw the expansion of the wooden cabin, new rooms being added to meet the growing requirements of the visitors. All through the summer there was dancing on the green in front of the building, first to a small orchestra consisting of a pianist, a cornet player and a violinist ; then boards were laid down on the grass, as the numbers of dancers increased, and with that increase the orchestra was augmented. In the sixties and seventies of the last century Uncle

Tom's Cabin was in the heyday of its success, but with the establishment of the Winter Gardens there came a change.

Visitors to Blackpool turned from the humble dancing floor upon which the figures on the roof smiled woodenly, to the veritable palaces erected for their pleasure. So Uncle Tom's Cabin gradually became a memory of the past. A tramway passed close by, but it brought only elderly folk who had known the delights of the place in their youth, and loved to return, and sit for awhile on the grass outside the curious conglomeration of old buildings. Nature completed what the change in fashion had begun. In the last ten years of the nineteenth century no less than forty yards of the cliff had been washed away by the action of the tides and the wind and rain. In June 1901 there was a heavy landslip which threatened the very foundations of the Cabin, and the place that had once given pleasure and delight to thousands became a menace to the safety of the public. It was necessary, therefore, to level it to the ground. But so long as it stood it served as an example of the pleasures of the earlier days of Blackpool, a striking contrast with the magnificent halls and buildings Blackpool has erected for the amusement of her visitors to-day.

"HELP THE BLIND"

SOME years ago visitors at Blackpool were one day much puzzled by an old woman who was playing a barrel-organ. At one end of the instrument was a notice—

"Help the Blind,"

and beneath it a second notice—

"I am the Father of seven Motherless Children."

The old woman wore a pair of blue spectacles, behind which her eyes were completely hidden.

A few streets further on the mystery of the inscription was cleared up, for there sat an old man grinding away at a barrel-organ as dilapidated as the one at which sat the old woman. He, too, wore blue glasses, and his organ bore this legend—

"Help the Blind,"

and underneath—

"I am the Mother of seven Fatherless Children."

A man stepped up to him and said, "Look here, my friend, next time you go out you had better get the right label on your organ."

The old man must have guessed what was wrong, for pushing his blue glasses up to his forehead, he glanced quickly up and down the street as if looking for a policeman. The street being clear, he leant over and read the sign.

"That's the old woman all over," he muttered, as he replaced his glasses and began to make preparations for a swift departure, "she's mixed them blooming organs up again."

CO=OPERATION IN LANCASHIRE

FEW stories in the industrial life of Lancashire tell of such courage in the face of adversity as the story of the foundation of co-operation in the county; and few movements, starting under such humble conditions, have achieved their object so fully as this system of mutual shopkeeping established in Rochdale sixty-seven years ago.

Co-operation was not an entirely untried system before it was started in Rochdale. There were various attempts in that direction as far back as 1777 in Birmingham. But none of the attempts were based upon the same principles as those of the Rochdale pioneers, as they are called. The most elaborate of these efforts was that of Robert Owen at New Lanark. Mr. Owen saw how the workpeople in his mills were being cheated by the shopkeepers, and that they were obliged to pay high prices for inferior and often bad materials; it thereupon occurred to him that this could be remedied by establishing stores in connection with his mill. As an experiment he bought food stuff, etc., in the best markets for ready money, selling them again to his workpeople at cost price. He found that his people thus saved twenty-five per cent. of their wages. As a natural outcome of the good food and of the extra money a great change came over the village of New Lanark. Drunkenness became less general, cleanliness more widespread; in fact, this system of co-operation between master and man made New Lanark a model village. As long ago as 1815, not content with the success of his scheme at New Lanark, Owen, who may be justly called the father of co-operation, used every endeavour to induce other manufacturers to follow his example, but neither the flourishing condition of New Lanark nor Owen's ceaseless campaign brought him any followers.

The one stumbling block to the establishment of a co-operative system was the lack of capital. Manufacturers and others, however deeply they might be interested in the condition of the working-classes, were scarcely prepared to give up a considerable sum of money like Mr. Owen, upon which they would get no interest. It was Charles Howarth of Rochdale who first conceived the idea of overcoming the difficulty.

The first co-operative store in Rochdale was the result of a strike. Flannel weaving was the staple industry of the town. During the year 1843 there was an unusually large demand and trade was brisk, whereupon the flannel weavers, deeming it their right to share in the increasing prosperity of the mill owners, demanded higher wages. Some of the masters were quite willing to meet this legitimate demand, but others opposed it strongly. The demand therefore was refused, and the workers went out on strike, thus robbing the masters and themselves of all the results of a year of unexampled prosperity. Labour in those days was unorganized, with the result that even those who were lucky enough to be taken back to their looms were reduced to great poverty, whilst a large number lost their situations altogether.

We who grumble against the condition of things in our own time can little realize the condition of working men and women, especially in manufacturing centres in Lancashire, sixty or seventy years ago. The hours of work were long, and it was frequently carried out under unhealthy conditions, for the protection and comfort of the workpeople were then left entirely to the consideration and humanity of the mill owner or manufacturer. There were no factory inspectors, no Workmen's Compensation Bill. Wages, too, were low. Lancashire we all know the ups and downs of the cotton trade and its attendant manufactures—the lowered wages reduced them to semi-starvation. A bad harvest, before the repeal of the Corn Laws in 1846, had

THE FIRST CO-OPERATIVE STORE

Quite a large proportion of the working-classes lived from hand to mouth, so that when a depression occurred in the trade in which they were employed—and in the same effect upon the pockets of the workers as lowered wages, for it sent up the price of bread. When trade depression and a bad harvest came together, the condition of the thousands of people engaged in Lancashire mills was pitiable. Little wonder, therefore, that with the miserable conditions of their lives and the constant menace of hunger and destitution before them, the Lancashire workers were in a state of unrest and discontent. Not only in Lancashire, but throughout the whole of England their sense of injustice as to the misery of their lot was making itself manifest in the working-classes. The introduction of machinery was making the fortune of the manufacturers, but the working people received no benefit. This agitation resulted in the Chartist movement, so called from the People's Charter, which was a demand that the working-classes should have the right to vote, and thus have some control upon the government of the country. In Lancashire this Chartist movement was particularly strong, the speeches of John Bright and Cobden, and the writings of Charles Kingsley and others, making a deep impression upon the quick and intelligent minds of the Lancashire workers. Many were the discussions at the various clubs and societies which had their birth in the Chartist movement, as to the best method of remedying the wrongs of working men and improving the conditions of their lives. But the most practical discussion, one which was to have a widespread influence upon future generations of Lancashire men and women, took place on a memorable Sunday afternoon in the year of the flannel strike at Rochdale.

There was a reading-room in the town called the Rochdale Temperance or Chartist Reading-room, and here, each Sunday, a debate was held by the weavers and others as to the methods by which they could best improve their own condition and that of their fellows. On this never-to-be-forgotten Sunday afternoon, one of the members of the little band, Charles Howarth, put before his comrades a suggestion which has resulted in hundreds of thousands of pounds passing into the pockets of Lancashire working men and women.

Howarth suggested that they should open a shop, and buying the goods wholesale, should sell them retail to one another, dividing the profits. But his plan roused no enthusiasm; co-operative shops, one or two said, had already been tried but had always failed.

"My plan has never been tried," said Howarth.

Then followed a conversation which Miss Isa Nicholson has preserved in her little book about the Co-operative Movement called *Our Story*.

"Just listen to me, mates," Howarth continued, "while I explain; but tell me first what you think was the reason all those union shops failed?"

"Folks getting things on strap (credit), and never paying for them," said one.

"The members buying their stuff at other shops, and not supporting their own," said another.

"Just so," said Mr. Howarth, "and my plan will do away with these difficulties. We will have no 'strap' at our shop; every customer must put his brass down when he takes his goods away, then there will be no bad debts."

"But it won't prevent members from going to a cheaper shop whenever they can," said another objector, "and women like big, smart shops, which we can't have."

"Not at first, but we will have some day," replied the hopeful pioneer, "and I'm going to tell you a plan I have in mind to help us all. You, John, have a big family, and at the end of half a year will have spent, say, ten pounds at the Store, while I have no children, and have probably only spent five pounds;

who has made most of the profit, you or I?"

"Oh, I have to be sure," said John.

"Yes. Well, now, my plan is this: as soon as the shop gets on its feet in a manner of speaking, we'll fix on a moderate interest—say two and a half per cent. per

scratched them in their efforts to take in this novel idea.

One man suddenly slapped his thigh, and gave a delighted chuckle. "Well," he said, "that beats all. Why, the more we spend the more we'll get. Our Mollie will like that."

JEERS AT THE EMPTY SHELVES

year—and then, after laying a bit aside for a dull season, and paying all expenses, divide the rest of the profits among the members, according to the money they have spent in the shop. That's the idea, mates. Just you think about it."

The men looked at each other, some nodded, some shook their heads, some

A serious debate followed upon this exposition of Howarth's views, the result being that it was decided that these twenty-eight men would form a Society and open a shop. But the necessary capital for such an undertaking presented a grave difficulty. It was decided that each of the twenty-eight should take a one pound share, but not a single one amongst them could have paid one pound any more than he could have paid a hundred pounds. Weekly subscriptions were then suggested, but it was found that none of the men, who were wool-sorters, weavers, cloggers, tailors, etc., could afford to pay more than twopence a week, and this was the sum decided upon. Three of the twenty-eight were appointed collectors, each taking a district, and for many months in all sorts of weather they tramped through the dust and the mud collecting the weekly dole. The tenacity of purpose of these twenty-eight men and their families was remarkable. To gather together twenty-eight pounds at the rate of twopence a week from each person, meant that a hundred and twenty weeks must elapse before their plan could be carried into execution, and even then the chance of any benefit to the subscribers was remote. Nevertheless they kept doggedly on. Time, instead of diminishing their enthusiasm increased it, for after a while the twopence a week was voluntarily increased to threepence ; and towards the end of 1844, the desired twenty-eight pounds had been collected. During all the months that the collecting had been going on, the scope of the work of the new Society had been seriously discussed amongst the members, and it speaks for the high intelligence of those twenty-eight Rochdale men that the plan evolved out of their many meetings, is the one which co-operative societies all over the country still follow. They determined :—

"They would establish a Store for the sale of provisions, clothing, etc. ; they would build and purchase good houses for their members to live in; they would manufacture such articles as the members required, and so provide work for other members who were out of employment ; they would rent or buy an estate, or estates of land to provide still more work for members, and for the benefit of the Society."

A wild dream, said the scoffers, seeing how painfully the Society had collected its twenty-eight pounds. The contrast between the high aims of the twenty-eight and their first shop, excited further mockery, but the dream came true.

A building in Toad Lane was chosen for the shop, a building which oddly enough was known by the name of the Pioneer Stores, having been used as a store-room years before by the Pioneer Regiment when stationed in the town. The ground floor was taken for three years at a rent of ten pounds a year, and shelves, etc., were put in. But when all the necessary expenses were paid it was found that only fourteen pounds were left wherewith to buy goods for sale. With the wisdom and foresight that distinguished these pioneers of co-operation, they laid in only flour, butter, sugar, and oatmeal, and with this slender store they opened the shop in Toad Lane on December 21, 1844. News had gone abroad that " t'owd weyvers " were going to open their shop that night, and a crowd of young men and boys gathered to see any fun that might be going. Inside the shop there was much discussion as to who should take down the shutters, none of the members caring to face the gibes and jeers of the crowd outside. There is a story that it was a woman who threw open the door, but that veteran of co-operation, the late Mr. G. J. Holyoake, said, " At length one bold fellow, reckless of consequences, rushed at the shutters, and in a minute Toad Lane was in a titter."

At first it was an uphill fight. Women

would go into the shop merely to ask for something they knew it could not stock, and then make galling and sneering remarks as to its limitations and the emptiness of the shelves. In addition, the men of the twenty-eight and their wives had much to bear from their neighbours in the way of ill-natured chaff.

sent so far away for things, instead of going into the shop next door. The mother explained that the profits made at the Store would come back to the members. She understood the lesson, and would come down in the morning to fetch the food for breakfast, and the family at home would wait till she

A SURPRISING RESULT OF THE " DIVI "

But they pursued their way unheeding. It was really due to the wives of the twenty-eight that the little shop became a success, and Mr. Holyoake tells a story which shows the spirit that inspired these brave and loyal women. " A mother who had always sent her little girl to the neighbouring shop, at length began to send her to the Store, which was more than a mile away from her house. The child asked her mother why she should be

returned, and both mother and child knew the reason why."

By reason of this whole-hearted support, by degrees, more and more articles were added to the shop in Toad Lane, and at the end of the first year, the Pioneers were in the proud position of being able to pay interest on their little capital and dividend upon purchases. From that time forth the word " divi" was permanently added to the vocabulary of Rochdale folk; gradually it passed into the vocabulary of the whole county.

With each year the "divi" grew larger and larger, and many pleasant things occurred in the lives of the shareholders in consequence. New clothes, new furniture, holidays at the seaside, and in times of slackness of work a little nest egg upon which to draw—all these things came from the formerly despised "owd weyvers' shop." But the climax of wonder was reached when one of the members bought a piano out of the profits accruing to him. Such a sight as a piano being carried into a cottage had never been seen in Rochdale; no commercial undertaking ever had such an advertisement.

In those early years of struggle the twenty-eight Pioneers never lost sight of the principles they had laid down during the long months of collecting the twenty-eight pounds—that of manufacturing clothing, food, etc., to be sold in their shop. Six years after the Society opened the shop in Toad Lane, a small flour mill was started in Rochdale, practically upon co-operative lines. Acting upon their principle of "assisting other Societies" the Toad Lane Pioneers not only took shares in the mill, but they also advanced it money from their savings, and bought their flour from it. Unfortunately there was a succession of three bad managers, and it seemed more than possible that not only was the mill going to fail but that the Store also would be involved in its ruin.

There was a panic amongst the members, and many of those who had invested their savings in the Store or had left their "divis" in it as capital, were much alarmed as to the safety of their money. One man had twenty-four pounds in the Store, made entirely out of profit sharing. He went to the shop, and feeling that it was mean to demand the whole sum, asked for sixteen pounds. The cashier told him that notice was required for the withdrawal of money; the man answered that he had come to give the notice and that he must have his money. Whereupon the cashier said that although the Society availed itself of the notice when it was likely to be short of funds, there was no such necessity then, and that the man had better take "t'brass" on the spot. He carried it away, kept it in the foot of an old stocking for two years, and at the end of that time, finding he was losing four per cent. on his money, he took it back to the Store.

A woman, too, came in a great state of mind demanding her money instantly. But when it was handed to her she refused to take it. She had been warned that she had lost it, but when she actually saw the gold and silver she was satisfied. Another woman, who had forty pounds in the Store, was warned that it was about to break, and that she would be wise to draw out her money at once. She answered—

"Well, if it does break, it will break with its own; it has all been saved out of my profits—all I have it has given me."

Such a spirit as this in its members enabled the Pioneers to weather out the storm, and brought the lasting success which has made the "Co-op." a feature in the industrial life of Lancashire to-day.

LANCASHIRE BEYOND THE SEAS

WHEREVER they go the Lancashire folk take with them an undying love of their native county; and in the olden days, when they went forth to seek their fortunes in the new countries beyond the seas, they expressed that love by christening the towns and villages they built upon land wrested from the primeval forest, or the savage desert, with the names of their native places. Scattered through America, Canada, Australia and the Colonies are the namesakes of almost every town in Lancashire, with the single exception of Blackburn, which may perhaps be taken as an indication that Blackburn folk have always been so prosperous that they have never emigrated in sufficiently large numbers to have a decisive vote in the choosing of a name for a new town. Manchester and Liverpool seem to have been the favourites, there being thirty-seven of the former in the United States and three in Canada. One Manchester in South Carolina is a " decayed village," but the Manchester in New Hampshire is a great and prosperous city, its staple trade being the manufacture of linen and woollen goods. Liverpool has fifteen namesakes in the United States, and two in Canada, one of them being the port of entry for Nova Scotia; the river upon which it is situated is called the Mersey. Preston comes next with a total of eighteen, and is followed by Prescot with eleven, whilst a Pendleton may be found in eight of the American States. In Australia Liverpool has given its name to a mountain range, a plain, and a river.

Elihu Burritt, who was called "The Learned Blacksmith," and who combined a taste for history with his useful trade, has left a touching picture of how the love of their native county prevailed amongst the early Lancashire settlers in America.

" A few men," he says, " with their axes, and their wives and children on ox-sleds, would venture out ten or twenty miles into the woods, and set to work building a little hamlet of log houses. Before a child was born in it, this infant town must be christened and have a name. I have often wondered how they made up their minds what to call it. Perhaps there was a good deal of earnest talk among them on this point, perhaps some voting, too, with ballots made of pine or whitewood chips, with town names written on them with coal, and then dropped into the old weather-beaten round-topped hat of one of the company. Who knows how many fireside debates, adjourned from house to house, took place before this important point was settled? One of their number, his wife and eldest son, might have been born in Colchester, another father or mother in Chelmsford, a third in Ipswich, two or three in Reading, and four or five in Lancaster, in England. 'Which of these names shall we give to the town we are building?' That is the question. Can you not imagine the group gathered around the great fire in that snow-covered cabin of logs? I fancy I can see them now—old men with grey hair and thoughtful faces, and strong, hard-handed men in their prime, and young men, and boys and girls, and mothers with babies in their arms, all sitting there in the firelight, some silently dwelling upon sunny memories of the fatherland, while one of the village fathers with his right finger pressed against the centre of the palm of his left hand is trying to show why Lancaster would be a better name than

Reading. Why it should be so it would be difficult for us to say if we had to decide the question. But he knows, or thinks he knows, why. See how his nut-brown face lights up with animation as he grows earnest in the matter. There are other faces that gleam with the same light as he goes on with his argument. The fact is there are more of the company born in old England's Lancaster than in Reading, and that decides the question; and Lancaster is the name of the meek little hamlet of huts planted in the midst of the wild woods, and eyed suspiciously not only by the thieving bears and growling wolves, but also by the Red Indians, who do not like such doings on their hunting grounds."

THE LAST WOLF

IT was on Humphrey Head on the northern shore of Morecambe Bay that, according to tradition, the last wolf was killed in England, its slayer being one of the Harringtons of Wraysholme Tower. In those days a few wolves still remained in Cartmel Forest, and these he gradually exterminated. During one of these wolf-hunts, Harrington had ridden on ahead of his companions, and losing sight of them had ascended to the top of Humphrey Head, which was near his own home, to see if he could discover their whereabouts. "Whilst traversing the forest on a fleet horse," says the legend, "he heard shrieks, and on reaching the spot from whence they proceeded, he beheld a young and lovely female, crouching in a cleft of the rock, while an enormous wolf was endeavouring to reach her, barking loudly, and with fierce flashing eyes. The knight succeeded in transfixing the furious animal with his hunting spear; and then dismounting, he assisted to release the lady from her rough and precarious asylum. The result may be anticipated. Gratitude was quickly succeeded by love; for the knight was young, handsome, brave, graceful, eloquent and kind. The neighbouring chapel soon received their exchanged vows. They lived long and happily, and soon a numerous progeny crowned their union. This wolf, says the tradition, was the last ever seen in England; on which account the knight assumed his crest. The happy pair, when they passed away, were laid together in a niche in Cartmel Church.

Their effigies were cut in stone, with a figure of the wolf at their feet. A few Runic knots, to mark the descent of the knight, were carved on the walls; but, without a word of inscription, their monument remains to perplex the modern antiquary."

A LANCASHIRE POETESS

WHO that passes through the busy streets of Warrington, with their ceaseless sounds of labour and ever-growing commerce, with their iron-foundries, glass-works and cotton-factories belching forth smoke and steam, and their great tanneries saturating the air with the acrid, pungent smell of hides and leather, would dream that this prosperous manufacturing town was once a literary centre and enjoyed the title of the "Athens of the North of England"? But so it was. And no provincial town in the country holds so high a rank in our literary history as Warrington. The first newspaper in Lancashire was issued there.

The Warrington Academy, founded in 1757, was famous amongst the Dissenters of England under the direction of such well-known scholars as Dr. Aikin (one of the earliest Unitarians), Dr. Priestley, Dr. Taylor (author of the Hebrew Concordance which is still a standard work of reference for Bible students), Dr. Enfield, and the Rev. Gilbert Wakefield, and for twenty-nine years it exercised a deep influence upon the education of Dissenters of the period; and was "the centre of the liberal politics and the literary taste of the county of Lancashire."

Anna Lætitia Barbauld—to give her her married name, by which she was known in literature—was the daughter of Dr. Aikin, who was appointed to the divinity tutorship of Warrington Academy in 1758. At that time his daughter was fifteen years of age. She was extremely clever, and could read with ease before she was three years old, and when quite a child had a wide acquaintance with the best English authors. She learned French and Italian; and such was her thirst for knowledge that her father taught her Greek and Latin, but only with reluctance. The life at Warrington was singularly happy. The tutors of the Academy and their families formed a delightful society, in which Anna Lætitia Aikin's precocious talents received every encouragement. Several times during the week there were literary gatherings at each other's houses; the elder ladies being carried from door to door in sedan chairs, whilst the younger ones with their thin shoes kept from the rough stones by pattens and their dresses carefully covered with a calash, the hood of which protected their powdered hair, performed the journey on foot, attended either by their gallants or by a servant carrying a lantern.

At Mrs. Priestley's parties the writing of verses was the great amusement. Sometimes the verses were written on the spot upon a given subject; at others, as each guest entered the room he or she dropped a poem into Mrs. Priestley's work-basket. When the number was completed the poems were read aloud, and it is said that it was after hearing some verses of Dr. Priestley's at one of these parties, that Anna Lætitia was fired to write verses herself. Notwithstanding her intellectual gifts, which were unusual for a young woman at that period, she was very modest and unassuming, and but for her brother it is probable that her poems would never have had a wider public than the admiring friends in Mrs. Priestley's parlour. There were many suggestions from kind Warrington friends that she should publish her poems, but it was her brother who succeeded in breaking down her timidity. She was thirty when she published her first volume of poems, which was printed at Warrington. The book—which included " Corsica," "The Mouse's Petition," and "An Address to the Deity"—met with an instant success, and ran into four editions in one year. With her brother, she wrote a volume of essays in imitation of the great Dr. Johnson, who said : " Although the imitators of my style have not hit it, Miss Aikin has done it the best, for she has imitated the sentiments as well as the diction."

In the year following this literary success Miss Aikin married the Rev. Rochemont Barbauld, one of the students at the Academy. His father, a clergyman of the Church of England, for some unexplained reason sent him to the Warrington Academy, where, as could only be expected, he took the religious views of his tutors and became a Dissenting minister. After the marriage the Barbaulds settled in Suffolk, where they started a boys' school, and here it was that Mrs. Barbauld wrote her *Hymns in Prose for Children*, which is her best work, and which has passed through numberless editions in England as well as being translated into other European languages. Thanks to Mrs. Barbauld's energy the school was a brilliant success, the first Lord Denman and Sir William Gell, the archæologist, being amongst its pupils. The marriage, although it prevented Mrs. Barbauld continuing her literary work, was a happy one, the only cloud being the husband's tendency to insanity—a tendency which

ended in his death in a mad-house in London in 1808.

Her husband's death was a lasting sorrow to Mrs. Barbauld, but it left her free to pursue her work. After editing an edition in fifty volumes of the best English novelists Mrs. Barbauld prepared a selection of the best passages from English poets and prose writers for the use of young ladies. This was called *The Female Speaker*, and few books have ever been so widely read or so popular. There was not a ladies' school in the kingdom, there was scarcely a household in which there were young girls, in which this book was not to be found, and perhaps it was owing to this book more than to her poetry that Mrs. Barbauld's name was a household word in the time of our great-grandmothers.

In the same year in which *The Female Speaker* was published Mrs. Barbauld wrote the most important of her poems called " Eighteen Hundred and Eleven." At that time the bitter struggle with Napoleon, and the heavy burden of taxation laid upon the people, had cast a gloom over the whole country. Of this poem a great friend of Mrs. Barbauld wrote : " Dear Mrs. Barbauld this year incurred great reproach on writing a poem entitled ' Eighteen Hundred and Eleven.' It prophesies that on some future day a traveller from the Antipodes will, from a broken arch of Blackfriars Bridge, contemplate the ruin of St. Paul's. (It was from Mrs. Barbauld, therefore, that Macaulay drew his oft-quoted fancy of the New Zealander apostrophizing upon the ruins of London.) This was written more in sorrow than in anger, but there was a disheartening and even a gloomy tone which I, even with all my love for her, could not quite excuse."

Mrs. Barbauld survived her husband seventeen years, passing a tranquil existence, happy in the companionship of her brother and in the society of the literary lions of her time, such as Mrs. Montagu, Hannah More, Maria Edgeworth, Howard the philanthropist, Sir Walter Scott, Wordsworth, Samuel Rogers and Joanna Baillie. Her epitaph in Stoke Newington says that : " She was endowed by the Giver of all good with wit, genius, poetic talent, and a vigorous understanding."

In this day and generation Mrs. Barbauld's poems would probably not run into four editions in one year; but in a more leisurely age our great-grandparents had time to enjoy what to us now appears somewhat pompous and long-winded. Mrs. Barbauld had wit, imagination and wide culture; but there is little doubt that it was the circumstances under which she spent the fifteen years of her life at Warrington before her marriage that stimulated talents which, but for the encouragement and sympathy of that kindly and intellectual circle, might have lain dormant.

NOTCHEL CRYING

THIS was a particularly unpleasant custom by which husbands made public announcement through the bellman that they would no longer be responsible for debts contracted by their wives. So late as 1859 the custom was observed at Accrington. In March of that year the public bellman went round the town announcing that a certain man from that day forward would not be answerable or accountable for any debts which his wife might contract. On the afternoon of the same day the inhabitants of Accrington heard the other side of the story, the bellman being employed by the wife to announce that, as she was up to that day straight with her husband, she would not be answerable for any debts he might contract. She added that she had only been allowed five shillings a week by her husband to find herself and him in food and lodging, also that he was not over-faithful, and that if he had brought home the money he had given to other women they could have lived in comfort. Great crowds followed the bellman through the streets, and owing to the scandal the practice happily fell into disuse. In some places small placards were pasted up on the walls of the town or village in which the parties lived. It is related that a wife whose name was publicly placarded replied with a counter announcement stating that as her husband had lived for years upon her earnings she declined to keep him any longer, and bade the tradesmen beware. In both these cases the ladies not only had the last word, but seem to have had the best of the argument.

MAB'S CROSS

A STORY OF WIGAN

"Then speech and thought and nature fail'd
a little,
And he lay tranced; but when he rose and
passed
Back towards his solitary home again,
All down the long and narrow street ne
went
Beating it in upon his weary brain,
As tho' it were the burden of a song,
'Not to tell her, never to let her know.'"

THUS did Tennyson's Enoch Arden
solve the tragedy that awaited his
return to England after being ship-
wrecked upon a desert island, and given up
by his family as dead. He found his wife
married to another:

"His wife his wife no more, and saw the
babe
Hers, yet not his, upon the father's knee."

Creeping away in the night, his one
thought, his one determination was that
he would keep the secret of his return,
"Not to tell her, never to let her know."
A similar tragedy befell Sir William
Bradshaigh, or Bradshaw, of Haigh Hall
near Wigan, in the reign of the second
Edward, but he met the situation in a
very different spirit.

Sir William, who was a knight of
renown, had married Mabel, the daughter
of Hugh Norris, of Haigh and Blackrod.
It was a love match, and some of the old
chronicles tell a romantic story of its
beginning. Sir William one day espied
a peasant girl drawing water from a well.
Struck by her beauty and her grace, he
reined in his horse and asked her for a

drink. This she gave him with a charming courtesy. Her delicate beauty and the gentleness of her bearing, marked her as no ordinary peasant girl, and Sir William fell over head and ears in love. The chroniclers relate, that he speedily discovered the girl was not the child of her supposed parents, and that further inquiries proved her to be the daughter of the wealthy Hugh Norris, from whose house she had been kidnapped when little more than an infant. The restoration of his long-lost daughter to her father, followed by her speedy marriage to Sir William, was only the natural conclusion of this romantic story, but unfortunately history has left no record upon which it could be based, and it appears to have been evolved out of some old legend, or else in the imagination of the chronicler. The true history of Sir William Bradshaigh and his wife is sufficiently romantic without the addition of kidnapping and restoration.

An entry in the genealogical tree of the Bradshaighs states that Sir William was a "great traveller and a souldger," and after his marriage was away for ten years in the "Holy Wars," meaning the Crusades, those expeditions to Palestine for the recovery of Jerusalem from the hands of the infidels, which between 1095 and 1270—the date of the first and last Crusades—drained Europe of millions of pounds' worth of treasure, and are estimated to have caused the death of two hundred millions of human beings. As Sir William was born about 1280, the war which kept him away for ten years from his wife and his home could not have been a Crusade, and with every probability it is supposed that the reference is to the disastrous war with Scotland in Edward II.'s reign, in which the English army was utterly defeated at the famous Battle of Bannockburn by Robert Bruce.

" In the moment of failure, the sight of a body of camp-followers whom they mistook for reinforcements to the enemy, spread panic through the English host. It broke into a headlong rout. Its thousands of brilliant horsemen were soon floundering in pits which had guarded the level ground to Bruce's left, or riding in wild haste for the border. Few, however, were fortunate enough to reach it. Edward himself, with a body of five hundred knights, succeeded in escaping to Dunbar and the sea. But the flower of his knighthood fell into the hands of the victors, whilst the Irishry and the footmen were ruthlessly cut down by the country folk as they fled. For centuries after, the rich plunder of the English camp left its traces on the treasure and vestment rolls of castle and abbey throughout the Lowlands." Amongst the English knights who were taken prisoner in their wild flight to the border is supposed to have been Sir William Bradshaigh, and he, with his companions in misfortune, was held in close captivity. It is known that many of the English knights taken at Bannockburn were kept in durance in Scotland for ten years, which would bring Sir William's return to Haigh Hall to 1324, the date assigned by Roby.

News travelled slowly in those days, and it was many weeks before word of the defeat at Bannockburn reached Lady Mabel. With it came a report that her husband was killed. Sir William sent no sign or message, doubtless because of his close captivity, and his wife had no alternative but to believe that he was dead. In such troublous times a widow possessed of so goodly a heritage as Lady Mabel was in a precarious position. The whole of Lancashire, at the bidding of Thomas, Earl of Lancaster, the cousin of Edward II., was seething with rebellion against that monarch. By reason of his royal birth, and his possession of the four earldoms of Lincoln, Leicester, Derby and Lancaster, Earl Thomas was the most powerful subject in the realm, and headed the barons in their struggle against the misgovernment of the favourite-ridden King. At one moment his power was more supreme than that of Edward himself. Lancashire was his absolute possession, and according to the feudal laws then in force, all the nobles and gentry who held land in the county were compelled to obey his summons to war. Each lord and knight held his estate on the condition that he should bring a certain number of men into the field when summoned to war by his overlord; the lords and knights granted farms and lands on their estates to yeomen on the same military tenure. Thus in the event of war, the king summoned the great nobles to bring the number of knights, esquires, and soldiers for which they were responsible to his standard, the great nobles called upon the lords, knights and esquires, who in their turn called upon the lesser gentry and yeomen.

Sir William Bradshaigh was responsible for fifty men. But whilst this tenure of land on a basis of military service provided the king with an army without the expense of its maintenance in times of peace, it likewise placed unlimited power in the hands of the great nobles, a power which, as in the case of Thomas, Earl of Lancaster, they frequently used against the monarch himself.

The revolt in Lancashire against Edward II. was taken advantage of by a Welsh knight, to whom Roby gives the name of Sir Osmund Nevill, to force Lady Mabel to marry him. As time passed and Sir William did not return and made no sign, the Welsh knight offered marriage to Lady Mabel, an offer she refused. Whereupon the knight informed her that in return for his great services, Thomas, Earl of Lancaster, had given him a grant of all the lands possessed by Sir William, and that unless she married him she must leave Haigh forthwith. The legend runs that the knight swore falsely when he said that Sir William's lands had been granted to him, but there is no doubt that he had lent the Earl assistance, and such an unjust grant of lands was by no means uncommon. Against such an authority as that of Thomas, Earl of Lancaster, the only appeal was to the king, but Edward the Second had by this time become a king in name only, and, in Lancashire especially, his writ no longer ran. Lady Mabel therefore had no appeal, and to save her children and herself from ruin and beggary was forced to marry the Welsh knight.

At the end of ten years, one day as Lady Mabel was giving her doles of bread and meat to the poor at Haigh Hall, she saw amongst the crowd of peasants and beggars a man in the dress of a palmer—the habit worn by all those who had made a pilgrimage to Jerusalem. When he approached to take his dole the palmer threw back his hood, and in his worn and emaciated features Lady Mabel recognized those of her long-lost husband, Sir William Bradshaigh. It was a painful moment. Lady Mabel burst into tears, upon which the Welsh knight fell upon her and beat her.

It is strange that Sir William did not fall upon the Welsh knight and beat him also for this treatment of his wife, but, in the record in the genealogical tree of the Bradshaigh family it merely states, "Sir William returning from the wars, came in a palmer's habit amongst the poor to Haghe, who, when she saw, and congetringe (conjecturing) that he favoured her former husband, wept, for which the knight chastised her, at which Sir William went to make him selfe known to his tenants—" a bald account of a most dramatic moment. Sir William was doubtless powerless to avenge this brutality to his wife, the Welsh knight being protected by his bowmen, and therefore sallying forth he invoked the assistance of his tenants. Returning to Haigh at the head of a good number of men, who were rejoiced at the return of their old master, however, were not at an end. As a punishment for slaying the Welsh knight, Sir William was outlawed for a year and a day, and Lady Mabel was commanded by her confessor to go barefoot and barelegged once a week, as long as she lived, from Haigh Hall to a cross near Wigan, as a penance for her unwitting bigamy. This weekly pilgrimage gave its name to the cross—the remains of which still stand at the top of Standishgate at the

HAIGH HALL

he found that the Welsh knight had fled. Arming himself and accompanied by a few attendants he set off in hot pursuit. " Such was the wrong Sir William had suffered," says Roby, "that his yet untamed spirit deemed it an offence too foul to be expiated by aught but the blood of his merciless foe." He overtook the Welsh knight at Newton Park, and challenging him to single combat, slew him after a fierce encounter.

The troubles of the unfortunate pair, entrance of Wigan Lane—Mab's Cross. Nothing is now left except the base of a pillar and a piece of a four-sided shaft, and these are much worn away.

After his outlawry was ended Sir William returned to Haigh, and he and Lady Mabel "lived happily ever after." They were buried in the Bradshaigh Chapel of Wigan Church, the chantry of which was built by Lady Mabel after Sir William's death in 1338, where their tomb may still be seen, with their sculptured effigies upon it, lying side by side. Sir William is clad in a coat of mail, with his shield upon his shoulder, his sword partially drawn out of its scabbard; Lady Mabel is in a long robe, with her hands joined in prayer.

A gallery at Haigh Hall, which was called " Mab's Gallery," was reputed to be haunted by Lady Mabel's ghost: this gallery was pulled down many years ago, and now all that remains to recall the story of the tragic separation and happy re-union of Sir William and his wife are the fragments of stone—most carefully preserved—in Standishgate, which witnessed her weekly penance, and their monument in the Bradshaigh Chapel in Wigan Church.

OLD MAY=DAY CUSTOMS IN THE FYLDE

THE old May-Day revels were a survival of a festival held by the Romans in honour of Flora, the goddess of spring, and in rejoicing that the rigours of the winter were over. They continued in Lancashire during fourteen centuries after the Roman occupation of that county, and nowhere were they celebrated with greater zest than in the Fylde. The great event of the day was an imposing piece of pageantry called " Bringing in May." A king and queen wearing wreaths of flowers, and followed by the youth and maidens of the village dressed as followers or mummers, bearing garlands and attended by a band of music, brought in " the May," a bough of hawthorn covered with blossom, as a sign of the coming of summer. As the procession passed through the town or village, the streets were strewn with flowers, the mummers sang and danced, receiving as their reward sweetmeats and ale and wine from the housewives. After the procession there were sports, races and wrestling bouts for the young men, and games for the young women, followed by dances round the Maypole until darkness fell. It was a day of hilarity, merrymaking and good-humour. Poulton-in-the-Fylde was especially noted for the excellence of its pageant of " Bringing in May," and for the care with which it was prepared.

It is difficult in these days of quick communication between even remote villages and the large towns to imagine the dreariness of a winter in country districts in the olden times. In the more remote parts villages and hamlets were cut off from the rest of the world for weeks together by the badly-made roads becoming impassable. Candles, made of rushes dipped in sheep's fat, were the only means of light in the cottages; there were no newspapers; there were no interests outside the circle of the home and village. The coming of spring, therefore, had a significance for our country forefathers which it does not possess for us, who are practically independent of distance and weather, since it meant not only a great material change in their year of toil, but a renewal of friendly and family ties which had ceased throughout the winter. Friends and relatives from distant hamlets, or from scattered dwellings, flocked into the village on May-Day to take part in the merry-making, the younger folk dancing upon the green whilst their elders sat round and gossiped upon all the events of the long winter. May-Day was not only a day of rejoicing; it was also a day of re-union.

DRESS IN OLD LANCASHIRE

THERE are some interesting particulars of the clothes worn by various classes in Lancashire in the reigns of Queen Elizabeth and James I. scattered amongst the records left by old writers. Thus Randle Holme, one of the county collectors of Lancashire, says that about the fortieth year of the reign of Elizabeth (1598), the old fashions, which were in use at the beginning of her reign, were again revived, but with the addition of double ruffs. "The men likewise, besides the double use of the cloak, had a certain kind of loose-hanging garment, called a *mandeville*, much like to our old jackets or jumpers but without sleeves, and having holes to put the arms through ; yet some were made with sleeves, but for no other use than to hang on the back." One of the fashions for men of quality in the early part of the reign of Elizabeth was most absurd and ridiculous : this was the wearing of great breeches stuffed with rags and horsehair to an enormous size. The coat worn with these puffed-out breeches fitted as tightly to the figure as a pair of stays, and in consequence was called the peascod doublet.

These breeches grew so extravagant in size, that Parliament was obliged to fix a regulation measure beyond which they were not to go. They were called " slops," and Bulver, in his pedigree of the " English Gallant," speaks of a man whom the judges accused of wearing breeches contrary to law, when he, for his excuse, drew out of his " slops " the contents—" as, first, a pair of sheets, two tablecloths, two napkins, four shirts, a brush, a glass, a comb, with nightcaps," and other useful articles. But Members of Parliament, despite their own legislation, appear to have been great offenders, for in the Harleian Manuscripts it is recorded that during the reign of Elizabeth a scaffold was erected round the inside of the House of Commons " for those members to sit in who used the wearing of great breeches stuffed with hair or bulging out like woolsacks." Nor were the women less grotesque. Following the example of the men in destroying all outline of the figure, they wore enormous hoops or farthingales and grotesquely puffed-out sleeves.

The ravings of a Lancashire lady, who was supposed to be possessed by a devil, afford a most graphic description of the dress of a gentlewoman of this time : " I will have a fine smock of silk, with a silk petticoat garded a foot high ; it shall be laid with good lace ; it shall have a French body, not of whalebone, for that is not stiff enough, but of horn, for that will hold it out. It shall come low before, to keep in my belly. I will have a French farthingale ; I will have it low before and high behind, and broad on either side that I may lay my arms upon it. My gown shall be black wrought velvet ; I will have my sleeves set out with wire, for sticks will break and are not stiff enough. I will have my perewincke [wig] so fine ; I will have my cap of black velvet with a feather in it with flowers of gold, and my hair shall be set with pearls. I will have a busk of whalebone ; it shall be tied with two silk points ; and I will have a drawn wrought stomacher embossed with gold and a girdle of gold. I will have my hose of orange colour ; this is in request ; and my cork shoes of red Spanish leather. I will have a scarf of red silk, with a gold lace about the edge. I will have a fan with a silver steel and a glass set in it. Bring me a pair of gloves of the finest leather that may be, with two gold laces about the thumb, and a fringe on the top with flowers and red silk underneath, that I may draw them through a gold ring, or else I will have none of them."

Here we have a complete picture of an Elizabethan lady drawn by a contemporary; and in these lines the dress of the spinning or factory girls—

" And in a chamber close beside
Two hundred maidens did abide,
In petticoats of flannel red,
And milk-white kerchers on their head ;
Their smock sleeves like to winter's snow,
That on the western mountains flow ;
And each sleeve with a silken band
Was fairly tièd at the hand.
Which pretty maids did never lin
But in that place all day did spin."

The sumptuary laws were still in vogue, and a person's rank and condition in life could immediately be determined by his dress. Thus, says Strutt in his *Ancient Manners and Customs of the English:* " The young gentleman was distinguished by his gay suit and apparel, his cloak and rapier ; the merchant's dress at that time was a plain, grave suit of clothes, with a black cloak ; and the rustic, when in his Sunday attire, had a leathern doublet with long points, and a pair of breeches primed up like pudding-bags, with yellow stockings, and his hat turned up with a silver clasp on the lee side."

These fashions were not confined to any particular district, they extended to the whole kingdom.

Speaking more particularly of Lancashire, another historian, John de Brentford, says : " The manners and customs of the inhabitants of Lancashire are similar to those of the neighbouring counties, except that the people eat with two-pronged forks. The men are masculine, and in general well-made ; they ride and hunt the same as in the most southern parts, but not with that grace, owing to the whip being carried in the left hand. The women are most handsome ; their eyes brown, black, hazel, blue or grey (one wonders what other colours they could have been) ; their noses, if not inclined to the aquiline, are mostly of the Grecian form, which gives a most beautiful archness to the countenance, such indeed as is not easy to be described. Their fascinating manners have long procured them the name of Lancashire witches."

Another chronicler, Leland, says : " The dress of the men chiefly consists of woollen garments, while the women wear those of silk, linen, or stuff. Their usual colours are green, blue, black, and sometimes brown. The military are dressed in red, which is vulgarly called scarlet."

The County Collector, Randle Holme, made a curious mistake when he wrote that hats were not generally worn in Lancashire until the reign of Charles II. They were in as general use there as in the south of England, and, in the south-east of the county, hat-manufacture existed two hundred years before the time of Charles II.—in the reign of Henry VI. That the industry was carried on prior to the reign of the unfortunate Lancastrian king is shown by a petition being presented to Parliament in his time by the Lancashire hatters, complaining of the introduction of machinery into their business, and representing that " hats, caps, etc., were wont to be fulled by manual labour ; but that of late fulling-mills had been introduced to effect this operation, to the prejudice of the workmen and the deterioration of the fabric." Even in the fifteenth century manufacturers had their grievances.

Silk stockings were unknown in England, or Lancashire, before the year 1560. On New Year's Day of that year Queen Elizabeth's silk-woman, Mrs. Montague, presented Her Majesty with the first pair that had come to the country. The Queen was so delighted with the difference between their ease and lightness and the clumsiness of the cloth stockings which had hitherto been worn by people of the highest birth, that she skipped and danced round her tiring-chamber until her beautiful silk stockings were in holes.

Ever afterwards the Queen wore silken hose, an example that was speedily imitated by her Court and all the people of quality throughout the country.

A CHARM AGAINST WITCHCRAFT

WHEN an old barn was pulled down at Healey in 1876, a small wooden box was found beneath one of the timbers of the roof. In the box was an old charm against witchcraft, written in cipher. At the top left-hand corner is a magic square dedicated to the sun, in which numbers are expressed by letters formed from the Greek alphabet. Any of the six numbers if added in a straight line, either upwards or across, make the number 111, the total forming the "number of the beast," 666 —taken from Revelation—" Let him that hath understanding count the number of the beast: for it is the number of a man, and his number is Six hundred threescore and six."

Next to the square are the symbols of the sun and moon, and under them the word "Machen," which signifies strife or contention. Below this is a Jerusalem cross and the sign of Jupiter with the word "Michael" beneath. No meaning can be found for the symbol in the centre; above it is the word "Intelligence." The remaining figure is the seal of the sun. Of the writing below, the first two lines are in Greek and have no meaning. The rest is in Latin and runs as follows, " I love God, the Lord God, the Hour, Christ, let it be done, let it be done, let it be done as it is said in the XVII chapter of St. Matthew and at the twentieth verse. By faith ye may remove mountains. Let it be according to your faith. If there is or shall. be, however, a bewitcher or a demon dwelling in, or in the habit of disturbing this person, this place, or this thing, I exorcise it to depart without any disturbance, trouble or the least tumult, in the name of the Father, and of the Son, and of the Holy Ghost." Then comes the Lord's Prayer.

On the back of the charm is written " Agla en Tetragrammaton." The four letters of " Agla " are the initial letters of a cabalistic word which means " Thou O Lord, art mighty for ever," whilst " Tetragrammaton " is the Hebrew for Jehovah.

These charms were in common use. Another charm used in certain parts of Lancashire was found under a brass plate on a tombstone, and a third was discovered in the roof of a barn near Clitheroe. Mr. Fishwick is of opinion that none of these exorcisms date back further than the earlier part of the eighteenth century, which shows how long the belief in witchcraft lingered in Lancashire.

ROCHDALE GRAMMAR SCHOOL

THE old grammar school at Rochdale was in existence for nearly three hundred years, receiving its first endowment from Matthew Parker, Archbishop of Canterbury, in 1565. When Edward VI. ascended the throne, one of his first acts was to assign the rectorial rights and revenues of Rochdale to the Archbishopric of Canterbury. The question of education was at that time strong in the minds of all thinking men, and schools were being established all over the country. Archbishop Parker was one of the foremost educationists of his day, and while still a young man had built and endowed a grammar school at Stoke in Suffolk. When he was appointed to the see of Canterbury in 1559, he made a strict inquiry as to the number of schools established amongst the widespread possessions of the Primacy, and finding Rochdale had no school he promised to endow a grammar school if the inhabitants would raise sufficient money amongst themselves to build it. This was in 1561.

In the following year the Vicar of Rochdale led the way by giving a piece of the glebe land, just outside the churchyard, for the site. His conveyance of the land, however, required the confirmation of the Archbishop, and this was not received until June 20, 1565. Owing, most probably, to the necessary funds not being subscribed, the building was not completed, and the Archbishop seems to have withheld his confirmation and endowment until, in May 1565, he heard from Francis and Charles Holt, and Charles Radcliffe of Todmorden Hall, that the building was finished. In the previous year, however, Archbishop Parker had arranged with the Masters and Fellows of Corpus Christi College, Cambridge, and the Vicar and churchwardens of Rochdale, for a perpetual stipend for a master and under-master, the first to be of fifteen pounds a year, the second two pounds a year, which were to be paid by the person who held the lease of the rectory. Sir John Byron held the lease, and the seventeen pounds a year was only obtained from him after a long lawsuit brought against him by the Archbishop.

The master was to be appointed by the Archbishop of Canterbury, and if the see was vacant, or an appointment was not made within three months of a vacancy occurring, the Master of Corpus Christi College was to appoint, but if neither the Archbishop nor the Master filled up the vacancy then the appointment was to be made by the Vicar of Rochdale. The foundation deed sets forth that the school was established by the Archbishop " for his good will to the inhabitants, that their youth might be brought up in the learning of true piety and the Latin tongue." The boys were to be taught free of charge if there were not more than one hundred and fifty, or less than fifty scholars daily.

When Sir John Byron received a renewal of the lease of the rectory in 1590, one of the conditions stipulated that he should pay the seventeen pounds a year to the two masters, but this was not done, and later the amount was charged upon the tithes.

In the course of time the school received various endowments, but none of any large amount. Jeremy Hargreaves, for example, left twenty pounds in 1696, the interest of which was to teach writing, and James Holt of Castleton Hall in 1712 left a hundred pounds for the then master on condition that he educated poor boys, not exceeding six in number, free of charge, their parents being settled inhabitants in the town. Girls as well as

ROCHDALE GRAMMAR SCHOOL IN 1840

boys were admitted to the school, but in 1826 there were only sixteen scholars, the master declining to take any more, as, without the services of an usher, he said he could not attend to a larger number. This same master, who was the Rev. William Hodgson, and occupied the post for nearly forty years, considered he was bound to teach boys who only wanted to learn " true piety and the Latin tongue " for nothing, but for the boys required to be instructed in other subjects, and for anything outside the expression of the founder, Mr. Hodgson contended he had a right to charge a fee.

The school, which was built of rough stone and covered with flag slates, was in use until 1846, when it was pulled down. It was only sixty feet long, by twenty feet in width. At one end were rooms to which access was gained by an outside stair. These, originally, had been the master's house, but latterly they were let to the person who cleaned the school.

The first head master was Robert Radcliffe, son of Charles Radcliffe of Todmorden Hall, and many of his successors were likewise the sons of neighbouring gentry.

HAIGH HALL

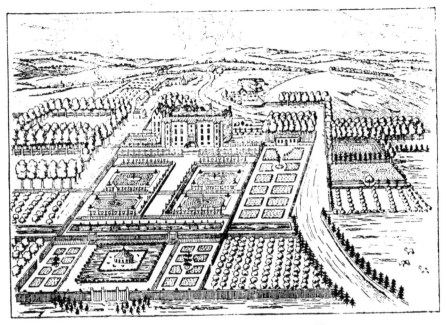

HAIGH HALL EARLY IN THE EIGHTEENTH CENTURY

THE Old Haigh Hall which stood upon the site of the stately mansion, now the residence of the Earl of Crawford, was the scene of the tragic home-coming of Sir William Bradshaw after his imprisonment in Scotland, when he found his wife, the Lady Mabel, married to a Welsh knight, believing Sir William to be dead.[1] For nearly five hundred and fifty years Haigh Hall remained in the Bradshaw family, and passed from them, as it came, through a woman.

Lady Mabel Bradshaw was a Norreys and her father's heiress, bringing with her, besides Haigh, the manors of Blackrod and Westley upon her marriage to Sir William Bradshaw. This was in the reign of Edward II. Over two hundred years later Sir William Norris, a descendant of Lady Mabel's family, gave a

[1] See "Mab's Cross."

curious piece of information in a declaration which has been preserved in the Harleian Manuscripts, and of which an old copy is treasured at Marple Hall. The document is dated 1563. After telling the story of Lady Mabel's marriage with the Welsh knight and his death at Sir William's hands, he adds, "But after this, Dame Mabel died without issue of her body to inherit her lands, and thinking that her husband Bradshaw would never have child gave by entitle to her husband Bradshaw her Manor of Haw, with all its appurtenances to him and to the heirs male of his body lawfully begotten—and for default of such issue of his body lawfully begotten then the said Manor of Haw and its appurtenances to her cousin Alan Norris of Spike and his heirs for ever. And for the fervent love and goodwill which she bare toward her said husband Bradshaw, of whom she

99

thought there would come none issue, and for the gentleness she found to William Bradshaw brother to her said husband, who was then full of children, she gave to the said William Bradshaw her brother-in-law, all the rest of her lands, that was the Manor of Blackrod and Westley, to the said William Bradshaw and his heirs for ever."

It is generally believed that a son of the devoted Lady Mabel and Sir William succeeded them at Haigh, but it was Sir William's brother John, miscalled William in Sir John Norris's declaration, to whom the whole of Lady Mabel's possessions passed—Haigh Hall by virtue of his heirship to his brother to whom she had given it, and the two manors of Blackrod and Westley by her own legacy. Thus this branch of the Bradshaw family became established at Haigh, and here they continued until 1780, one of the most important of the Lancashire country gentry. In the reign of Charles II. the then owner of Haigh, Roger Bradshaw, was created a baronet. Three Sir Rogers suceeded him, but the fourth died without male issue. His only daughter, Elizabeth, was dead, as also was her daughter, like-wise named Elizabeth, who had married Charles Dalrymple of Berwick, therefore Haigh and the Bradshaw property devolved upon his great-granddaughter, a third Elizabeth.

The Bradshaws could have echoed King William IV.'s famous saying, " My crown came from a lass " (meaning the Electress Sophia of Hanover), " it will go to a lass," for with the marriage in 1780 of Elizabeth Bradshaigh Dalrymple to her cousin, Alexander Lindsay, sixth Earl of Balcarres, Haigh Hall and its estates passed into that family. In 1808 the Earl of Balcarres, who had been Governor of Jamaica, became the twenty-third Earl of Crawford, and thenceforward was known by the older title. He died in 1825, his heiress-wife having predeceased him by nine years. Their son, the seventh Earl of Balcarres and twenty-fourth Earl of Crawford, was created Baron Wigan of Haigh Hall, a peerage which gave him the right to sit in the House of Lords. His grandson, the twenty-sixth Earl of Crawford, now reigns at Haigh Hall, and the title of Balcarres is borne by his eldest son, who has done the country signal service by protecting her ancient buildings from destruction.

Haigh Hall stands upon a high hill—from its windows thirteen counties may be seen, as well as the Irish Sea and the Isle of Man. Above the doorway are the arms of the Bradshaw family quartered with those of the Earls of Derby, thus recording the marriage of a Bradshaw to a Stanley.

For nearly three hundred years the cannel coal at Haigh was regarded as one of the curiosities of nature, and is mentioned in more than one of the old chronicles. In 1676, Francis North, Lord Guildford, was in Lancaster on circuit, and his son, Roger North, has left this interesting account of their visit to Haigh :—

" In the return homewards from Lancaster his Lordship took all the advantage he could of seeing great Towns and places of note. He staid some days with Sir Roger Bradshaw, whose lordship is famous for yielding the canal (or candle) coal. It is so term'd, I guess, because the manufacturers in that country use no candle, but work by the light of the coalfire. The property of it is to burn and flame till it is all consumed, without leaving any cinder. It is lighted by a candle like amber, and the grate stands not against the back of a large chimney, as common coal grates, but in the middle, where ballads are pasted round, and the folk sit about it, working or merry-making. His Lordship saw the pits, where vast piles of that coal were raised; and it is pity the place wants water-carriage, else London would be, in the better part, served by it. But the greatest wonder his Lordship saw was that which they call the Burning Well. The manner of it is this. First, in some place, where they know the sulphurous vapour perspires (often in a ditch) they dig up a turf, and clap it down in its place again; and then they are ready for projection. When the Shew Company are come, a man takes up the turf, and after a little puffing of a brown paper match gives fire, and instantly the hole is filled with a blue, spirituous flame like brandy. It seem'd to waste, and I believe would not have burnt in that manner long; but while it was burning they put water in the hole, and the flame continued upon the water as if it had been spirits. And some people said they used to boil eggs there. That which seem'd most strange was that the vapour should come through the water and burn, and no bubbling of the water appear. It seems to infer that the vapour permeates the body of the water, as water through sands."

The Burning Well, which so greatly excited Lord Guildford's wonder, was about a mile from Hindley Hall, and has long since disappeared. There are many accounts of it in the "Transactions" of learned societies, detailing various experiments, but they all describe practically the same phenomena. Mr. Stirling wrote of the well being in one place only, and that the water boiled and rose up like water in a pot upon a fire, and although he put his hand into it he felt no warmth. The flame rose up in a cone-like form with a circular base, about the circumference of the brim of a man's hat. The "Burning Well" was still in existence in 1835, when it was described thus: "The gas ascends out of a small hole through a heap of clay, near a little rill, and takes fire on the application of the flame of a candle, the carbonated (carburetted) hydrogen—a black, oily liquid—boiling up and bubbling continually at the bottom, while the flame ascends about half a yard high."

"RIDING THE STANG"

This custom is still observed in some of the out-of-the-way Lancashire villages when, reversing the usual procedure, a wife has beaten her husband. The neighbours put a small boy on a "stang" or pole, and carry him through the streets in the neighbourhood where the beating has taken place. Every now and again the procession stops and the boy recites this doggerel, to an accompaniment of pans and kettles struck by the crowd—

"Ting, tong to the sign o' the pan!
She has beat her good man.

It was neither for boiled nor roast,
But she up with her fist an'
Knocked down mesther post!"

It was notorious in one town that a six-foot collier, sturdy and strong in proportion to his height, was constantly thrashed by his wife, who was a diminutive person with the temper of a spitfire. One day a friend reproached him saying he wondered he allowed her to beat him, and that it was making quite a scandal. "Aw don't care," replied the good-natured giant, "it pleases her, an' it don't hurt me!"

OLD LANCASHIRE CUSTOMS AND GAMES

SOME fifty or sixty years ago the custom of Souling was still prevalent in Lancashire on the eve of All Souls' Day. The custom dated to the times before the Reformation, since in the Roman Catholic Church it is the custom to pray for the souls of the dead on All Souls' Day, or All Hallows, as it was called in England. As Mr. Fletcher Moss says, "It is difficult to see the precise connection between the soul mass cake, as it was formerly termed, and the mass for the souls, but the poorer people may have virtually said to their richer neighbours, 'Give us cakes that we may feast to-day and fast to-morrow, and pray for the repose of the souls of your forefathers and ours.'"

The "Soulers," or "Sowlers," as they came to be called, went round the village, stopping at all the houses of the well-to-do and singing—

"A soul cake, a soul cake,
I prithee, good missus, a soul cake,
One for Peter, two for Paul,
And three for Him who made us all.
A soul cake, a soul cake."

The origin of the custom was of course entirely unknown to the more modern "soulers." It served as an opportunity for free feasting. If the "soul" cakes were not forthcoming, they had another verse which ran—

"An apple, or pear, or cherry,
Or aught as 'll mak' us all merry;
Up wi' th' kettles an' down wi' th' pon,
Gi' us good ale an' we'll be gone."

If cakes and apples or pears were not produced the "soulers" lowered their demands—

"If you ha' ner a penny a hawpenny 'll do;
Gi' us a cake or an apple or two."

In a letter to a Manchester newspaper in 1895, a correspondent says that over fifty years ago, "I went soul-caking myself in a little hamlet on the Lancashire side of the Mersey not far from Warrington. We were entirely the children of the labourers and our houses of call were those of the farmers who employed our parents." He had no recollection of the verses quoted above being used, the only request being, "Pray, dame, a soul cake." "They were a kind of soft cake like a pancake," he says, "and probably caused some confusion in our minds as to whether we had obtained a 'soul cake,' or a 'sole cake,' such was its leathery feel." He also went "pace-egging" at Easter, as "peace-egging" was called, and then the request was the same, "Pray, dame, a pace egg." But if the Easter egg were not forthcoming the housewife was greeted with this threat—

"Pray, dame, a pace egg! If yo'll give us none,
Yo'r cock will stand a-straddle leg, an' yo'r hens will lay a stone."

There was also an old game played by girls and boys. A ring was formed, a boy being placed in the centre. The others then moved round, singing—

"All go round and choose your own,
And choose my fairest daughter."

When the choice had been made, the couple were greeted with—

"My daughter's got married and tied to a peg,
And tied to a peg.
My daughter's got married and tied to a peg,
She's married a man with a wooden leg."

Another game was played by boys only. A circle was formed, the biggest boy being chosen as leader. Each lad would then say one of the following words, the leader starting with the word "One," the next saying "hammer," and so on—

"One hammer on a block,
My man, John,
Riddle the can,
Blow, bellows, blow,
Fire away, lads,
For an hour or so."

There are twenty-two words, and no matter how many or how few took part in the game, the boy who had to say the last word " so," was fallen upon and thumped by the others until the leader gave the order to stop.

The game of " Three Dukes a-riding " has had a longer life than others, and so late as 1893 was played in Heaton Norris and the neighbourhood. It was also known as " Ransom, tansom, titty-fy-day." In other parts it has completely disappeared, but formerly it was not only played by children but by young men and women at the wakes and fairs. It was a " choosing partners " game ; the boys formed in one line, and the girls in another, the two lines advancing and retiring alternately, and singing the following lines :—

Boys (advancing).
  " Here comes a Duke a-riding
     To my ransom, tansom, titty-fy-day.
  „ *(retiring).*
  Here comes a Duke a-riding
     To my ransom, tansom, titty-fy-day.
Girls (advancing).
  Pray, what is your will, sir ?
     To my ransom, tansom, titty-fy-day.
  „ *(retiring).*
  Pray, what is your will, sir ?
     To my ransom, tansom, titty-fy-day."

Each of the following lines was repeated twice as the two sides advanced and retired, with the " To my ransom, etc." added.

Boys. " My will is for to marry.
Girls. Our house is lined with silver.
Boys. My house is lined with gold.
Girls. Pray take one of my daughters.
Boys. They're all too black and blowsy.
Girls (indignantly). They're good enough for you, sir.
Boys. They're all as stiff as pokers.
Girls. They can bend as well as you, sir.
Boys. The fairest one that I can see
    To my ransom, tansom, titty-fy-day,
  Is pretty ——. Come to me.
    To my ransom, tansom tay."

The girl mentioned by name would then go over to the boys, and the game would begin all over again, but this time it would be " Here come two Dukes a-riding," and so on until all the girls had been chosen. When all the girls had been chosen and only one remained—a distinctly galling position—she had the consolation of being able to choose any boy she pleased. But this would be a case of Hobson's choice if the boys and girls were equal in number.

The words were sung to a pretty air, and in some places the continual advancing and retiring were varied by dancing. There were several variants of the game, one of which was that a boy alone represented the duke a-riding, and having chosen his partner from a line of boys and girls, the girl then made her choice, and so alternately until there was only one boy or girl left to be chosen.

Another version of the game, the words of which were sung to the same air, is particularly interesting as it points to its origin—the marriage of Queen Mary Tudor with Philip of Spain, a union that was profoundly unpopular throughout the whole country. There were the same advancings and retirings to these words :—

" There come three Spaniards out of Spain,
  Who come to court your daughter Jane."

" My daughter Jane she is too young,
  She has not learnt your Spanish tongue."

" Whether she be young or whether she be old,
  It is for her beauty, she must be sold ;
  So fare you well, my lady gay,
  We'll call again another day."

" Turn back, turn back, ye Spanish knights,
  And rub your spurs till they are bright."

" Our spurs are bright and richly wrought,
  For in this land they were not bought ;
  Nor in this land they shan't be sold,
  Neither for silver nor for gold."

" Turn back, turn back, ye Spanish knights,
  And choose the fairest in your sight."

"If we must choose from east to west,
If we must choose one we like best,
The fairest one that we can see
Is pretty ——. Come to me."

One who played the "Three Dukes" in childhood says, "The Three Dukes formed in a line, the rest (a varying number) represented the maidens, also drawn up in line opposite. The Dukes (in some sort of coranto or cinq-pace) dance up to the maidens and then dance backwards, keeping their faces to their fair *vis-à-vis*. The maidens dance up to the Dukes and similarly retreat. The Dukes advance again, and the dialogue goes on right through, till at the end a maiden is chosen and joins the line of Dukes. The whole dialogue is repeated until all the maidens except one have been taken into the Dukes' company. Then around this non-elected demoiselle all the others form a circle and shout rather than sing—

"'Through the kitchen, through the hall,
She's the fairest of them all.'

As they do this the prisoner tries to escape, the result of which is a rough kind of Sir Roger de Coverley figure which closes the proceedings. Even now I can feel the pit-a-pat with which one *named* the little girl whom, in ducal capacity, was the one selected. In the last verse there is a change of rhythm, but the tune can be, and no doubt was, accommodated to it. If you are the happy possessor of a family circle, do try it this Christmas. There can only be three Dukes, but they can change about, and the number of maidens is unlimited. The Sir Roger de Coverley business is rather *ad libitum*, but with a lot of nicely dressed children you might reduce it to some sort of form, and with the wild break-up of the group, which is such a relief and delight to children, the effect would be charming."

Another ring game which was played by both girls and boys was accompanied by the following rhymes :—

"Up streets and down streets, windows made of glass,
Isn't Betsy Taylor a handsome young lass?
Isn't Johnnie Simpson as handsome as she?
They shall be married if they can agree.

Betsy made a pudding, so nice and so sweet,
She daren't stick a fork in till he came home at neet,
Then taste, love, taste love, don't be afraid,
For next Monday morning will be your wedding-day."

These words were sung to a beautiful old English air, as were also the words of another round game in which a girl stood in the centre of a circle of boys and girls, who, with joined hands, marched round and round singing—

"Rise ! Sally Waters, rise, if you can,
Rise ! Sally. Rise ! Sally, follow young man.
Choose to the east, choose to the west,
Choose to the bonnie lad that you love the best."

The choice having been made, the next verse was—

"Now, Sally, you're married, I hope you'll enjoy,
First of a girl, and second of a boy,
Seven years, and afterwards seven years of love,
Pray, young couple, a kiss and go."

A similar game was conducted to this chant—

"Silly old man, he walks alone, he walks alone, he walks alone,
Silly old man, he walks alone, he wants a wife, and can't find one.
All go round and choose your own,
And choose your own, and choose your own,
All go round and choose your own,
And choose a good 'un, or let it alone."

The choice having been made, came this information—

"Now you're coupled and got together
Your father and mother you must obey.
Love one another like sister and brother,
And pray, young couple, to kiss together.

It is not necessary to add that these "kissing" games were very popular.

A great favourite amongst girls was one in which the supposed mother of a circle of other girls sang—

"Here comes a man who wants a wife,
Who wants a wife, who wants a wife,
Which will he choose to be his wife
Out of you all, my daughters?"

In reply the girls show their qualifications—

"This is the way we wash the clothes,
Wash the clothes, wash the clothes,
This is the way we wash the clothes
All in the morning early."

Then followed—

"This is the way we wring the clothes,
This is the way we iron the clothes,
This is the way we knead the dough,
This is the way we bake the bread,"

each in the four-line verse. Many other domestic duties were added, and always expressed in pantomime.

Finally the "mother" sang—

"Here stands a man who wants a wife,
Wants a wife, wants a wife:
Which will he choose to be his wife?
Choose one, choose two,
Choose my fairest daughter."

The girl in the centre then made a choice, and the game began all over again.

Girls had many special games of their own in older Lancashire. Thus, "Blackthorn" was exclusively their own. A line of girls on one side of a lane or street represented a flock of geese, whilst another girl stood alone on the opposite side. The geese called out to her—

"Blackthorn!
Buttermilk and Barleycorn;
How many geese have you to-day?
More than you can catch and fly away!"

and scattering far apart ran across the roadway, their object being to evade capture by "Blackthorn." They crossed backwards and forwards until all the "geese" had been taken, and when only one remained, it was her lot to become "Blackthorn."

A ring-song which used to be a great favourite at Burnley was as follows:—

"I'll buy a horse and steal a gig,
And all the world shall have a jig,
And I'll do all that ever I can
To push the business on.
To push the business on,
And I'll do all that ever I can
To push the business on."

"Waiting for a partner!
Waiting for a partner!
Go round the ring and choose one in,
And kiss her when you get her in."

The lady having been chosen, the gentleman was told—

"Now you're married you must obey,
You must be true to all you say;
You must be kind, you must be good,
And help your wife to chop the wood."

Here and there these old games and songs may still be heard in Lancashire, but to the majority of the present generation they are unknown.

PEA SOUP YEAR

AT the beginning of the eighteenth century Blackpool consisted of about two hundred cottages, built of clay from the cliffs, and cobblestones from the beach. Its inhabitants, the majority of whom were both fishermen and agricultural labourers, at the best of times gained but a hard living, depending during the winter mainly upon the products of their small fields. The summer of 1799 was long remembered in Lancashire, being what is called a "blighted summer." The potato crop failed entirely; the cornfields yielded so poor and miserable a harvest that it was scarcely worth the gathering; and with the scarcity of corn prices went up to famine rates. Keen as was the distress in other parts of the country, in Blackpool the people were faced with absolute starvation; the long winter lay before them, and there were no stores of potatoes and barley! Food was only to be had by making a long journey inland, but the prices were prohibitive. Even before the winter commenced gaunt hunger had made itself felt in the little clay and cobble cottages. It was an appalling prospect; and they could do nothing but wait for the starvation that seemed inevitable.

In the midst of their misery a terrific storm broke upon the coast, raging for a whole day. Cottages were unthatched, the roaring sea swept inland for half a mile, flooding the houses; to the hungry people it seemed as if the end of all things had come. But the tempest which threatened their utter ruin in reality was their salvation.

As the evening drew on, a vessel, her sails torn to ribbons, was seen off the shore. She was entirely at the mercy of the wind and waves, and was being driven towards the beach. That she was doomed was beyond all doubt; her rudder was gone, and each great breaker brought her nearer. The men rushed down to the beach to give what help they could. In a little while the vessel grounded on the sand. Wave after wave broke over her, crashing down the mainmast and the bulwarks. Through the mist of flying spray her crew could be seen clinging to the broken bulwarks, but it was impossible for any one to venture into the wild and raging sea to attempt their rescue. Then, suddenly, when all hope seemed gone, a mighty wave lifted the vessel and bore her higher up the beach. The next moment the brave Blackpool men had dashed into the boiling surf, and with the help of ropes succeeded in rescuing every one of the crew. Scarcely was the last man drawn ashore when the vessel began to break up, and in a little while the beach was strewn with bags and packages. The vessel was carrying a cargo of provisions, the larger part of which was peas.

The shipwreck saved Blackpool from starvation. All through that winter peas from the vessel were the food of the people, varied only by fish occasionally, and cockles from the South Shore beds. Extraordinary ingenuity was shown in cooking this lucky gift of the sea, in order to vary the monotony of peas for every meal, and for years afterwards that time was known as "Pea Soup Year."

Mr. Allen Clarke (Teddy Ashton), tells us in his "Tales of Old Blackpool and the Fylde," that an old fisherman, questioned on the matter long afterwards, said, "Oh, ay, I recollect it weel, we were fair starved o' peas. We couldn't stomach 'em for years after i' Blackpool. Still th' peas were a blessing. We should ha' clemmed but for that wreck, an' I don't want to seem ungrateful, but I do know that I did say, after I'd had peas fro' morn till neet for two months, 'Well, it were aw very nice o' Providence to send us the pea wreck, but I think it wouldn't be no wus—wi' aw respect to Providence—if he'd just send us a bacon wreck as weel, so that we could have a bit of a change o' diet.'"

Some fifty years later Blackpool had become a favourite seaside resort, but the following account of the place written in 1843, gives a vivid contrast between the Blackpool of the early years of Queen Victoria's reign, and the present City of Lancashire Pleasure.

"About four miles south-west of Poul-ton-le-Fylde we reached Blackpool, the principal watering-place in the county according to some local authorities. Passing down a street that ran nearly east and west, the end of which opened upon the sea, consisting of that ever, and yet never varying style of buildings which spring up in such localities, we reached the corner house, which forms the left angle of this street and an esplanade facing the sea of considerable extent. Here visible tokens of character came at once upon the view. A long space of road, having the sea upon the right hand, passed down from north to south, and at a short depth under a bank or elevation, consisting of dark peaty earth, crumbling down in masses upon the sand, there lay a very fine level beach, from which a shallow sea had retired more than a quarter of a mile; two or three gaily painted boats high and dry upon the hard sand; beyond the beach an extensive ocean line, the horizon north-wards or southwards unrelieved by a single headland, and the road above the sand protracted to the extreme point of view, which might be about a mile or a mile and a half, and lined on the eastern side with houses, nearest to which, within the carriage-road, were rails and garden-seats thinly scattered, and scantily occupied by silent sitters, who seemed to gaze upon the sea for want of occupation, or out of pure vacancy of thought—such was our first introduction to the Brighton of Lancashire. . . . The house at the end at the angle of the street before spoken of is an

OLD BLACKPOOL

hotel and boarding-house, and bears the name of ' Lane-end Hotel,' a very extensive establishment counting ten windows on a floor upon the sea-front, three storeys high, with eight upon the north front.". The prices at this "very extensive establishment" are in as great a contrast with those of to-day as is the old hotel itself with the present palatial hostelries. A good sitting-room, and a bedroom and dinner cost three pounds thirteen and sixpence a week !

At Little Martin, to the east of Blackpool, the same writer tells us, there was a subterranean forest "by digging out the oaks from which many poor people make a living." The wood was fine enough to make furniture, and was also used for the roofs of barns and for fences.

THE PRIDE OF THE LANCASHIRE WITCHES

The following is taken from an old ballad-sheet sold in the streets.

I N vain I attempt to describe
    The charms of my favourite fair ;
    She's the sweetest of Mother Eve's tribe,
With her there is none to compare.
She's a pride of beauty so bright,
    Her image my fancy enriches ;
My charmer's the village delight,
    And the pride of the Lancashire witches.
        Then hurrah for the Lancashire witches,
        Whose smile every bosom enriches,
            O dearly I prize
            The pretty blue eyes
        Of the pride of the Lancashire witches.

They may talk of the dark eyes of Spain—
    'Tis useless to boast as they do—
They attempt to compare them in vain
    With the Lancashire ladies of blue.
Only view the dear heavenly belles,
    You're soon seized with love's sudden twitches,

Which none could create but the spells
    From the eyes of the Lancashire witches.
    Then hurrah for the Lancashire witches,
    Whose smile every bosom enriches,
        O dearly I prize
        The pretty blue eyes
    Of the pride of the Lancashire witches.

The Lancashire witches, believe me,
    Are beautiful, every one ;
But mine, or my fancy deceives me,
    Is the prettiest under the sun.
If the wealth of the Indies, I swear,
    Were mine, and I wallowed in riches,
How gladly my future I'd share
    With the pride of the Lancashire witches.
    Then hurrah for the Lancashire witches,
    Whose smile every bosom enriches,
        O dearly I prize
        The pretty blue eyes
    Of the pride of the Lancashire witches.

"THE LOYND WIFE"

THE EAGLE'S CRAG

ON the road between Todmorden and Burnley there stands the Eagle's Crag, so intimately associated with the history of the Stanley family. A legend of witchcraft also hung about the spot, dating from the reign of Charles I.

Giles Robinson, a farmer who lived in Pendle Forest, had been called upon to make a payment by nine o'clock in the morning of All Saints' day (November 1) at a place near Burnley. He had experienced great difficulty in procuring the money and in consequence it was late at night when he came through the valley in which stands the Eagle's Crag. Giles was in anything but a happy frame of mind ; the path was rugged, the place had the reputation of being haunted, and apart from his personal discomforts and fears he considered the claim which he had been called to meet an unjust one. His one desire was to reach his destination, pay the money, and return to his own home before nightfall on the following day. But suddenly and without any warning a flash of light blazed across the path, followed by a terrific crash as if the Eagle's Crag had been rent in twain. Giles's first idea was that he was beset by robbers, and he folded his arms round his body to protect his money, which was hidden in a bag concealed under his jerkin. The light and crash were followed by an intense silence, and finding himself unassailed, Giles began to recover from his alarm. But chancing to look upwards on the left he saw a sight which froze his blood with horror. Perched upon a crag which stood out sheer above the precipice was the Loynd Wife, a witch whose name was a terror throughout the whole of Blackburnshire. To add to Giles's terror, a violent storm came on. The thunder roared and echoed on all sides, seeming to come from the very bowels of the mountain; the rain fell in torrents. Giles tried to find some place of shelter from the downpour, when he found something smooth and hard rubbing against his legs, and looking down he saw a huge black cat, from the eyes of which darted sparks of fire. This was the Loynd Wife's "familiar."

"Thou cursed my mistress two days ago," said the cat. "She will meet thee two days hence at Malkin Tower."

Then it disappeared, darting more quickly than thought to the top of the precipice, where Giles saw it jump on to the Loynd Wife's shoulder, she then sitting astride of the Eagle's Crag. The moment the cat had taken its place the witch drew a huge torch from the mountain and waving it round and round her head, flew away into the night towards the northeast.

"True enough," said Giles to himself "she is gone to Pendle Forest. Horrid scenes will surely take place there before the sun rises."

Such was Giles Robinson's story.

Now Giles had a son called Ned, who on the previous evening had left his home for a ramble in the woods. He had only gone a few hundred yards through the thickets when he saw two greyhounds running towards him. When they came up both the dogs fawned upon him, and to his great surprise the boy saw they wore collars of gold. It was a good opportunity for a hunt, and a hare appearing in a field in front, Ned set both dogs at it.

"Loo! Loo!" he cried, but neither of them moved, and in spite of his cries and persuasions they would not stir a step. Ned, naturally, was enraged, and having a cudgel in his hand he belaboured both animals soundly. The beating produced a miraculous effect, for instead of two greyhounds there stood before him, Moll Dickenson, a neighbour, and a little boy. Ned turned to flee, but the woman placed her hand upon his shoulder, and he was as if rooted to the ground.

"Here," she said, giving him a purse of silver; "take this and hold thy peace."

"Aroint thee, witch!" cried Ned. "Thinkest I know thee not?"

Upon this Moll took a piece of string from her pocket, and throwing it on the little boy's neck, he was at once changed into a white horse, and the next moment Ned found himself on the horse's back with the witch behind him. Away they went through the air until they arrived at a new house called Hoarestones, higher up the mountain. The door was beset by beings human in shape but demoniacal in aspect, and from all quarters others were coming up on fiery horses, but the largest number came from the Cliviger side of the county.

Ned had heard of the "Witches' Sabbath," and with fright and horror he realised that he was about to witness one of these horrible gatherings.

What he saw he afterwards described in a Court of Justice. Three-score hags crowded the place and began to prepare a feast. At a word, fires were kindled and whole carcasses set to roast before them. In a few moments the meat was ready, and the witches were in the midst of their banquet. Then, as if at a secret signal, they all rose and uttered piercing shrieks.

"Feed him! Feed the wretch!" cried Moll Dickenson.

A pretty young woman thereupon came to Ned bearing a delicious-looking steak upon a golden dish. He took one bite and fell back overcome with disgust. The next minute he found himself standing upright in a barn! Before him knelt six hags pulling at six ropes fastened to the roof. Down the ropes came roasted lamb, lumps of butter and the richest cream, falling into basins and dishes placed to receive them. These witches were soon replaced by six others, who applied themselves to the same work. "But who can describe the hideous features which they all wore, or the horrid discord, which came as from twelve church bells all broken," says the chronicler, "while owls hooted in secluded corners of the barn, and shrieks and groans thickened around it from without?"

Next a huge cauldron rose out of the barn-floor in the midst of lurid and scorching flames. More witches appeared, amongst whom Ned recognised the Loynd Wife. The hags, under her direction, threw various things into the cauldron, saying—

" 1st Witch. Here's the blood of a bat.
Loynd Wife. Put in that, O put in that.
2nd Witch. Here's libbard bane.
Loynd Wife. Put in again.

1st Witch. The juice of toad, the oil of adder.
2nd Witch. That will make the yonker madder.
Loynd Wife. Put in; there's all, and rid the stench.
Firestone. Nay, here's three ounces of the red-haired wench.
All. Round, around, around."

A hideous dance followed round the cauldron.

"It takes! It takes!" the witches suddenly shrieked. "Her flesh has done it," and the trembling Ned saw the figures of his mother and father rise out of the ground in the opposite corner of the barn.

"Wretches!" cried the Loynd Wife, "we know and can punish our enemies. You are here to see the fate of your own boy——"

Before she could finish her sentence, Ned, maddened by fear, had darted from the barn and was running at full speed towards his home, with but one thought in his head.

"Could I get past the Boggart-hole, I should be safe."

Close behind him came the troop of witches, led by the Loynd Wife. She had stretched out her long, bony hands to seize him when Ned gave a great leap, and landed two yards below the Boggart-hole. At that moment two horsemen came up, and the witches beat a hasty retreat into the forest. Ned was taken to his home by the two men, but for a whole week afterwards he did nothing but rave.

His father, who returned from Burnley shortly after his son had been brought back, found that the sole object of the gathering of the witches had been to punish and do evil to himself and his house. For days he did no work, sitting silent and almost motionless, planning how he could be revenged, until at last he suddenly burst out, with—

"Wife, there is a law against these demons, and I will have it. The lad is getting better, and his evidence with mine will hang them all!"

Eighteen persons were brought up for trial at Lancaster, seventeen of them being found guilty on the evidence of Giles Robinson and his son, and condemned to death as witches!

For some reason, however—probably the fantastic absurdity of the boy's story—the judge reprieved the prisoners and reported the case to King Charles in council. They were handed over to the Bishop of Chester for examination, and when he had given his opinion, four of them were sent to London, and there examined, first by the King's physicians and afterwards by the King himself. The result of these careful examinations was that strong suspicions were excited against Giles and his son. They were subjected to a most searching interrogation, which brought out the truth, showing that whether the father had been scared by a thunderstorm or not, the son had been instructed and suborned by him to give the horrible evidence which had brought seventeen people under sentence of death. Robinson's motive was revenge, a revenge that was chiefly directed against the Loynd Wife. Her supposed appearance sitting astride the Eagle's Crag, and flying away in the midst of the storm, was a piece of evidence cleverly concocted by Giles to substantiate the story he had instructed the boy to tell.

An amazing fact in this story is that one of the women, Margaret Johnson, actually confessed her guilt, stating [1]—as is related elsewhere in this work—in the most definite manner how, when, where, and for what purpose she had become a witch.

[1] See " The Confession of a Witch."

SPRAWNGING

A LANCASHIRE lad heard a Welshman boasting of the height of Snowdon. "Hasti' never bin i' Owdham?" he asked. Receiving a reply in the negative, he went on, "Then tha's never seen Platt's chimbley, 'at's so high tha canna see't top for smook. When it gets out o' order, they han to send up a steeple-jack to fettle it; an' one day, one o' these felleys, bein' a chap fond o' trying o' sorts o' dodges, covered hissel' all o'er wi' indy-rubber, so at he's be o' reet if he fell. Well, up he goes to fettle t'chimbley, an' sure enough deawn he comes. An' what does ti' think? Astid o' gettin' kilt, he just started bouncin', an' he kept on bouncin', and he bounced for days. If tha'll believe me, he bounced so long 'at they had to shoot him at last to stop him fro' clemmin' to 't dyeath."

Mr. Frank Ormerod tells this amusing story in his *Lancashire Life and Character.*

THE CLEGG HALL BOGGART

TRADITION has woven many strange stories round Clegg Hall, the old house near Rochdale, built in the reign of James I. upon the site of an ancient dwelling erected by the Cleggs in the reign of King Stephen. At that time, as so frequently happened in Lancashire, the representative of the family, Bernulf de Clegg, was succeeded by his daughter, Quenilda. By a curious mistake on the part of the chroniclers, Bernulf and Quenilda are spoken of as man and wife, but Dr. Whitaker found a deed signed by Quenilda de Clegg in which she granted to Michael Hunrisfield for his homage and service, and two marks of silver paid to her in advance, "all the land that she held from Adam her husband, before marriage, and which he held of Suard de Hunrisfield, rendering thence per annum 6ᵈ. and one pair of white gloves at the feast of St. Oswald"; this proves that she was the lady of the manor.

Whether the father Bernulf, or the daughter Quenilda and her husband Adam, built the first Clegg Hall, is not known. It was very unlike its successor, built in the reign of the first James. The original Clegg Hall was low and dark, being built of wood and of a shape not unlike the hull of a great ship. Huge timbers formed the framework; to these ribs of wood were attached, the spaces in between being filled with a composition of clay and chopped straw. This primitive architecture was the only alternative to the stone-built and strongly fortified castle for the English gentry in the twelfth century who wished to build a dwelling-place upon their estate. Such buildings were little better than glorified hovels, but it was only the powerful nobles who could afford to build castles. For five centuries Clegg Hall withstood the assaults of time, but each century saw some alteration, some addition to the old building. In the reign of the sixth Edward it passed to William Ashton by marriage. It was his son who built the second Clegg Hall, and when he died unmarried, it went to the Haworths of Haworth.

But the old building had an uncanny reputation. All round about in the district it was firmly believed that it was haunted by an evil spirit, or boggart, which was chained to the spot because of a deed of unspeakable evil it had committed when in the flesh. Legend had it that an uncle being left guardian to two orphan children, who were heirs to the estate, threw them over a balcony into the moat, and so gained their inheritance for himself, and that in consequence his ghost was doomed to haunt Clegg Hall ever afterwards. This tragedy, whether it was based upon any actual happenings or purely upon local imaginings, together with the ghost, were so firmly believed in by the country-folk that when any untoward circumstance arose it was invariably attributed to the Clegg Hall Boggart.

During the first year of the Commonwealth, a sturdy old beggar, who vouchsafed neither his name nor anything of his past history, suddenly made his appearance at the Hall, which was then occupied by the Haworths. He returned from time to time and finally was allowed to sleep in one of the rooms of the old house, which had not been destroyed, and was used for a lumber-room. Some one had dubbed the mysterious beggar Norman, and as Norman he became known to all the country-side.

Now, it was confidently affirmed that the pulling down of the greater portion of the old house had not driven forth the boggart, and that it still continued to haunt the new dwelling. Vague, mysterious stories which had long been floating about amongst the credulous neighbours began to take a definite shape, even to the Haworths, after the arrival of Norman. Strange noises were heard in the old lumber-room and curious sounds of tapping from underground whenever he was there. And on the morrow he had thrilling stories to tell of ghostly manifestations. Such was the superstitious belief of the time that none of the Haworths or their servants dare go near the lumber-room, nor did they doubt for one moment the truth of the beggar's descriptions of the boggart's visits. But as the spirit appeared to Norman whenever he slept in the room, a conviction gradually spread amongst the servants, and one not unshared by their masters, that he was a wizard, who possessed the power of conjuring up ghosts. He was therefore both hated and feared, and out of dread of the evil he might wreak upon the house if annoyed or sent away, he was allowed to come and go without let or hindrance, and occupy the haunted chamber at will.

And so matters might have gone on for years, had not Love intervened, a factor the beggar Norman had not taken into account.

The daughter of the house, Lucy Haworth, was a pretty girl, of a very romantic temperament, and strongly imbued with all the current belief in witches, good and bad spirits, and fairies. She had already been impressed by a stranger whom she had met several times, in the woods and lanes, and about the house itself. Although he had never spoken to her the man's demeanour left no doubt as to his admiration. Lucy made many inquiries, but no one knew the stranger, where he lived, or whence he came. The mystery surrounding her secret and silent admirer added not a little to Lucy's romantic interest.

The romance was heightened further by a strange happening at the marriage-feast of Dorothy Holt of Castleton and Stubley and John Entwistle of Foxholes, to which Lucy and her brother Nicholas Haworth were bidden. In the midst of the dancing and merry-making two men dressed as Turks, their faces masked, entered the hall at Stubley, and when one of them began to do conjuring tricks of surprising cleverness the guests thought it was a further diversion provided by their host. One of the men carried a box, and after performing a variety of tricks, he asked Lucy Haworth, to whom both strangers had paid particular attention, whether it was her wish that it should be opened. Upon her expressing her assent, he unlocked the box, the lid flew open, and up rose a peacock, so realistically made that for a moment the company thought it was a real bird. Being placed on the floor it was flapping its wings and spreading its tail to the wonder of everybody, when a little door in its breast opened, and out came a white pigeon, from the breast of which in the same manner came a nightingale, which fluttered its wings and sang so sweetly that the wedding party again thought they saw and heard a real bird. But the breast of the nightingale opened and out hopped a humming-bird of wonderful plumage, with a piece of paper in its beak, which it presented to Lucy. Having read the billet she thrust it into the bosom of her dress. An awed silence fell upon the company whilst the two Turks collected the automatic birds together and put them back into the box. Then they made their salaams and disappeared round the oak screen in the hall as mysteriously as they had arrived. Some of the guests declared that the conjurors were followed by lines of fire.

Everybody congratulated the host, Robert Holt, upon the entertainment he had provided, but he disclaimed all knowledge of the jugglers and laid their coming entirely at the door of the bridegroom, Entwistle of Foxholes. But the latter protested his ignorance, and then it was discovered that no one in the assembly knew anything about the masked Turks, and that no one was responsible for their coming to Stubley. Lucy was closely questioned as to what was written in the note presented to her by the humming-bird, but she only made answer that it was a " stale conceit appropriate to the masque."

The mystery worked quickly upon the superstitions of the wedding-party, and the Turks were roundly declared to be emissaries of Satan.

When Lucy Haworth had told her friends that the missive was only a " stale conceit " she had not spoken the truth. In one of the Turks she saw a close resemblance to the silent admirer who had already impressed her romantic mind, and this, together with the words upon the paper, roused her curiosity. The message ran as follows, according to Roby :—

" *To-morrow at midnight, in the haunted chamber ! If thou hast courage tarry there a while. Its occupant will protect thee. Peril threatens thy house, which thy coming can alone prevent. Shouldest thou reveal but one word of this warning, thy life, and those dear to thee, will be the forfeit. From thine unknown monitor.*

" THESE."

The occupant of the haunted chamber was Norman, and when on the following morning he showed Lucy that he knew of her receipt of the note, her curiosity became inexpressible; overcoming even her superstitious fear of the boggart. Accordingly that night when all the house was wrapped in slumber, Lucy crept from her bedroom to the boggart chamber, which was in the part of the old Clegg Hall that had not been pulled down.

Immediately she entered the room Norman closed and bolted the door. Lucy not unnaturally began to feel some alarm; the old chamber, lighted only by the candle she carried and filled with the lumber of years, was most eerie and ghost-like; then, to add to her rising fears, Norman suddenly disappeared behind a great oak bedstead. Terrified, Lucy called out to him, but there was no reply.

Suddenly her light was blown out and she felt her arms seized.

" Be silent on thy life ! " some one whispered in her ear. The invisible hands gently dragged her forward, and too frightened to exert any will-power, she was led through cold, dark passages, downwards and downwards. Her guide evidently was well accustomed to these passages beneath the house, for despite the darkness he passed on swiftly. At length a streak of light showed a doorway. There was the clank of chains and the rattle of iron, a flood of light, and after a whispered " No harm should befall thee " from her invisible companion, Lucy found herself in a vaulted chamber, and the door closed upon her.

An iron lamp hung from the vaulted ceiling and by its light Lucy saw that she was in a treasure house. Round the walls stood coffers, each with its lid set wide open, and showing within piles and piles of golden coins—the stores of Crœsus in a cellar of Clegg Hall!

Whilst she was lost in wonderment the door opened and the mysterious stranger who had awakened her interest by his strange demeanour and silence, entered, but to her passionate inquiry as to why she had been brought to the cellar, and what peril affected her house, he made no answer. He only pointed to the money-filled coffers, then to himself, by which she understood that he was in love with her and was placing himself and all this wealth at her feet.

When Lucy did not appear on the following morning at breakfast, and when as the day passed no tidings could be gleaned of her whereabouts, or traces found of her having left the house, all those at Clegg Hall, especially her brother Nicholas, were filled with consternation and dismay. Returning from a vain quest to Foxholes, Stubley and Pike House, Nicholas met the old beggar Norman, who with an air of the deepest mystery told him that his sister had departed. When questioned by Nicholas he replied :

" Ask the little devilkins I saw yesternight. I have told ye oft o' the sights and terrible things that have visited me i' the boggart chamber, and that the ghost begged hard for a victim."

Nicholas was half persuaded that the Clegg Hall boggart had carried away his sister, but suspecting Norman of having dealings with evil spirits he threatened to hale him before the magistrates for " practising with forbidden and devilish devices." But Norman found it an easy matter to impose on the young squire's credulity, and in order to prove that he was in no way in league with the boggart, he offered to cast him out. Although reassured Haworth was still suspicious, and when the beggar offered to lay the ghost on the morrow he shut him up all night in the kitchen as a means of precaution.

No one slept that night at Clegg Hall. Hitherto the mysterious sounds, the tappings, the rattlings of chains, had been confined to that portion of the house near the Boggart's Chamber, but this night all over the house were heard loud rumblings, shrieks, howlings, and alarming sounds as if heavy weights were falling from a height. But when Nicholas and the terrified servants went to the kitchen, where Norman had been secured, they found him sleeping peacefully. At this moment two of the farm-hands rushed in gibbering with fright. They had found all the cart-horses harnessed in their stalls, and the bull perched up on top of the haystack. All were convinced that Satan and his myrmidons had visited the house during the night.

Nicholas Haworth, beside himself with rage and fear, commanded Norman to rid the house of the evil spirits, on pain of instant denunciation to the authorities. To this Norman agreed, on the stipulation that he must first be alone in the Boggart Chamber for a time.

Accordingly he was locked in and a watch was set to prevent his escape. At the end of an hour he announced his readiness to begin his exorcism, and in the very Boggart Chamber itself.

Drawing a line with his crutch through the thick dust on the floor, Norman sternly ordered that no one should pass beyond it, and that no one should speak save himself. Then he began mumbling meaningless incantations, which were answered by low rumblings from beneath. He knocked upon the floor, and to each knock came another from below the floor. Then in bombastic and high-flown language he conjured the spirit to say why it was disquieted and what would be the price of its departure. Shrieks and yells were the response. After a while in response to further questions from Norman a faint murmuring was heard beneath the floor which he translated to the terrified onlookers as a statement that the spirits were those of the two Clegg children who,

so long ago, had been thrown by their uncle into the moat. A further message he declared to be:

"They must have a living body sacrificed, and in four quarters it must be laid; then shall these wicked spirits not return hither until what is severed be joined together. With this hard condition we must be content."

Nicholas Haworth's suspicions of Norman being in some way connected with his sister's disappearance were in no way allayed by the incantations he had heard and their uncanny answers, and he immediately suggested that the beggar should be offered up as the sacrifice required by the tormenting spirit. Norman saw that he ran a grave danger, and with great resource cried out that no human victim was needed. "Bring hither the first brute animal ye behold," he cried to the trembling and affrighted servants, "any one of you, on crossing the threshold of the portal."

The messenger who was dispatched in obedience to the order and who went with all speed, being glad to be free of the haunted room, returned with a barn-door fowl. Forthwith, Norman led the way to the courtyard, where with more incantations, the bird was killed and cut into four pieces. By the beggar's directions one quarter was buried at Little Clegg in a field, the second at Beil Bridge, the third under one of the hearthstones in the hall, and the fourth under the floor of the barn.

Scarcely, however, had the last piece of fowl been buried, when a loud explosion shook Clegg Hall to its very foundations, and smoke was seen pouring from one of the outbuildings on the other side of the moat. With a loud cry of alarm Norman began to run in the direction of the smoke, then stopping suddenly he paused and seemed to be considering what he should do. After a moment's reflection he hurried to the kitchen and thence by a staircase to the Boggart Chamber, Nicholas and several of the servants following him. Quickly moving a pile of lumber, Norman raised a trap-door in the floor, which concealed a flight of steps. Down these he disappeared, Nicholas pressing hard upon his heels. In the pitch blackness of the passage, into which the steps led, his only guide was the sound of Norman's footsteps. This he was following cautiously when he heard a loud shriek, and convinced that it came from his sister he ran swiftly along the passage until he found his way barred by a door. Beyond the door there were cries and sounds of much confusion. Suddenly the door opened and out came Norman bearing the senseless Lucy in his arms, dense smoke and flames following them.

When they reached the upper air, Norman laid the fainting girl upon a bench and turning to Nicholas said:

" There, at the peril of all I possess, and of life too, I have rescued her. My hopes are gone—my schemes for ever blasted—and I am a ruined, wretched old man, without a home or a morsel of bread."

Nicholas was too busy helping to restore his sister, to notice that Norman then walked straight out of the house.

It was afterwards said that two strangers had been seen to appear in the avenue, as if from the bowels of the earth, and being joined by Norman, all three had disappeared.

When she recovered consciousness, Lucy had a curious story to tell. But for the explosion she would have been kept a close prisoner in the cellars of her own home, because she would not consent to marry the mysterious stranger who had lured her there, and who had sought to dazzle her by the display of his vast wealth. The secret of the cellar now being known to her, her captors did not dare to release her.

The ghostly sounds, the clanking of chains, and all the supposed evidence of the boggart at Clegg Hall, were now explained.

Norman was a descendant of the Clegg family. During a long residence abroad he had become an adept coiner, and in addition had learnt many of the tricks of the alchemists. These tricks, although only based upon simple experiments in chemistry, were regarded as magic by the ignorant. In his youth Clegg had spent some time at Clegg Hall, and when he and his son and a confederate decided to carry on the coining of false money on a large scale, he remembered the old vaults and cellars and the secret entrance to them from the Boggart's Chamber. The stories of the boggart being heard from time to time in the house, also favoured the choice, since any underground noises would be put down to the presence of the ghost. By dressing as a beggar, the elder Clegg easily got admission to the house, and permission to sleep in the Boggart Chamber during his periodical visits. Gradually, all the necessary material for the manufacture of counterfeit coin was introduced into the old cellars; and an entrance to them having been discovered in the avenue, the younger Clegg and the confederate could come and go in safety, and unperceived. Each time Norman left the Hall presumably on a begging round, his leather wallet was well filled with false coin, which with the help of agents was gradually circulated throughout the country.

Finding his stories of the supposed appearances of the boggart implicitly believed, Clegg had arranged a plan by which to drive the Haworths from Clegg Hall. A reign of terror was to be instituted in the shape of ghostly manifestations, which would make the house uninhabitable. A sample of what would have been carried on was given on the night of Lucy Haworth's disappearance. But just as the plan was to be carried into execution the younger Clegg saw Lucy, and fell in love with her. Being half Spanish, his love was violent in its nature, and his father hoping that if a union took place between them Clegg Hall might yet again belong to a Clegg, helped his son, not only in the masquerade as Turks at Stubley, but also to persuade Lucy to go with him to the cellar.

The younger Clegg fondly imagined that he had only to snow Lucy his supposed treasure to win her hand. But it had precisely the contrary effect. She refused and repulsed him. But for the accident which caused the explosion Lucy Haworth would probably have died in the old cellars of her own home, a few feet away from those whose days were spent in searching the country-side for some trace of her.

The vaults and cellars were found to extend a considerable distance both under and beyond the moat. Nicholas Haworth caused them to be walled up, and the remains of the original Clegg Hall to be pulled down. The instruments for coining and a vast hoard of counterfeit money were also destroyed.

Notwithstanding these plain hard facts of actuality, for generations afterwards Norman figured in many tales of the ghostly and marvellous all about the district, and the existence of the Clegg Hall Boggart was believed in as firmly as ever.

A GRADELY PRAYER

BY

TEDDY ASHTON (ALLEN CLARKE)

GIVE us, Lord,
    A bit o' sun,
    A bit o' wark,
  An' a bit o' fun.
Give us aw,
  In th' struggle an' splutter,
Eaur daily bread—
  An' a bit o' butter.

Give us health
  Eaur keep to make,
An' a bit to spare
  For poor folks' sake.
Give us sense
  (For we're some of us duffers)
An' a heart to feel
  For aw that suffers.

Give us, too,
  A bit of a song,
An' a tale, an' a book,
  To help us along.
An' give us eaur share
  O' sorrow's lesson,
That we may prove
  Heaw grief's a blessin'.

Give us, Lord,
  A chance to be
Eaur very best;
  Brave, wise, an' free—
Eaur very best
  For eaursels an' others,
Till aw men larn
  To live as brothers.

THE STORY OF WHALLEY ABBEY

THE GATEWAY, WHALLEY ABBEY

THE Abbey of Whalley owed its existence to the great de Lacy family, whose progenitor had fought with William the Conqueror at the Battle of Hastings. John de Lacy, Constable of Chester, founded a Cistercian abbey at Stanlaw in Cheshire in 1175, endowing it richly. His son, grandson, and great-grandson in succession, added to the possessions of the Abbey, and in the fourth generation, Henry de Lacy, Earl of Lincoln, not only gave the monks the advowson of the church of Whalley and land at Castleton, but likewise granted them permission to remove from Stanlaw. The situation of the latter place was a bad one. During the spring tides it was practically inaccessible, the abbey itself being sometimes flooded to a depth of three feet; in addition the sea made continual encroachments upon the land.

In the course of the century after its foundation the chief portion of the estates of the Abbey of Stanlaw—owing to the generosity of successive de Lacies—had come to lie in Lancashire, and the monks naturally desired to live nearer their lands. Blackburn, however, was only a bed of sand. Rochdale was surrounded by morasses. Neither of these places therefore offered any improvement upon Stanlaw. But when Henry de Lacy gave them the advowson of Whalley, in 1283, they found themselves provided with a site which answered all the Cistercian ideals of a monastic dwelling-place. It has been said of this Order, " Though the Cistercians affected to plant themselves in the solitude of woods which were to be gradually essarted by the labour of their own hands, and though they obtained an exemption from the payment of tithes on that specific plea, yet they were excellent judges of the quality of land, however concealed, and never set about their laborious task without the assurance of an ample recompense." In describing the Whalley given by the Earl of Lincoln to the Stanlaw monks, Dr. Whitaker says : " A copious stream to the south, a moderate expanse of rich meadow and pasture around, and an amphitheatre of sheltering hills, clad in the verdant covering of their native woods, beyond ; these were features in the face of Nature which the earlier Cistercians courted with instinctive fondness. Where these combined it does not appear that they ever abandoned a situation which they had once chosen ; and when these were wanting, it is certain they never long or willingly remained."

Monks, however, were not allowed to change their habitation in the reign of the first Edward at their own sweet will, or by the permission of a great lord who gave them land. The consent of the Pope was necessary, and thus thirteen years elapsed between the gift of Whalley and the receipt of the Papal Bull granting the monks of Stanlaw authority to migrate to that place. The move was not made, however, without bitter opposition on the part of the monks of Salley Abbey, some six or eight miles away from Whalley. Salley Abbey was likewise a Cistercian house and had been founded thirty years before the Abbey at Stanlaw. But it was not so richly endowed. Its members viewed with no little apprehension, not perhaps unmixed with jealousy, the establishment of a larger monastery than their own so close to their doors, a monastery too, which would grow corn and other necessaries that they themselves could not produce, the land about Salley being suitable only for cattle-grazing. They contended that the introduction of a large number of people into a district scarcely able to support its existing inhabitants would send up the price of provisions. Matters between the old and the new monasteries became so strained that the monks of Whalley in 1306 seriously thought of removing once more, to Toxteth. At this juncture, several neighbouring abbots were called in to settle the differences between the two houses, which had developed into a scandal. By their decision the monks of Whalley remained undisturbed.

Others suffered besides the monks of Salley by the migration from Stanlaw ; these were the priests who held the various livings comprised in the rectory of Whalley, the secular clergy, as they were called to distinguish them from the monks. " Whalley, previously venerable for its ecclesiastical antiquity, became the seat of a flourishing establishment which continued for two centuries and a half to exercise unbounded hospitality and charity, to adorn the site which had been chosen with a succession of magnificent buildings, to protect the tenants of its ample domains in the enjoyment of independence and plenty, to educate and provide for their children, to employ, clothe, feed and pay many labourers, herdsmen, and shepherds, to exercise the arts, and cultivate the learning of the times, yet unfortunately at the expense of the secular incumbents, whose endowments they had swallowed up, and whose functions they had degraded into those of pensionary vicars or mendicant chaplains."

But many of the dwellers on the Abbey lands, serfs as they were called, were actually slaves, as is shown by an old deed, in which a native of Whalley bought the freedom of himself and his family. The of our successors have given, granted and delivered to our beloved in Christ John G. and his assignees, R. son of I. son of A de W, our native, with all his family and all his effects for 100 shillings

THE LAVATORIUM, WHALLEY ABBEY

mere fact of a peasant being born upon the Abbey lands made him *ipso facto* the slave of the Abbot; this explains the phrase in the deed that no claim shall be made upon the man in the future on account of his "nativity." The deed, translated from its old Latin, runs thus :—

"To all etc. Gregory Abbot and the Convent of Whalley, health. Be it known that we for ourselves and each

sterling to us by the said John delivered and paid : so that the said John with all his family be free, discharged, and quit of all challenge. So that neither we nor our successors for the future shall be able to claim any right in the aforesaid on account of his nativity saving to us our right and challenge with respect to any others, our natives. It witness whereof we have affixed our seals."

The Abbots also hired servants for life, which was practically slavery, as is shown by another deed, in which the Abbot undertakes to give one " Galf, called K. board and raiment in our house at Whalley for the whole term of his life, as long as he behaves himself faithfully and honestly," because of the " service he has hitherto performed, and shall in future perform for us." He was to have "such victuals and dress as is usual for one of the grooms of the Abbot's stable," and in the event of being incapacitated from work by illness or old age, he was to have the " right to his keep among our servants in the infirmary of the lay brothers."

After their settlement at Whalley, a breach occurred between the monks and their munificent patron Henry de Lacy, and he, considering he had dealt with too bountiful a hand towards them, seized the chapel of St. Michael in Clitheroe Castle, and detached it from the mother-church of Whalley. The Abbot and his monks protested, and when his successor continued the spoliation they petitioned King Edward III., declaring that Henry de Lacy had taken the chapel " not by right but by the magnitude and force of his domination," giving it to another " at the peril of his soul." For three years they pestered the King and the Parliament, until, ultimately, the chapel was restored to them by letters patent, and in their possession it remained until the time of Henry VIII.

The early years of the Cistercian fathers at Whalley were spent in building ; it was twelve years after their arrival from Stanlaw before the Abbey was ready for consecration. Additions were made to the buildings for more than a hundred and forty years afterwards. The original cost of the monastery was three thousand pounds, a prodigious sum for those days when an artisan's wages were twopence a

day, and when all the timber required was taken from their own woods, six miles in length and four in breadth, and the stone quarries of Read and Symonstone were quite near.

" Happy is the nation that has no history "; happy also the monastery of which the same can be said. From the time of the Abbot, Robert Topcliffe, who successfully petitioned for the return of Clitheroe Chapel, down to the last Abbot, John Paslew, Whalley has no records beyond those of increasing prosperity. Once, in the reign of Henry VI., a serious scandal stirred the happy calm of the monastery. Adjoining the Abbey was a hermitage for two recluses, founded and well endowed by Henry, the " good Duke of Lancaster." To this hermitage women were admitted who took the conventual vows. For a hundred years or so all went well, then Isole de Heton, a widow " of the county of Lancaster " who had solemnly sworn that she would be an anchorite in that place for the rest of her life, broke her vows and left her cell. Whether the widow made complaint to the Abbot in breaking her vows, or whether her abrupt departure caused matters to be inquired into, we do not know, but an inquiry was made and as a result a petition was presented to Henry VI., stating, " That divers of the women that have been servants there in the hermitage, and attendyng to the recluses afortym have been misgovernyd . . . within the sayd plase halowyd to the grete displeasaunce of hurt and disclander (scandal) of the abbeye aforeseyd." Henry hearkened to the petition and dissolved the hermitage, appointing in its place two chaplains to say mass daily in the parish church of Whalley for the repose of the soul of Henry, Duke of Lancaster, its founder, and of the souls of his ancestors.

At the height of its prosperity the

monastery of Whalley contained some one hundred and twenty persons. There was the Lord Abbot, the prior, and twenty monks, an uncertain number of novices, hundred and fifty quarters of malt, eight pipes of wine, one hundred and thirty-two oxen and cows, one hundred and twenty sheep, sixty calves, thirty lambs and four

HENRY VIII
(After a portrait generally attributed to Holbein)

and ninety servants, twenty of whom were for the personal service of the Abbot. These people, together with the guests of the Abbey, and the mendicants constantly within its gates, consumed in one year two hundred quarters of wheat, one porkers. Of this three-fifths went to the Abbot's table. The Cistercian rule was very strict. There were no sheets on the monks' beds, they wore no shirts and slept in their woollen dresses. Cleanliness was not accounted a virtue, and Dr. Whitaker puts the condition of the monks in this delicate fashion: They "never availed themselves of a practice, from which they do not appear to have been prohibited, and which alone rendered the same habits tolerable in the ancients, namely a constant use of warm baths, which would have removed all impurities from the skin." Little wonder, therefore, that repulsive skin diseases were rife among them.

THOMAS CROMWELL
(From Holland's " Heroölogia")

When Henry VIII. decided upon the suppression of the monasteries by the advice of Thomas Cromwell, Whalley, by reason of its wealth, was one of the earliest to be visited by the King's Commissioners. An inventory was made which is now at the Record Office in London, but the relaxation of discipline and the gross immorality, which gave Henry and Cromwell the excuse for suppressing so many of the religious houses, clearly did not exist at Whalley, as no mention is made of any irregularity, and no action was immediately taken against the monks.

The suppression of the monasteries

caused widespread and bitter discontent in the North of England. Henry and Cromwell began with the lesser houses. " The religious feelings as well as the temporal interests of a large body of men were deeply involved in the suppression of the lesser monasteries, which measure was considered with much justice, as the precursor of a still more sweeping appropriation of church property. The families of distinction, whose ancestors had founded monasteries, or whose sons were provided for by spiritual offices, complained of being deprived of their patronage and emoluments, and the poor, for whom there was then no parochial provision in infancy or in old age, and whose wants had been supplied at the doors of the convents, were equally loud in their complaints ; while persons under the influence of higher motives felt shocked and outraged by the spoliation and overthrow of the altars of their fathers." These feelings very naturally found expression in rebellion. Twenty thousand men rose in Lincolnshire, but were dispersed by a proclamation of the king's pardon. In Lancashire and Yorkshire the rising was more formidable, being headed by many of the great nobles. It was called the Pilgrimage of Grace. At the head of the insurgent army marched a body of priests with the banner of the Cross, on which was depicted the figure of the Saviour with the chalice and the host. Each soldier bore on his sleeve a representation of the five wounds of Christ with the word " Jesu," in the centre, and every man had to take this oath, " that he entered into this pilgrimage for the love of God, the preservation of the king's person and issue, the purifying the nobility, and driving away all base-born and ill councillors, and for no particular profit of his own, not to do displeasure to anyone, nor to kill anyone for envy ; but to take before them the cross of Christ, his faith, the restitution of the churches, and the suppression of heretics and their opinions."

In an evil hour for himself and his house Abbot Paslew of Whalley joined the Pilgrimage of Grace. There is a tradition that he was an unwilling participant. An arrangement had been made by which the country-folk should be called to arms by the firing of a beacon. But Abbot Paslew, anxious to see which way success would go before finally committing himself, hesitated, so it is said, to light the beacon on the hill above Whalley; and one of his followers therefore set it on fire. The signal was thus given, and willingly or unwillingly the Abbot with his following went to Doncaster to join the rebel army.

Henry VIII. had dispatched the Duke of Norfolk against the Pilgrimage of Grace. Twice the rebel leaders tried to ford the Don to attack the royal forces, but each time the waters of the river rose suddenly, and made their passage impossible. To the "pilgrims of grace" this appeared as an evil omen, and their forces gradually melted away on a promise of a general pardon, a promise that was not kept. When the pilgrimage was dissolved Henry sent a manifesto which was more calculated to excite another rebellion than to allay the unrest. In answer to the part of the petition of the "pilgrims" which referred to the removal of his ministers, Thomas Cromwell being meant, the haughty Tudor monarch wrote, "And we, with our whole council think it right strange that ye, who be but brutes and inexpert folk, do take upon you to appoint us who be meet or not for our council. We will therefore bear no such meddling at your hands, it being inconsistent with the duty of good subjects to interfere in such matters."

After Abbot Paslew's departure to Doncaster, the Lord Lieutenant of Lancashire took possession of Whalley Abbey, co-operating with the Earl of Derby in crushing the rising in Lancashire. For a brief space the rebels gained possession of the Abbey during the long-drawn-out negotiations between the insurgent and royal leaders, but were finally driven out by the Earl of Derby.

When the Pilgrimage of Grace, and all the minor risings in Lancashire in connection with it, had been suppressed, the punishments, despite the king's promise of pardon, began. The headsman and the hangman were set to work. Abbot Paslew and many of his monks were haled before the Assizes at Lancaster upon a charge of high treason. He was condemned to be hanged, drawn and quartered, his execution to take place at Whalley. A gallows was erected in front of the monastery, and there on March 12, 1537, the last Abbot of Whalley looked for the last time upon the place where his word had been absolute, and where he had enjoyed both temporal splendour and spiritual pre-eminence. Before the shuddering eyes of the country-folk, to whom he had been as a father, John Paslew was thrown from the ladder. A few convulsive movements and there was no longer any Abbot of Whalley. Out of regard for his rank Paslew was spared the drawing and quartering, but upon John Eastgate, one of his monks who suffered with him, all the horrors of the sentence were carried out. Another monk of Whalley, called William Heydock, was executed the following day at Padiham. Thus ended the history of Whalley Abbey. The monks were dispersed and the Abbey lands were seized by Henry VIII. They were leased to John Bradyll of Bradyll, who a few years later in partnership with Richard Assheton of Downham purchased

THE RUINS OF WHALLEY ABBEY

the whole property from the Crown, Assheton taking the house, and Bradyll a large portion of the land.

When Mary Tudor came to the throne one of her earliest actions was to attempt to restore the old abbeys. Those who had bought monastic buildings, or to whom they had been granted by Henry VIII., replied with a vigorous use of the pickaxe. "Such as possessed them," says Fuller, " plucked out their eyes by levelling to the ground, and shaving from them as much as they could, all abbey characters." It was then that the demolition of Whalley Abbey began, a demolition which was completed by Sir Ralph Assheton in 1661, after the Restoration of Charles II. To prevent the building ever being used as a fortress he pulled down the walls of the close, part of the church and steeple, and fourteen yards of the high cloister wall.

The various records of Whalley give a complete account of the rents and values of land in the reign of Henry VIII.; and these, in contrast with those of later centuries, are both curious and interesting. In the time of Abbot Paslew the rent of land at Whalley was about two shillings an acre, and the rent of a cottage from one to two shillings per annum. A hundred years later land was from four to five shillings an acre; in the reign of Queen Anne it had advanced to eight shillings, and at the end of the reign of George II. (1760) it had risen to one pound an acre. In 1835, the rental was three pounds an acre.

NORTH LANCASHIRE WEATHER PROVERBS

IN remote country districts even in our time the predictions of local weather prophets are more firmly believed in than the official announcements of the Meteorological Office. Their knowledge is based partly upon experience and the observation of Nature, and partly upon traditions handed down in verse or proverbs through the centuries. North Lancashire is especially rich in these sayings and proverbs, which predict the weather from the appearance of the sun and moon, the state of the winds, the appearance of plants and the actions of animals, etc.

In Chambers's *Book of Days*, Dr. Jenner set forth an epitome in verse of the signs betokening bad weather. The majority of these were firmly believed in North Lancashire.

" SIGNS OF FOUL WEATHER.

"The *hollow winds* begin to blow ;
  The *clouds look black*, the glass is *low ;*
  The *soot falls down*, the *spaniels sleep ;*
  And *spiders* from *their cobwebs* peep.
  Last night the *sun* went *pale to bed ;*
  The *moon* in *halos* hides her head.
  The boding shepherd heaves a sigh,
  For, see ! a *rainbow* spans the sky.
  The walls are damp, the *ditches smell*,
  Closed is the pink-eyed *pimpernel*,
  Hark ! how the *chairs* and *tables* crack,
  Old Betty's joints are on the rack,
  Her *corns* with *shooting pains* torment her,
  And to her bed untimely sent her.
  Loud *quack the ducks*, the *sea-fowl cry*,
  The *distant hills* are *looking nigh.*
  How restless are the *snorting swine !*
  The *busy flies* disturb the *kine.*
  Low o'er the grass the *swallow wings*,
  The *cricket*, too, how *sharp he sings !*
  Puss on the hearth with *velvet paws*
  Sits wiping o'er her *whisker'd jaws.*
  The *smoke* from chimneys *right ascends*,
  Then spreading, *back to earth it bends.*
  The *wind* unsteady, *veers around*,
  Or settling, in the South is found,
  Through the clear stream the *fishes rise*
  And nimbly catch the incautious *flies.*

The *glow worms* num'rous, clear and bright,
Illum'd the *dewy hill* last night.
At dusk the squalid *toad* was seen
Like *quadruped* stalk o'er the green.
The whirling wind the dust obeys,
And in the *rapid eddy* plays.
The *frog* has chang'd his *yellow vest*,
And in a *russet coat* is drest.
The *sky is green*, the air is still,
The *mallow* blackbird's voice is shrill.
The *dog* so alter'd in his taste,
Quits mutton bones on *grass* to feast.
Behold the *rooks*, how odd their flight,
They imitate the *gliding kite*,
And seem *precipitate to fall*
As if they felt the piercing ball.
The *tender colts on back do lie*
Nor heed the traveller passing by.
In *firey red* the *sun* doth rise,
Then *wades through clouds* to mount the skies,
'Twill *surely rain*, we see't with sorrow,
No *working in the fields to-morrow*."

There were other signs of purely local significance. Thus, if the sun broke out suddenly through a stormy sky, it was said to be making holes for the wind to blow through. The setting of the sun also betokened the direction of the wind—

" When the sun sets in a bank
    A Westerly wind we shall not want."

" When the sun sets bright and clear
    An Easterly wind you need not fear."

But if the sun when rising or setting was of a dull yellowish brick-dust colour, it was said rain or wind would follow. It is also said that if on looking at the large buildings east of Lancaster, when the sun is reflected in their windows, should it be of a rich deep golden colour, this is a sign of fine weather ; should it be of a pale silvery or leaden colour rain is threatening.

The halo sometimes seen round the moon is called a " bor." or " burr," and when it is near the moon the rain is far off, but when the " burr " is far from the moon then the rain is near—

    " Near bur.   Far rain."

It is also put thus—

"If the Rim round the Moon be near, the
    storm will be far,
If the Rim far, the storm near,"

and

"When the wheel is far the storm is n'ar;
    When the wheel is n'ar the storm is far."

When the horns of the crescent moon
are turned upwards she is said, locally,
"to be on her back," and the more perfectly she shows in this position, the finer
and more settled the weather will be, so
long as she remains in that quarter.

The wind was full of presages to the
observant weather prophet, the north-
west wind being especially favourable.

"Do business with men when the wind
is in the north-west," says one proverb,
whilst this rhyme gives the character of
the four winds—

"The West wind always brings wet weather,
The East wind cold and wet together,
The South wind surely brings us rain,
The North wind blows it back again."

If there is an east wind a few days before,
and on the 21st March, three months' dry
weather may be expected. But if the
wind is in the west and the thunder packs
extend up Lunesdale and towards Yorkshire, continual wet weather may be regarded as certain. If the storm clouds
are driven southwards and ride over
Bleasdale and Bottom Fells, wet weather
will be heard of in Derbyshire and the
surrounding districts.

"East winds and honest men go to bed
together," is another proverb, in reference
to the east wind generally dying away
early in the evening.

"When the smoke goes west,
    Good weather is past,
When the smoke goes east
    Fine weather comes neist" (next).

If a rainbow appears in the eye of the
wind, rain is sure to follow, and if its
predominating hue is green more rain
may be expected; if red, then wind as
well as rain.

The clouds formed another weather-
glass, as it were. A perfectly cloudless
sky is almost always followed by rain.
Before strong east winds set in, a
heavy bank of clouds is seen to rest
behind the fells above Bowland; these
clouds remain stationary for hours, until
breaking away in detached pieces, they
come down the hills towards the sea in
heavy gusts and squalls, hence the
rhyme—

"When the scud flies high,
    You may let your kites fly;
When the scud flies low
    Then prepare for a blow."

In spring and autumn if the morning
mist rises from rivers and low ground the
day will be fine, and the sun is said to be
"rolling up his blanket." If, however,
the mist instead of disappearing covers
the sky, and the clear blue of the early
morning is changed to a leaden sky, there
will be rain. The sun is then said to
have spread out his blanket, or to have
gone to bed. A watery, leaden sky is
often called a "blanket sky."

The coming of rain is likewise denoted
to the weather-wise by the action of
plants. The small bindweed, the scarlet
pimpernel, shut up their flowers before
approaching rain; the latter flower is
often called the "Poor man's weather-
glass." If the convolvulus shuts up its
leaves in the morning a thunderstorm may
be expected, whilst chickweed expands its
leaves boldly and fully when fine weather
is to follow.

When sounds are heard with great dis-
tinctness on the countryside, it is taken
as betokening rain—

"A good hearing day is a sign of wet,
    Much sound in the air is a sign of rain."

At Glasson, for example, if railway trains
are heard distinctly on the main-line,
there will be open weather to the east-
ward, and easterly winds. And when in
still weather the sea is heard upon Rossall

reef, there is a saying in Glasson, "Rossall's wife is churning." This is an unfailing sign of coming south-west storms. When the guns at Fleetwood are clearly heard it is common to say that the sky is open to the south-westward and to expect a change in the weather, with wind blowing from that direction.

Of the sayings attaching to the months of the year, March has the larger proportion, it being believed that the weather in that month was an indication of the following summer—

"A wet March makes a sad harvest."

"Never come March
Never come winter."

"A peck of March dust
And a shower in May,
Make the corn green
And the fields gay."

Of April it was said—

"April borrows of March again
Three days of wind and rain,"

whilst "A cold May enriches no one," is borne out by "A dry May and a dripping June bring all things in tune," but the latter saying is contradicted by—

"June if sunny, brings harvests early."

Portents also attached to the weather upon certain days of the week, thus, "A wet Sunday, 'tis wet all the week." Wednesday is another important day—

"Wednesday is aye weather true
Whether the Moon be old or new."

When the Welsh mountains are clearly seen from Glasson Dock it is said that a severe gale is sure to follow from the south-west; and when Blackcombe is visible and clear from Lancaster, fine weather will follow, but rain is coming when it is capped with cloud. Rain too, may be expected when the Isle of Man, or the Welsh mountains can be seen from Lancaster churchyard or Blackpool; or when the Lake mountains are particularly clear and distinct.

There is a saying, "A bee was never caught in a shower."

"If Bees stay at home,
Rain will soon come;
If they fly away,
Fine will be the day."

And here is another rhyme about bees—

"A swarm of bees in May
Is worth a load of hay;
A swarm of bees in June
Is worth a silver spoon;
But a swarm in July
Is not worth a fly."

Animals, birds and insects all exhibit signs of restlessness before a change in the weather—

"When oxen low and midges bite
We all do know 'twill rain to-night."

"When dogs eat grass there will be rain."

"When cattle lie much rain is expected."

"When cattle walk much fine weather is looked for."

Crows on the sand or curlews on the land are signs of rain. When sea-gulls come screaming on the low land, bad weather may be expected—

"Sea gull, sea gull, get thee on t' sand,
'Twill never be fine whilst thou'rt on land."

There are innumerable sayings and proverbs showing how the ordinary matters of life were regarded as weather signs. As for example, "When the smoke rises straight up from the chimney, it will be fine, but when smoke donks [1] it will rain."

When the fire burns faster than usual, and with a blue flame frosty weather may be expected.

"If it raineth at tide's flow
You may safely go and mow,
But if it raineth at the ebb
Then if you like, go off to bed,"

gives the belief that rain with an ebb tide was likely to be continuous.

Pain, too, was looked upon as a sign of bad weather—

"A coming storm your shooting corns presage
And aches will throb, your hollow tooth will rage."

[1] Falls.

OLD GRAMMAR SCHOOL, LANCASTER

LANCASTER, unlike many other places in the County Palatine, had not to wait until the Tudor period for its school. This is proved by a deed of the thirteenth century, one of the witnesses to which was Thomas de Kyrkeham, "master of the school at Lancaster." There is no date to this deed, but in 1384 there is a record that "Emma, wife of Thomas, the schoolmaster of Lancaster," appeared as a defendant in a case at the Assizes. But the grammar school proper did not come into existence until 1472, when one, John Gardyner, not only established it but gave it an endowment of six marks a year charged upon Newton Mill. Gardyner's will was proved in 1483 and some twenty years later an arrangement was made between his surviving trustee and the Mayor of Lancaster, by which the nomination of the schoolmaster was vested in the Corporation. During the next seventy years the youth of Lancaster received its education at John Gardyner's school. Then a calamity affected its fortunes.

The mill from which it drew its modest endowment of six marks a year was destroyed by a flood, or as the old chronicle puts it, was by "a great rage of waters utterly decayed." No payment therefore could be made and consequently the school ceased to exist. How the boys of Lancaster were educated during the next forty years is not recorded. No mention is made of any school in the town until 1615, when Randal Carter of "the parish of St. Savior in Southwark, in the county of Surrey, a citizen and tallow chandeler of London," left an annuity of ten pounds a year in his will, "towards the meyntenance of an usher in the free schoole of Lancaster." This annuity was a charge upon land in Whitecross Street, "without

Cripplegate," in London. It was paid for over two centuries and a half to the Corporation of Lancaster. In 1886 the land which produced the ten pounds annuity was sold to the Metropolitan Board of Works for £328 7s. 2d., this sum being placed in the hands of the Charity Commissioners.

Three years before the death of King Charles II. the school, which was sadly out of repair, was found to be too small and dark. It was therefore rebuilt. At that time there were only two masters—the head-master who received a salary of thirty pounds a year, and an usher who received fifteen pounds a year. The head-master or the usher apparently had to teach the young Lancastrians how to write, for a writing master was not appointed until 1768. His salary was ten pounds a year. The head-master, following the agreement made in 1500 between the trustees of John Gardyner's will and the then Mayor, was always appointed by the Mayor and Corporation of Lancaster. In the report of the Corporation in 1824 it was stated that there were then sixty-four boys in the school, forty-six of these being the sons of freemen.

Besides their salaries, the head-masters and ushers of the old Grammar School received "cock-pennies" from the boys on Shrove Tuesday. This was a payment made by the scholars to the masters in place of the perquisites they obtained formerly from a barbarous game played by the boys upon this particular holiday. On Shrove Tuesday the boys were allowed to have cock-fights, when all the birds that were killed became the perquisite of the master. There was also a barbarous game played upon the same day called "throwing at cocks," when each boy, armed with a stick of a certain length and thickness—called in the sixteenth century a " cock-stele "—threw it at a cock penned in an enclosure; the boy who killed the cock won the game, but, as in the cock-fighting, the body of the bird went to the master's kitchen. In some places the cock was partially buried in the ground, its head and tail only being exposed to the throwing of the sticks.

This brutal game is said to have had its origin in the reign of Edward III., penny." At Lancaster the " cock-penny " was paid until 1824; in that year it was decided by the Corporation that it should be given up, and in its place the usher was to receive ten shillings a quarter for every boy in his charge, whilst the head-master was to be paid fifteen shillings a quarter for each boy on the lower benches and twenty shillings a quarter for each boy on the upper benches. At the same

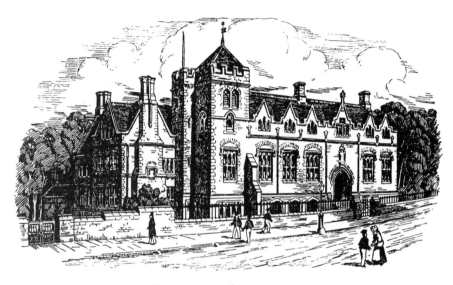

THE GRAMMAR SCHOOL, LANCASTER

when the fierce and bitter war with France was raging. The Latin word *gallus* means not only a cock but also a French-man—hence the word Gallic as applied to the French nation. The school-boys of that time, seizing upon the double meaning of the word, vented their patriotic feelings upon cocks, every bird killed by their sticks representing a Frenchman. When cock-fighting and throwing at cocks fell into well-merited disfavour, the larders of the school-masters suffered. In order to make good the deficiency each scholar had to pay a penny on Shrove Tuesday, a donation which was called a " cock-

time it was decided that there should no longer be any free education in the Lan-caster Grammar School, " there being ample provision for that kind of education in the national and other schools."

Upon the lengthy roll of its scholars the Lancaster Grammar School shows two great names, those of Sir Richard Owen and William Whewell. Sir Richard Owen, who became the greatest anatomist in England and one of her foremost men of science, went to the Lancaster Grammar School when he was six years old. Like so many boys who in later life become distinguished and brilliant men, Owen showed no signs of his great talents at school. His only hobby was heraldry, a subject far removed from the surgery and science with which his name will always be associated. In 1820 after having been ten years at the Lancaster Grammar School and being then aged sixteen, Owen was apprenticed to a Lancaster surgeon and apothecary called Dickson. Two years later Dickson died, and the youth was transferred to another Lancaster doctor called Joseph Seed, who in 1823 became a naval surgeon. Owen was then transferred, for the second time, to James Stockdale Harrison. The apprentices or pupils of this doctor had access to the gaol in Lancaster Castle, and had the privilege given them of carrying out post-mortem examinations there. Owen speedily became interested in the study of anatomy, and from these first experiences in Lancaster Castle may be dated the beginnings of that profound knowledge of the human body which made Owen's name famous in medical circles throughout the world. Queen Victoria had a special regard for Sir Richard Owen, and gave him a delightful house, called Sheen Lodge in Richmond Park, as a residence. Here he lived until his death in 1892.

William Whewell and Richard Owen were school-fellows at Lancaster, and remained lifelong friends, although men of very different temperaments. Whewell, the son of a master carpenter, was born in Brook Street, Lancaster, in 1794. He was sent to the " Blue School, " but Joseph Rowley, the master of the Grammar School, chancing one day to talk to the boy, was so struck by his intelligence and

ability that he offered to teach him without charge at the Grammar School. The elder Whewell had intended to apprentice his son to his own trade, but after some hesitation consented to the master's suggestion. Mr. Rowley's opinion of Whewell's talents was fully justified by his after life. He went to Cambridge and after a brilliant career there became one of the leading scientific writers of his day. In 1825 he was ordained a priest, and until 1841 was one of the leading tutors at the University. In October of that year he was appointed Master of Trinity College, one of the highest honours at Cambridge. This office he held until his death in 1866. It has been written of Whewell, " During his term of the mastership he was incomparably superior to any of the other heads of colleges, very few of whom had any reputation outside of Cambridge, while none showed any intellectual power at all of the same order. Whewell's force of character, as well as his knowledge and abilities, soon gave him the most prominent position in the University, and no master . . . had been so worthy to preside over the greatest of English colleges. Happily too, although masterful and rejoicing in argument, he was thoroughly magnanimous." A year after his election both Whewell and Owen were entertained at a public dinner in their native town of Lancaster. Whewell was a man of splendid physical development, and there was a story told at Cambridge of the Master of Trinity being thus addressed by a prize-fighter, " What a man was lost when they made you a parson."

A Famous Lancashire Steeple-jack

THERE died at Rochdale nine years ago a man who was justly called "the most famous steeple-jack in the world." Wherever there were tall chimneys the name of Joseph Smith was well known; hundreds of articles were written about him in magazines and newspapers, as well as a book, *The Lancashire Steeple-Jack*, which described his methods of work and many of his adventures.

He enjoyed the reputation of having felled more chimneys than any other member of his calling, and although he repaired and destroyed chimneys and steeples all over the country and abroad, no serious accident ever happened to him or to the many men in his employment. But he himself had some narrow escapes. Perhaps his worst experience was a struggle with one of his own workmen who suddenly went mad whilst he and his master were working on the top of a tall chimney at a corn mill near the old railway station at Rochdale.

Without any warning the man suddenly uttered a loud cry and leaped into the air. "As he disappeared," says the author of *The Lancashire Steeple-Jack*, his employer seized him by the ankle, and the unfortunate madman hung, a dead weight, in mid-air. It was a desperate situation, and no man but one of iron strength and courage could have faced and overcome it.

"A most terrible struggle ensued, a struggle which, as one may readily believe, was as likely to prove disastrous to the rescuer as the rescued. By an almost superhuman effort Mr. Smith managed to pull the hanging body up until he could seize the man's belt. Having got hold of this he dragged the still struggling workman on to the platform, where the battle was renewed more furiously than ever.

"Remember that these two men had to fight it out between themselves upon a narrow scaffolding on a high mill chimney far beyond the reach of all prompt human aid. So desperate was the madman that, finding his repeated attempts to throw himself over ineffectual, he tried to bite himself free, and to this day the Lancashire steeple-jack bears marks of this appalling contest." (The story was written in Mr. Smith's lifetime.) "At last becoming weak himself, and knowing that he must adopt the most extreme measures for their joint safety, he seized a small crowbar and with it struck the struggling lunatic a stunning blow on the head. But even this was not enough, and before the unhappy wretch could be sufficiently subdued another was needed. Then the Lancashire steeple-jack found that it was possible to lower his assailant to the ground by means of a rope attached to his belt.

"By the time the ground was reached the maniac had almost recovered consciousness, and the terrible nature of his attack may be understood when it is stated that, on a stone bottle containing brandy being applied to his lips as a restorative, he bit the neck off with his teeth. The man eventually recovered. This terrible encounter was witnessed by a considerable number of people at Rochdale station, who were waiting for their trains."

During the course of his dangerous calling, Smith's presence of mind had grown into what was practically an instinct. Once, he was working on the top of a tall chimney which was very much out of the plumb. Suddenly he heard the ominous sound that precedes the fall of brickwork raised to a great height, and the next instant was sliding down the life-line like a cat. Long experience had told him which way the chimney would fall, and when he reached the ground he darted in the opposite direction. Scarcely had he run ten yards when the chimney collapsed with a roar like a whole battery of guns being fired at once.

On another occasion he was employed in removing a dangerous coping, when it suddenly fell, carrying away the scaffolding upon which he was standing. By a happy chance the coping was at the very top of the chimney. As the scaffolding fell, Smith seized the edge of the chimney-top, and drawing himself up, lay upon it, his legs dangling outside, his head and shoulders over the inside. He was badly scorched by the hot bricks, and almost suffocated by the smoke and hot air, but nevertheless he gradually worked his way round the edge of the chimney until he got to the ladder, and then reached the ground in safety.

His worst fall was from a chimney seventy-five feet high. Whilst he was fixing the last section of laddering at the top, part of the ladder below collapsed, and Smith fell straight to the ground. The horrified spectators rushed to him, expecting to find him dead, but although badly hurt, he was still breathing. But not a single bone was broken, and beyond a few bad bruises, the steeple-jack was none the worse.

The laddering of a tall chimney is a perilous proceeding. An iron dog or "holdfast" tipped with steel is driven firmly into the brickwork. To this is lashed an eighteen-foot ladder which the steeple-jack mounts, taking with him another ladder, the bottom of which he lashes to the top of the first ladder.

"I can fix," Smith once said, "with the assistance of one labourer, sixty yards of laddering in forty-five minutes. It is true that as the top end of each ladder is loose it sways a bit as you mount, but it is safe enough. There are few people, of course, who would care to sit cross-legged on the top rung of a swinging ladder twenty feet from the ground; but the position is the only one which gives the leverage you want for driving in the holdfasts. Yet, careful as I always am, the unexpected is always happening. I remember once as I was walking round the coping of a two-hundred-foot chimney the whole of the coping gave way under my feet. Down I went with the débris, but we parted company on the road, for fortunately I fell close to the ladders, which I clutched and so saved myself."

The most hazardous feat he ever attempted was fixing a flag to the lance of the wooden St. George, which stood on the spire of the old Rochdale Town Hall—a distance of two hundred and sixty-five feet from the ground—in honour of John Bright's birthday. "After I had started climbing," Smith said, " hand over hand, I found, to my dismay, that the lightning conductor was in a very insecure state. However, there was no help for it, so I persevered. Arrived at the summit, a still more dangerous task awaited me. This was to get a footing on the shoulders of the wooden man and lash a pole eighteen feet long with a banner attached, to the lance of St. George. I succeeded in doing this, but I should not care to tackle the job again."

For some ten years, Smith lived in a kind of Pullman Car, which he fitted up with much comfort and some little luxury. He disliked lodgings, and had an overwhelming fear of damp beds. By living in this unusual kind of habitation, he could travel up and down the country— literally a movable house on wheels— without ever leaving his home. But his wife grew tired of it; likewise " some difficulty arose with the Corporation, who did not appear to be quite able to classify the structure," and very reluctantly the great steeple-jack was obliged to go to a more conventional dwelling. However, he continued to use his luxurious caravan for his work.

Smith was a short man, only five feet five and a half inches in height, but he had a striking personality. It was written of him, " His clear-cut features demonstrated the old saying, ' There goes a man who would tackle the devil himself.' He did not smoke, and was a total abstainer, not from any reason of fad or principle, but because of the nature of his perilous calling.

" A man that has to do the jobs that I do," he said, " can't drink and be successful."

RINGING THE PAN

IN the neighbourhood of Burnley there still lingers a curious idea that it is wrong for an engaged couple to " court" on Friday night, and in former times public opinion upon the subject was expressed in a very unpleasant manner. The offending pair were treated to what was called " Ringing the Pan." A band of young people, chiefly young men, armed with frying-pans, pokers, tongs, shovels, and pieces of tin, formed a procession, and, headed by a pretended bellman, proceeded to the house where the couple were " courting," the bellman calling out at intervals—

" Oh, dear a me !
A B and C D (mentioning the names of the couple)
Court six neets out o' seven,
Un corn'd let Friday neet olooan."

Arrived at the house, the unfortunate pair were treated to a serenade—a deafening din—upon the frying-pans and shovels, etc.

THE STORY OF RICHARD HURST

THE story of Richard Hurst gives us one of those instances, unhappily too frequent in the history of religious differences, in which a man was hanged because of his faith, and not because of any crime he had committed.

Richard Hurst was a yeoman of considerable means who farmed his own small estate near Preston, early in the reign of Charles I. He was a Roman Catholic, and not having obeyed the law against recusants, the Bishop of Chester sent a pursuivant called Christopher Noncross to arrest him. Noncross took with him two men named Wilkinson and Dewhurst, the latter of whom was a "notorious ruffian," and for whose apprehension and commitment to the House of Correction the parish constable at that very moment held a warrant.

They found Hurst ploughing near his house, with a boy leading the horse; a maid-servant was harrowing in the same field. Noncross and his assistant advanced towards Hurst with the warrant, and Wilkinson struck him with his staff, a most unjustifiable proceeding. Seeing Hurst thus struck, the maid-servant ran towards the house screaming "They're killing the master! They're killing the master!" Whereupon, Mrs. Hurst, a man-servant, and a friend called Bullen, who chanced to be in the house, hurried out and were immediately attacked by Wilkinson, who "floored the two men." They sprang to their feet, however, and Dewhurst ran to Wilkinson's assistance, but as he passed the maid-servant she gave him a blow on the head. The blow had no effect whatever, but before he reached his companion, the "notorious ruffian" tripped over one of the newly ploughed furrows, and falling heavily upon the hard ground, broke his leg. Then, we are told,

"Not receiving proper attention the hurt in his leg struck up into his body and within a fortnight he died."

Before he died Dewhurst made a solemn declaration, to the hearing of which two witnesses testified on oath, that "the occasion of his death was by no other hurt than his fall, the blow on the head having nothing to do with it, and Hurst being in no way responsible for it, either by direction or management."

No evidence could be clearer or more fully substantiated. But at this juncture it had been determined that a severe example should be made of recusants. In the opinion of the authorities, the circumstances of Dewhurst's death made Hurst's case one which would be an object lesson to all those recusants who proposed to resist the law; they actually used this case as intimidation against resistance.

Hurst was therefore charged with the death of Dewhurst. At once he petitioned the King for a "pardon," a petition supported by his friends and many others who knew the actual circumstances. Queen Henrietta Maria, too, was "an earnest suitor for his life." Even in the early years of his reign the open protection of a Roman Catholic, although it might be from cruel injustice, was more than Charles I. could venture upon; he therefore decided that before the "pardon" could be granted Hurst must stand his legal trial. The unfortunate man, "trusting in the innocency of his cause, yielded himself up for trial before Sir Henry Yelverton."

At the coroner's inquest upon Dewhurst it had been proved that his only hurt was his broken leg, and this was also proved to have been the cause of his death. His declaration upon his death-bed that he had broken it himself, was likewise given before the coroner, who mentioned it in his verdict, as well as in the depositions of witnesses examined by Sir Ralph Assheton, the magistrate who committed Hurst for trial.

At the trial at Lancaster, all this went authority, and directed that they must find him guilty as "an example." In the lack of all evidence of Hurst's responsibility for Dewhurst's death, and the

RICHARD HURST

for nothing, and although the only fresh evidence then produced was that Hurst was five or six rods from Dewhurst when he fell, Sir Henry Yelverton, the judge, "contrary to all show of justice," told the jury that the prisoner was a recusant who had resisted the Bishop of Chester's latter's dying declaration, the jury hesitated to bring in such a verdict. They therefore deputed the foreman and two others to wait upon the judge in his chamber after dinner.

Yelverton listened to their pleading, and then " took the foreman by the hand

and repeated that the verdict must be murder, as an example to the other recusants." Hurst was therefore condemned —a political as well as a religious martyr— and "upon the judge's certificate to the Lord Keeper the royal pardon was stayed."

The day after this unjust sentence, Hurst was ordered to attend the church at Lancaster with other prisoners, to hear a sermon. He declined, and resisting stubbornly was dragged by the legs by the order of the High Sheriff "over a rugged and stony road for twenty or thirty yards from the prison to the church." But in the church he threw himself flat upon the ground and thrust his fingers into his ears that he might not hear the sermon. The following day was fixed for his execution.

At the foot of the gallows he was offered his life if he would take the oath of allegiance to King Charles, but as certain clauses of the oath were directly opposed to his faith Hurst replied that being a Catholic he could "not take such an oath, as it was incompatible with his belief and hence unlawful." When mounted upon the fatal ladder he was given another chance, but, reiterating his refusal, was cast off, the date being 29th August, 1628.

There is no other instance in the history of Lancashire in which the law was deliberately prostituted to strike terror into a sect or party, besides this case of Richard Hurst. The Roman Catholics by their brave adherence to their faith, were causing the authorities no little anxiety. By hanging Hurst they sought to terrify his co-religionists into obedience and allegiance; this they could only do by a false charge of murder.

The illustration, reproduced from a print of the time, is very curious. It gives the whole history of the case. In the foreground Hurst stands with clasped hands, a halter round his neck. On the left, in the background, he is seen at his plough, whilst Wilkinson is in the act of striking him with his staff. Beyond, Dewhurst is shown, fallen to the ground, and Hurst standing at some distance from him. On the right is the gallows with Hurst at the foot of the ladder, refusing to save his life by taking an oath which he believed was not compatible with his religion.

CHARLES I

(From a miniature drawing by Matthew Snelling, 1647)

THE SAMLESBURY WITCHES

DURING the summer of 1612 no less than nineteen persons were lying in the prisons of Lancaster Castle on the charge of witchcraft, ten from the Pendle Forest district, one from Gisburn in Craven, one from Windle near Prescot, and eight from Samlesbury. But of these last eight only three were brought to trial at the Assizes—Jennet Bierley, Ellen Bierley and Jane Southworth. The charge against them was that they had "feloniously practised, exercised, and used diverse, devilish and wicked arts, called Witchcraft, Inchauntments, Charmes, and Sorceries, in and upon one Grace Sowerbutts, so that by means thereof her body wasted and consumed." This Grace Sowerbutts was a girl of fourteen, the daughter of a husbandman called Thomas Sowerbutts. She was the principal witness against these three women, one of whom, Jennet Bierley, was her grandmother, who were standing their trial for their lives. Jane Southworth was a natural daughter of Sir Richard Sherburne of Stonyhurst, and the widow of the grandson of Sir John Southworth, lord of the manor of Samlesbury. Ellen Bierley was apparently a relative by marriage of the girl Sowerbutts.

Grace Sowerbutts' evidence has been preserved, and is a strange record of the lengths to which superstition and the fixed belief in the powers and practices of witches could be carried. She swore upon oath that :—

"For the space of some years now last past she hath been haunted and vexed with some women who have used to come to her ; which women she sayeth were Jennet Bierley, the Informant's grandmother, Ellen Bierley, wife to Henry Bierley ; Jane Southworth, late the wife of John Southworth ; and an Old Doewife, all of Samlesburie aforesaid. And she saith, that now lately these foure women did violently draw her by the haire of the head, and laid her on the toppe of a Hay-mowe, in the said Henry Bierley's Barn. And she saith, further, that not long after, the said Jennet Bierley did meet (her) near unto the place where she dwelleth, and first appeared in her own likeness, and after that in the likeness of a black Dog, and as (witness) did go over a style, she picked (pitched or pushed) her off ; howbeit she saith she had no hurt then, but rose again, and went to her Aunt's in Osbaldeston, and returned back again to her Father's house the same night, being fetched home by her father. That in her way homewards she did then tell her father how she had been dealt withall both then and at sundry times before that ; and before that time she never told anybody thereof ; and being examined why she did not, she saith she could not speak thereof, though she desired so to do. And she further sayeth that upon Saturday, being the fourth of this instant April (witness) going toward Samlesbury bote (boat) to meet her mother coming from Preston, she saw the said Jennet Bierley who met (her) at a place called the Two Brigges, first in her own shape, and afterwards in the likeness of a black Dog, with two legges, which dog went close by the left side of (witness) till they came to a Pit of Water, and then the said Dog spake, and persuaded the Examinate to drown herself there, saying it was a fair and an easie death. Whereupon this Examinate thought there came one to her in a white sheet and carried her away from the said pit, upon the coming whereof the said black dog departed away ; and shortly after the said white thing departed also. And after (she) had gone further on her way, about the length of two or three fields, the said black dog did meet her again, and going on her left side, as aforesaid, did carry her into a barn of one Hugh

Walshman's, near thereby, and layed (her) upon the barn floor, and covered (her) with straw on her body, and hay on her head, and the dog itself lay on the top of the said straw, but how long the dog lay there this examinate cannot tell, nor how long herself lay there, for she sayth, that upon her lying down there, as aforesaid, her speech and senses were taken from her, and the first time she knew where she was, she was layed upon a bed in the said Walshman's house, which (as she hath since been told) was upon the Monday at night following; and she was also told that she was found and taken from the place where she first lay, by some of her friends, and carried into the said Walshman's house, within a few hours after she was layed in the barn, as aforesaid. And she further sayth, that upon the day following, being Tuesday, near night of the same day, she was fetched by her father and mother from the said Walshman's house to her father's house. And she sayth, that at the place before specified, called the Two Brigges, the said Jennet Bierley and Ellen Bierley did appear unto her in their own shapes; whereupon (witness) fell down, and after that was not able to speak or go, till the Friday following; during which time, as she lay in her father's house, the said Jennet Bierley and Ellen Bierley did once appear unto her in their own shapes, but they did nothing unto her there, neither did she ever see them since. And she further sayth that a good while before this (she) did go with the said Jennet Bierley, her grandmother, and the said Ellen Bierley, her aunt, at the bidding of her said grandmother, to the house of one Thomas Walsham, in Samlesbury aforesaid. And coming thither in the night, when all the household was a-bed, the doors being shut, the said Jennet Bierley did open them, but this Examinate knoweth not how;

and being come into the said house (witness) and the said Ellen Bierley stayed there, and the said Jennet Bierley went into the chamber where the said Walshman and his wife lay, and from thence brought a little child, which this Examinate thinketh was in the bed with its father and mother; and after the said Jennet Bierley had set her down by the fire with the said child, she did thrust a nail into the navel of the said child, and afterwards did take a (quill) pen and put it in at the said place, and did suck there a good space, and afterwards laid the child in bed again, and then the said Jennet and the said Ellen returned to their own houses, (witness) with them. And she thinks that neither the said Thomas Walshman nor his wife knew that the said child was taken out of the bed from them. And she saith also, that the said child did not cry when it was hurt, as aforesaid; but she saith, that she thinketh that the said child did thenceforth languish, and not long after died. And after the death of the said child, the next night after the burial thereof, the said Jennet Bierley and Ellen Bierley taking (witness) with them went to Samlesbury Church and there did take up the said child, and the said Jennet did carry it out the churchyard in her arms, and there did put it in her lap and carried it home to her own house, and having it there did boil some thereof in a Pot, and some did broil on the coals, of both of which the said Jane and Ellen did eat, and would have had this Examinate and one Grace Bierley, daughter of the said Ellen, to have eaten with them, but they refused so to do; and afterwards the said Jennet and Ellen did seethe the bones of the said child in a pot, and with the fat that came out of the said bones they said they would anoint themselves, that thereby they might sometimes change themselves into other shapes. And after all this being done, they said they would lay the bones again in the grave the next night following, but whether they did so or not the Examinate knoweth not; neither doth she know how they got it out of the grave at the first taking of it up. And being further sworn and examined, she deposed and saith, that about half a year ago, the said Jennet Bierley, Ellen Bierley, and Jane Southworth, and this (witness) (who went by the appointment of the said Jennet, her grandmother) did meet at a place called Red Banck, upon the North side of the water of Ribble, every Thursday and Sunday at night by the space of a fortnight, and at the waterside there came unto them, as they went thither, four black things, going upright and yet not like men in the face; which four did carry the said three women and (witness) over the Water, and when they came to the said Red Banck they found something there which they did eat. But (witness) saith she never saw such meat; and therefore she durst not eat thereof, although her said Grandmother did bid her eat. And after they had eaten, the said three Women and (witness) danced every one of them.

" (Witness) further saith upon her oath, that about ten days after her Examination taken at Blackburn, she being then come to her Father's house again, after she had been certain days at her Uncle's house in Houghton, Jane Southworth, widow, did meet (witness) at her Father's house door and did carry her into the loft and there did lay her upon the floor, where she was shortly found by her Father, and brought down and laid in a bed, as afterwards she was told; for she saith, that from the first meeting of the said Jane Southworth she (witness) had her speech and senses taken from her. But the next day, she saith, she came somewhat to herself, and then the said Widow Southworth came again to (witness) to her bed-side, and took her out of bed, and said to (her) that she now would after do to her, and thereupon put her upon a hay-stack standing some three or four yards high from the earth, where she was found after great search made by a neighbour's Wife near dwelling, and then laid in her bed again, where she remained speechless and senseless as before, by the space of two or three days. And being recovered within a week after, she saith, that the said Jane Southworth did come again to (witness) at her father's house, and did take her away, and laid her in a ditch near to the house upon her face, and left her there, when she was found shortly after and laid upon a bed, but had not her senses again for a day and a night or thereabouts. And she further saith, That upon Tuesday last before the taking of this her Examination the said Jane Southworth came to (witness's) Father's house, and finding (witness) without the door, took her and carried her into the Barn, and thrust her head amongst a companie of boards that were there standing, where she was shortly after found and laid in a bed, and remained in her old fit till the Thursday at night following. On being further examined touching her being at Red Banck, she saith, That the three women, by her before named, were carried back again over the Ribble by the same black things that carried them thither; and saith that at their said meeting in the Red Banck, there did come also divers other women, and did meet them there, some old, some young, which (witness) thinketh did dwell upon the North side of the Ribble, because she saw them not come over the water, but (she) knew none of them; neither did she see them eat or dance, or do anything else that the rest did, saving that they were there and looked on."

Such was the extraordinary and circumstantial story told by the girl Grace Sowerbutts. The grandmother changing herself into a black dog, and the four women being carried over the Ribble by four mysterious beings, and the eating of the flesh of the dead child were all common superstitions with regard to witches; but this part of the story received support from the testimony of Thomas Walshman, who swore upon oath that "he had a child died about Lent twelvemonth who had been sicke by the space of a fortnight or three weeks, and was afterwards buried in Samlesburie church; which child when it died was a year old, but how it came to the death of it (witness) knoweth not. And he further said that about the fifteenth of April last, or thereabouts, the said Grace Sowerbutts was found in (his) father's farm, laid under a little hay and straw, and from thence was carried into (his) house, and there laid until the Monday at night following, during which time she did not speak, but lay as if she had been dead."

Another witness, John Singleton, a yeoman, a few days before the Assizes, made a deposition to Robert Holden of Holden Hall, and Justice of the Peace, swearing that he had "often heard his old master, Sir John Southworth, knight, now deceased, say touching the late wife of John Southworth (his grandson) now in the gaol, for suspicion of witchcraft, that the said wife was as he thought an evill woman, and a Witch, and he said he was sorry for her husband, that was his kinsman, for he thought she would kill him." This witness further declared, "that the said Sir John Southworth, in his coming or going between his own house at Samlesbury and the town of Preston, did for the most part forbear to pass by the house where the said wife dwelled, though it was his nearest and best way; and rode another way, only for the fear of the said wife, as (witness) verily thinketh." William Alker, another Samlesbury yeoman, corroborated this statement as to the grandfather of Jane Southworth's husband believing her to be a witch. Alker swore "that he hath seen the said Sir John Southworth shun to meet the wife of John Southworth, now Prisoner in the Gaol, when he came near where she was; and hath heard the said Sir John Southworth say that he liked her not, and that he doubted she would bewitch him."

This evidence was a grotesque fabrication, for Sir John Southworth died in 1595, seventeen years before this trial, and his will shows that six weeks prior to his death, his grandson John (the husband of the lady accused of witchcraft) was still unmarried. As a matter of fact John Southworth could only have been about fourteen years of age at the time of the old knight's death, whose will states the giving of certain property to the wife of his son Thomas, "or to such wife as Johne Southworth, sonne and heir apparent of the said Thomas shall marrie." It was therefore impossible for the old Sir John to have believed Jane Southworth to be a witch, or to have avoided her house at Lower Hall, Samlesbury, as these two men so glibly and untruthfully declared. John Southworth had died a few months before the accusation made against his wife, the real cause of which would appear to have arisen from religious differences in the family.

The only evidence against the three unhappy women that in any way corroborated the amazing story of Grace Sowerbutts, was the testimony of these two perjurers, and the death of Walshman's child, but no proof could be adduced that the Bierleys had anything to do with it. The girl's father, Thomas Sowerbutts, was called, but he could only say that he had found "the wench upon the hay in one of her counterfeit fits."

This concluded the case for the prosecution, and the presiding judge demanded what answers the prisoners had to make, and they "humbly upon their knees with weeping tears desired him for God's cause to examine Grace Sowerbutts, who set her on, or by whose means this accusation came against them."

A curious scene followed. The suggestion that they had been "set on" evidently found the accusers unprepared, for "immediately the countenance of Grace Sowerbutts changed, the witnesses, being behind, began to quarrel and accuse one another." The judge himself examined the girl Sowerbutts, "who could not for her life give any direct answer, but strangely amazed, told him she was put to a master to learn, but he told her nothing of this." Her father was re-examined as to "what master taught his daughter," but he denied every question upon the point. Some of those present in court then told the judge the truth; and the prisoners themselves stated that Grace Sowerbutts "had gone to learn with one Thompson, a Seminary priest, who had instructed and taught her this accusation against them, because they were once obstinate Papists and now came to church." In her evidence, Jane Southworth drew aside the curtain from a family tragedy. "Jane Southworth saith, she saw Master Thompson, alias Southworth, the Priest, a month or six weeks before she was committed to the gaol; and had conference with him in a place called Barn-hay Lane, where and when she challenged him for slandering her to be a Witch; whereunto he answered that what he had heard thereof he heard from her mother and her aunt; yet, she, this Examinate, thinketh in her heart it was

by his procurement, is so moved to think, for that she would not be persuaded from the (Protestant) Church."

"Master Thompson, alias Southworth," was Christopher Southworth, the fourth son of Sir John Southworth, and therefore the uncle of Jane Southworth's husband. He was a Roman Catholic priest, and had been imprisoned in Wisbeach Castle during the reign of Queen Elizabeth. The Southworths were staunch Roman Catholics, old Sir John himself having suffered imprisonment for his faith's sake at Manchester. In the reign of Queen Mary Tudor, Sir John had been held in high esteem and was High Sheriff of Lancashire, even after the accession of Queen Elizabeth. During the last year (1557) of Mary's reign, he was warmly commended because of his desire to remain in the Queen's service with his hundred men, and "being a toward and tall gentleman," it was requested that his "honest suit" should be favoured. But eleven years later "for not repairing to Church, nor receiving the sacrament, and for speaking against the Book of Common Prayer," Sir John was thrown into the New Fleet Prison at Manchester, and only gained his liberty on the payment of a fine of five hundred pounds.

Jane Southworth had recently entered the Protestant Church and, seeing the bitter religious controversy of the time, there is some reason for accepting the sinister suggestion made to the court that her relative had sought to bring about her utter destruction, and that of the Bierleys, by inciting Grace Sowerbutts to accuse them of witchcraft—a charge more easily proved than disproved in those days of crude superstition.

By the judge's order the girl was taken out of her father's charge and "committed to Mr. Leigh, a very religious preacher, and Mr. Chisnell, two Justices

of the Peace, to be carefully examined."
After being subjected to a close interrogation Grace Sowerbutts confessed that all her statements about the witchcraft of the prisoners was false, and that "one Master Thompson, which she taketh to be Master Christopher Southworth, to whom she was sent to learn her prayers, did persuade, counsell, and advise her" to make these horrible charges against her grandmother and her aunt and against Mrs. Jane Southworth.

The three women were acquitted; but there is no record of any punishment being meted out to those who had endeavoured to swear away their lives.

AN OLD ADVERTISEMENT OF SILHOUETTE CUTTING

THE SIEGES OF BLACKBURN

WHEN the Civil War between King Charles I. and the Parliament broke out in 1642, Blackburn and Salford and their neighbourhoods were strong for the Parliament, whilst West Derby, Leyland, Amounderness, and Lonsdale were Royalist. Manchester was the political and military head-quarters of the Roundheads, as the Parliamentarians were called, and was strongly defended. Bolton also was partially fortified, but Blackburn, although very much exposed to the enemy, had no fortifications. Indeed, in the whole of the Hundred of Blackburn the only fortified place was Clitheroe Castle, and each of the other market towns, Burnley, Colne, and Haslingden, was better protected than Blackburn itself, by reason of the roughness and badness of the roads that led to them.

In September 1642 the Roman Catholic gentlemen of Lancashire had petitioned King Charles to relax the law which forbade them—they were called Recusants—to keep arms in their houses, and asked that the arms previously taken from them might be " redelivered in this time of actuall war." Happily for them the permission was immediately granted, the loyal " Recusants " being bidden to " provide sufficient arms for themselves, their servants and their tenants, to be used in defence of their own persons and property and of the royal interests. The following month the Parliamentarians in order " to keep their soldiers in exercise " sent some of their captains into the Blackburn Hundred, and their first action was to make a raid upon the Townley estate with the object of capturing Townley Hall. Both sides were, however, fearful of each other's designs. The Royalists about Preston were afraid lest the Blackburn and Salford Roundheads should come down upon them

unawares. whilst the Parliamentarians about Padiham were afraid lest the Royalists from Preston should attack them, they being still unprepared. Richard Shuttleworth of Gawthorpe, a member of Parliament, was the leader of the Parliamentarians. The Sheriff of the county put an end to these doubts and fears by ordering all the Royalist gentry of the Leyland district and their tenants to be in readiness to take the field " upon four and twenty howres further notice and warninge, on pain and forfeiture of their lives and estates." " Fforasmuch," ran the writ of summons, " as the rebellious Route under the conduct of Richard Shuttleworth Esq. and others within this County palatine of Lancaster, doe daylie swell and increase in a greater rebellious body, which commit severall outrages and notorious wicked acts and offences, ffor speedie redresse and suppression whereof I am required to raise and have in readiness the power of the County." In obedience to this summons Sir Gilbert Hoghton, the brilliant courtier of James I., together with William Farrington of Worden, had been busily employed during the months of October and November in getting their levies into fighting order.

When the Roman Catholics in the Hundred of Blackburn had been disarmed some little time before by the order of the Parliament, the arms so taken had been deposited at Whalley. Now, Blackburn, surrounded on all sides by low hills, and with no defences or fortifications of any kind, was completely dominated by Sir Gilbert, either from Hoghton Tower or from Walton. He therefore decided to seize the arms stored at Whalley and to take them to Blackburn, making the place an advanced Royalist post. Accordingly, towards the end of November he marched his men to Whalley, seized the arms, and then fell back upon Blackburn, which he had already caused to be occupied by a body of foot soldiers. So far his manœuvre had been most successful, the people of Blackburn making no resistance. But Sir Gilbert reckoned without the enemy. Colonel Shuttleworth having received word of his intention, "had a Rendavous of the Clubmen of Blackburne Hundred upon Houley (Healey) Moor, where they held a consultation which course to take about those Armes, the general vote being not to let them goe out of their Hundred, but eyther Reskewe them or adventure themselves to the hazard. Soe at night," continues the Puritan chronicler, "hearing that Sir Gilbert with his Companie and the Armes had taken up their quarters at Blackburne, they silently fell down upon Blackburne beating up their quarters, took many of Sir Gilbert's soldiers prisoners (and) seased upon the Armes."

Sir Gilbert, utterly surprised and overcome by this sudden and unexpected night attack, fled out of the town. The prisoners were taken before Colonel Shuttleworth, who released them, with the advice " to be honest men and keep at home."

Such was the true story of the events at Whalley and Blackburn on that November day—the seizure of the arms, the peaceful occupation of Blackburn, and the night surprise and flight. The following account shows the colour party and religious rancour can give. It was written by Thomas Jesland, a rabid Puritan and Parliamentarian :—

" Now the men of Blackburn, Paduam, Burneley, Clitheroe and Colne, with those sturdy churles in the two forests of Pendle and Rossendale, have raised their spirits and have resolved to fight it out rather than their Beef and fatt Bacon shall be taken from them. For the last Weeke,

Sir Gilbert Hoghton set his Beacon on fire, which stood upon the top of Hoghton Tower and was the signal to the countrey for the Papists and Malignants to arise in the Field (Fylde), and in Lealand Hundred ; whereupon great multitudes accordingly resorted to him at Preston in Andernesse, and ran to Blackburne, and so through the countrey disarming all, and pillaging some ; which Master Shuttleworth, a Parliament man, and Master Starkie hearing of, presently had gotten together out of the places formerly mentioned about 8,000 men, met with Sir Gilbert and his Catholique Malignants at Hinfield Moor, put them to flight, tooke away many of their armes, and pursued Sir Gilbert so hotley that he quit his Horse, leaped into a field, and by the coming of night escaped through fur (furze) bushes and by-wayes to Preston, and there makes great defence by chaining up the Ribble Bridge and getting what force he can into the Towne for its securitie, out of which the countrie swears they will have him by God's help, with all his adherents either quicke or dead ; so that by the next post I hope I shall certifie of some good fortune that the countrey will be in. O that Parliament had but sent downe their one thousand Dragoniers into the countrey— we would not have left a Masse-monger nor Malignant of note but we could have provided a lodging for him."

The number given by Jesland of the Roundhead forces—eight thousand—is grotesque. But of the many scribes who set pen to paper during those troubled days, not one upon either side has given the reason of the peasantry taking sides in the fray, with such outspoken frankness as Jesland. The small farmers, the labourers, and the "sturdy churles of Pendle and Rossendale," did not join the Roundhead forces from any agreement with the Puritan ideas of morals or religion, or because they hated the tyranny of King Charles. They fought simply to save "their Beefe and fatt Bacon," which they were told, and believed—and not without reason—that the Royalists intended to take. They were fighting on the Parliamentary side in order to defend their goods and their herds of cattle and swine.

Four weeks after his forced flight from Blackburn, Sir Gilbert Hoghton made another descent upon the town. But during those four weeks the few hundreds of the Parliamentarian Militia which had been left there as a garrison, had made some attempt to fortify the place, by casting up rough earthworks to guard the four entrances—one at the top of Northgate on the Ribchester road, one beyond Astleygate on the road to Preston ; one somewhere between Salford Bridge and Bottonngate, and another on the road to Darwen. It was on Christmas Eve, 1642, that Sir Gilbert made his attack, but avoiding the earthworks he got his men close to the town by an old lane leading from Mellor to Samlesbury. It was an abortive affair on both sides, but as contemporary accounts give more vivid pictures, and more reality to these far-away happenings than any recital of the facts, here is the whole scene in an account in the *Discourse of the Warr in Lancashire*, which says :—

"The Hundred of Blackburne being put into a Warlike posture, many companies of Resolut Soldiers being raised within it. The Colonels Ould Shuttleworth and Starkie, having a speciall eye to Blackburne towne, being soe neare unto Preston, as also fearing inroads into the Hundred by the enimie besydes Plundering, laid some Companies of souldiers in it, and caused some fortifications to be made about it, in some measure to secure it, and so till Christmas 1642 it continued in a quiet, reasonable condition. But

Blackburne lying within three miles of Hoghton Tower, the principal house of Sir Gilbert Hoghton, a Deputie Lieutenant for the Earle of Derbie and a commissioner of Array. He tooke it into consideration how unsafe it was for him in respect of his person and estait about Hoghton, but especiallie how dishonourable it might prove to his reputation with the King, if he suffered a Garrison of the Enimie soe neare unto his house and used no means to dissipate it, was moved about the latter end of December 1642 to thinke upon reducing that Garrison to the King's part. And thereupon resolved to set upon it, having the assistance of most of the Popish affected gentlemen in Amounderness Hundred with their Tenants in Armes, the Trained Bands, and the Clubmen of the Field (Fylde) and other parts. He marched forward from Preston the twenty-fourth daye of December, being Christmas time, up the way to Mellor to a head, soe upon the North syd of Blackburne ; set downe most of his forces about and neare the house of . . . . a husbandman by a bye-name called Duke of the Banke, and having a small piece of Ordnance plaid most of that night and the day following against the Towne, the greatest execution that it did, as was heard of, a bullet shot out of it entered into a house upon the South side of the Churchyard and burst out the bottom of a fryen pan. There was noe nearer assault to the Towne then a quarter of a mile. They were afraid of comming near one another. The Souldiers within the Towne went out of it and dischardged their muskets towards them at randome, for any thing was knowne there was not a man slayne or hurt. Upon Christmas Day at night Sir Gilbert withdrew his forces being weary of his siege, and his soldiers and Clubmen were glad of it that they might eate their

Christmas pyes at home. But they did the good man about whose house they lay great harm, not only in eating his provision of Meale and Beefe and the like, as also in burninge his barne doors with his Carts, wheels, and other husbandry stuff. This was all the expedition of Sir Gilbert Hoghton against Blackburne."

During the next three months the Royalists left Blackburn in peace, then it was temporarily occupied by James, Earl of Derby. But notwithstanding their freedom from attack, the garrison and townspeople had frequent alarms, the most serious of which was provided by Sir John Talbot of Salesbury Hall. Sir John was a Roman Catholic, and whilst affecting an attitude of strict neutrality was secretly Royalist in sympathy. In order to benefit the King's cause he laid a plot, which admits of no defence. Making a vaunt of his neutrality he invited some of the leading Parliament men to Salesbury Hall from Blackburn, " promisinge them very kind usage and some other courtesies by way of complyance with them," with the design of making them all prisoners. But suspicion being aroused, a small party of horse was sent to Salesbury to see what preparations he had made for the entertainment of the Parliamentary leaders. The men found over a hundred horses in his stable, saddled and fully accoutred, their riders being hidden near by, ready to fall upon and seize Sir John's guests. Being too few to deal with this number of men the reconnoitring party returned to Blackburn, whence, shortly afterwards, some three hundred troopers set out for Salesbury. On their arrival they found Sir John Talbot and all his company in full flight. Following in hot pursuit, the Roundheads soon came up with the fleeing Royalists, and after killing several of them, and driving some of the horses into the Ribble, where their riders were drowned, they returned to Salesbury Hall " where they found good pillage." The house was seized and sacked from top to bottom.

Sir John paid dearly for his attempted treachery. His estate was sequestrated, and he only obtained possession of it again by the payment of a heavy fine.

SELLING A WIFE

FROM time to time cases in the police court show that there is still a belief, especially amongst colliers, that a man may legally sell his wife. Formerly the error was widespread amongst the lower classes in Lancashire, it being thought to be a purely legal transaction if the wife was taken to the place of sale with a halter round her neck, and the buyer was given a written receipt by the husband for the money paid. Quite late in the nineteenth century a man pleaded in a Lancashire county court that he was not liable for his wife's debts as he had sold her to another man for half-a-crown long before the debts in question were contracted, and *had given a receipt for the money!*

THE LANCASHIRE WITCHES

IN the early part of the seventeenth century the inhabitants of the Forest of Pendle, with few exceptions, must have been miserably poor and ignorant, since they had little communication with the outside world. Superstition exists in the district to this day. When James I. was on the throne it held absolute domination over the simple minds of the inhabitants. And no belief was stronger than that in witchcraft. Upon this belief two old women, called Elizabeth Southerns and Anne Whittle, but better known in the chronicles of witchcraft as Old Demdike and Old Chattox, had played for many years with great success. Both these women were old, and both pretended to possess supernatural powers, and were therefore bitterly opposed to one another. Each woman had her following amongst the credulous peasantry, and in their anxiety to outvie one another each represented herself as more death-dealing, destructive and powerful than her neighbour, and the one who could show the most damage done to man or beast (whether real or not was quite immaterial) was more likely to get a larger custom for her charms and philtres, and horrible incantations.

It is a curious fact that, despite the bitter rivalry existing between these two women, the son-in-law of one of them, whose own wife was afterwards executed as a witch, paid the other an annual dole of meal to be exempt from her charms and witchcraft. As one of the many writers on the subject says, " Where the possession of a commission from the powers of darkness was thus eagerly and ostentatiously paraded, every death, the cause of which was not perfectly obvious, whether it ended in a sudden termination or a slow and gradual decline, would be placed to the general account of one of the two agents for the devil, in those parts, as the party

responsible for these unclaimed dividends of mortality. Did a cow go mad, or was a horse unaccountably affected with the staggers, the same solution was always at hand to clear negligence and save the trouble of inquiry ; and so far from modestly disclaiming these atrocities, the only struggle on the parts of Mothers Demdike and Chattox would be which should first appropriate them. And in all this it must not be forgotten that their own credulity was at least as great as the credulity of their neighbours, and that each had the power in question was so much an admitted point that she had long ceased, in all probability, to entertain any doubt on the subject."

Little wonder therefore that the doings, real or imaginary, of these two old women should become a scandal throughout the Forest of Pendle, and when James I. launched forth his famous treatise on witchcraft and demonology, " one of His Majesty's Justices in those parts, a very religious honest gentleman painful in the Service of his country," Roger Nowell, took up the case of these self-accused witches. They were brought before him and both having made confession, they were committed to take their trial at the next Lancaster Assizes on charges of various murders and witchcrafts. At that time the Clerk of the Assize Courts was one Master Thomas Potts, who left a full record of the proceedings. Besides Mother Demdike and Mother Chattox, their two daughters, Alison Device and Anne Redfern, were also committed. Master Potts tells us that the four women had not been in Lancaster Castle a week " when their children and friends being abroad at libertie, laboured a speciall meeting at Malking Tower in the Forrest of Pendle, upon good-fryday within a weeke after they were committed, of all the most dangerous, wicked, and damnable witches in the country, farre and neare. Upon good-fryday they met, according to solemne appoyntment, solemnized this greate festivall day according to their former order, with great cheare, merry company, and much conference. In the end, in this great assemblie it was decreed that M. Covell (he was the gaoler of Lancaster Castle) by reason of his Office, shall be slaine before the next Assises, the Castle of Lancaster to be blown up." The evidence that this great meeting of witches ever took place was based solely upon the testimony of a child of nine, Jennet Device, the granddaughter of Mother Demdike. The child was intelligent and cunning and there is an ugly suspicion that she glibly repeated a lesson she had been taught. Who taught her the lesson can never be known, but the activity which Roger Nowell displayed in arresting all those who were said to have attended the witches' convention on Good Friday, casts considerable doubts upon his motives. Amongst those arrested was Alice Nutter, a lady of good family and a fair estate at Rough Lea. There is every reason to believe that she was in no way implicated in the doings of the so-called witches, and that the child Jennet Device was bribed by some of her relatives, who in the event of her death would inherit her property, to introduce her name. In addition to this Roger Nowell was one of her bitterest enemies : Alice Nutter won a lawsuit against him with regard to the boundary of their respective properties, he having claimed a portion of her land. The only charges made against her were that she had been present at the meeting at Malkin Tower on Good Friday, and had joined with Mother Demdike and Elizabeth Device in bewitching to death an old man called Mitton. The only witnesses against her were Elizabeth Device and her two children James and Jennet.

As a result of Jennet Device's evidence Mr. Justice Nowell sent as prisoners to Lancaster, Elizabeth Device, daughter of Old Demdike, and her son James, Catherine Hewitt, John and Jane Bulrock, Isabel Robey, and Margaret Pearson, as well as Alice Nutter, making in all twelve persons accused of "the most barbarous and damnable Practises, Murthers wicked and devilish conspiracies."

The confession made by Mother Demdike to Roger Nowell on the second of April could only have sprung from hallucination or have been deliberate lying. Master Potts says, "She was a very old woman, about the age of Fourscore yeares, and had been a Witch for fiftie yeares. She dwelt in the Forrest of Pendle, in waste places, fitte for her profession. What she's commited in her time no man knows." Mother Demdike in her confession fixed the period of her practice in witchcraft at twenty years. She said that one day as she was returning home from a begging expedition she met, near a stone pit in Gouldshey, a spirit or a devil in the shape of a boy, one half of his coat black and the other brown. He bade her stay, saying to her that if she would give him her soul, she should have anything she wanted. Old Demdike inquired the spirit's name and was told it was Tib, and "in hope of such gaine as was promised by the sayd Devill or Tib, was contented to give her Soule to the said Spirit." During the next five or six years Tib appeared to Mother Demdike at various times and always "about Daylight-Gate," that is towards the evening, asking her what she would have or do. She always answered nothing. But about the end of the sixth year, one Sunday morning as she sat asleep with a child upon her knee, the spirit appeared to her in the shape of a brown dog, and as she was only wearing a smock it succeeded in drawing blood from under her left arm. Awaking suddenly she cried, " Jesus, save my child," but she had no power to say " Jesus save me," whereupon the brown dog vanished and for a space of eight weeks, she was " almost stark mad."

The only name mentioned in Mother Demdike's confession is that of a man called Baldwyn, who, when she and her granddaughter Alison Device, went to ask for money, called them witches and drove them away. Mother Demdike was blind, but as her granddaughter was leading her away, Tib appeared and said to her " Revenge thee of him," to which Old Demdike replied " Revenge thee either of him or his." The spirit vanished out of her sight and she never saw him again.

The most curious fact about this case is the diabolical readiness with which the Device family not only confessed they were witches, but testified against other people and against their own flesh and blood. Old Demdike in her confession said nothing as to any evil befalling Richard Baldwyn, but her granddaughter, Alison Device, said that the day after Baldwyn ordered them off his land, she heard that one of his children had fallen ill, and that after languishing for about a year, had died, and upon oath this woman stated she verily thought " that her said grandmother did bewitch the said child to death."

Old Demdike at the end of her confession said, " That the speediest way to take a man's life away by Witchcraft, is to make a Picture of Clay, like unto the shape of the person whom they mean to kill, and dry it thoroughly ; and when they would have them to be ill in any one place more than another, then take a Thorne or Pinne, and prick it in that part of the Picture you would so have to be ill: and when you would have any part of the Body to consume away, then take that part of the Picture and burne it. And when they would have the whole Body to consume away, then take the remnant of the said Picture and burne it: and so thereupon by that means, the Body shall die."

Mother Chattox whom Master Potts describes as " a very old, withered, spent, and decrepit creature, her sight almost gone," made her confession after a few weeks' imprisonment in Lancaster Castle. She declared that she was " seduced to condescend and agree to become subject unto that devilish abominable profession of Witchcraft" through the wicked persuasion and counsel of Mother Demdike. She also had her familiar spirit, who was called Fancie. She declared that at the time of the initiation she heard Tib say to Mother Demdike that she should have " gold, Silver, worldly Wealth at her will. And at the same time she saith, there was victuals viz. Flesh, Butter, Cheese, Bread, and Drink and bid them eat enough. And after their eating, the devil called *Fancie*, and the other spirit calling himself Tib, carried the remnant away. And she saith that although they did eat, they were never the fuller, nor better for the same ; and that at their said Banquet, the said spirits gave them light to see what they did, although they neither had fire nor candle light ; and that there were both the spirits and devils."

The old woman admitted having bewitched to death one man.

Nor were women alone concerned in this chapter of horrors. James Device, Old Demdike's grandson, not only confessed to his own participation in the craft, but testified against his mother, his grandmother and his sister Alison. His evidence was given in the matter-of-fact way which distinguishes that of all those who made confessions. They all speak as if witchcraft were an ordinary every-day reality, and as if evil spirits went about the country-side in various disguises. James Device declared that on a certain to bring it away with him, and hand it to "such a Thing" as he should meet on his

AT MALKIN TOWER

Shrove Tuesday, his grandmother bade him go to church to receive the sacrament. He was not to eat the sacred bread but way homeward. But he disobeyed and ate the wafer. On his way home, when about fifty yards from the church, he was met by a " Thing in the shape of a hare " which asked him if he had brought the bread according to his grandmother's directions. He answered that he had not, whereupon the Thing threatened to tear him to pieces, but when he called upon the name of God, it disappeared. A few days later a thing in the shape of a brown dog met him near the new church in Pendle. It asked him for his soul, promising him in return that he should be avenged on his enemies. To this Device made answer that his soul was not his to give but was his Saviour Jesus Christ's, yet as much as was his to give he was contented to yield to the spirit. Within two or three days of this meeting, James Device went to Carre Hall, where Mrs. Townley, after charging him and his mother with having stolen some of her turf, bade him begone. As he went " forth of the door the said Mistress Townley gave him a knock between the shoulders." A day or two later a black dog met him, and reminding him of the insult put upon him by Mrs. Townley, directed him to make a clay image like Mrs. Townley and he would help him to destroy her. Bidding Device to call him Dandy, the spirit disappeared. The next morning he made an image of clay of Mrs. Townley, and dried it the same night by the fire. Every day he crumbled away a piece of this image. At the end of a week it was all gone and two days later Mrs. Townley died. In the following Lent, one John Duckworth of the *Lawnde* promised James Device an old shirt, but when he went to get the gift, Duckworth refused to give it to him, and he was driven away. As he was going out of the house, the spirit Dandy appeared to him, and said " Thou didst touch the said Duckworth." This James Device denied but the spirit answered, " Thou didst touch him and therefore I have power of him."

Whereupon Device expressed his wish to the spirit that Duckworth might be killed. Within a week Duckworth was dead.

" Who but Witches can be proofes, and so witnesses of the doings of Witches ? " asks Master Potts, " since all their Meetings, Conspiracies, Practices, and Murthers are the works of darkness ? But to discover this wicked fury God hath not only raised meanes beyond expectation by the voluntarie Confession and Accusation of all that are gone before to accuse this Witch (being Witches, and thereby witnesses of her doings), but after they were committed by meanes of a child to discover her to be one and a Principall in that wicked assembly at Malking Tower, and so devise such a damnable course for the deliverance of their friends from Lancaster, as to kill the Gaoler and blow up the Castle, wherein the Devill did but labour to assemble them together, and so being known, to send them all one way." Such was the arraignment of Catherine Hewitt.

She was accused of being present at the famous convention of Witches on the previous Good Friday at Malkin Tower. The only evidence against her was that of the Devices—mother, son, and daughter. James Device swore that not only was Catherine Hewitt present at the meeting at Malkin Tower, but had there confessed that she had killed the child of a man named Foulds at Colne. Elizabeth Device gave the same evidence. That imp of unspeakable wickedness, Jennet Device, whom Master Potts conceived to have been divinely inspired for the rooting out of witches, completed the chain of evidence against the unhappy woman. Called into court, she was directed by the judge to identify Catherine Hewitt. Without the least hesitation, the child went up to her and, taking her by the hand, accused her of being a witch. She described the place in which she had sat at the witches' feast on Good Friday at Malkin Tower, and then proceeded to relate their conversation, "without any manner of contrarieties." Upon this evidence Catherine Hewitt was condemned to death, and because she protested her innocence to the end was branded as an impenitent.

Old Mother Demdike died in prison before the trials took place, a victim of ill-treatment. The "confessions" made by this old woman, her daughter, and two grandchildren, as well as that of Old Chattox, were, in all probability, given under the promise that if they told the truth their lives would be spared. · There is no record of any of the Lancashire witches being put to the torture, although this horrible means of extorting confessions was resorted to in other parts of the country. Yet remembering the superstitious belief in witchcraft which characterised the age, a belief that in the opinion of some of the most enlightened men warranted any means being used to extract the truth, Master Potts' description of James Device's appearance when he was brought to trial, gives rise to the assumption that in his case, at any rate, torture had been employed. We must remember that Master Potts was an official of the court, and that great stress was laid, both in his account and in the judge's summing up, of the fact that the confessions were "voluntarie." Of James Device he says, "This wicked and miser-Wretch, whether by practise, or meanes, to bring himself to some untimely death and thereby to avoid his Tryall by his Countrey, and just judgement of the law; or ashamed to bee openly charged with so many devilish practises, and so much innocent blood as hee had spilt; or by reason of his imprisonment so long time before his Trial (which was with more favour, comisaration and reliefe than hee

deserved) I know not : But being brought forward to the Barre, to receive his Tryall before this worthie judge, and so Honourable and Worshipfulle an assembly of justices for this service, was so insensible, weake and unable in all thinges as he could neither speake, heare, or stand, but was holden up when hee was brought to the place of his arraignement to receive his triall."

James Device certainly deserved his fate, for, in addition to testifying against his mother, Elizabeth Device and his sister Alison, he was instrumental in sending three absolutely innocent women to their death—Catherine Hewitt, whose case has been already mentioned, Anne Redfern, and Alice Nutter. There seems every reason to believe that these two last women were accused of witchcraft by the Nutter family. Anne Redfern was the daughter of Old Chattox, but there was nothing to show that she had taken any part in her mother's supposed magic arts of witchcraft. Some eighteen years previously a young man, named Robert Nutter, had made improper advances to Anne Redfern and had been repulsed. Six months later he died of a languishing sickness, and this was the evidence on which Anne Redfern was hanged! Old Demdike declared to Justice Nowell that she had seen Anne Redfern and Old Chattox making three clay figures of Robert Nutter, his wife, and his father. James Device said that he saw three figures of clay, half a yard in length, at the end of the Redferns' house ; one of these figures Anne Redfern was crumbling in her hands. He could not say who the figures represented. Robert Nutter's sister declared that there had been a quarrel between her brother and Anne Redfern about Whitsuntide, some eighteen or nineteen years before. Her brother had told her of the quarrel, and within a week or a fortnight he had fallen ill, "and so languished until about Candlemas then next after, and then died." During the time of his sickness Robert Nutter "did a hundred times at least say that the said Anne Redfern and her associates had bewitched him to death." She also said that her father, Christopher Nutter, shortly after her brother's death, also fell sick, and after languishing for some months he, too, died. The elder Nutter likewise "did sundry times say that he was bewitched, but named nobodie that should have done the same." The evidence of John Nutter, Robert's brother, completed the case against the unhappy Anne Redfern. He said that about Christmas time some eighteen or nineteen years previously, whilst riding from Burnley with his brother Robert and his father, he heard the former say—

"Father, I am sure I am bewitched by the Chattoxes, Anne Chattox and Anne Redfern her daughter; I pray you cause them to be layd in Lancaster Castle." To this the elder Nutter replied—

"Thou art a foolish lad, it is not so, it is thy miscarriage."

Then Robert Nutter, weeping, said, "Nay, I am sure that I am bewitched by them, and if ever I come again (he was then ready to go to Sir Richard Shuttleworth in whose service he was), I will procure them to be layd where they shall be glad to bite lice in two with their teeth."

At this point occurred one of the most moving scenes in this horrible trial. Old Chattox was brought forward to be examined. She admitted making the clay figures, and falling upon her knees she confessed, and, with tears streaming down her withered cheeks, implored the mercy of the court for her daughter, whose innocence she protested. This appeal had no influence upon the besotted prejudices of the judge and jury who condemned this woman to death for the "murder" of Robert Nutter upon evidence that was only hearsay, and was clearly inspired by the spite of enemies.

A shadow even more sinister rests upon the case of Alice Nutter. In those days to be accused of witchcraft was practically to be condemned. The ordinary rules of evidence were of little or no avail to the accused. She might bring the most convincing proof that she was fifty miles away from the spot on which she was declared to have taken part in the witches' orgy. The firm belief in the power of witches to ride through the air, to transport themselves where they would in a few moments, discounted all such evidence. Amongst this band of wretched women Alice Nutter was the only person of any condition or degree. The Demdikes and Chattoxes were practically mendicants. Alice Nutter was a lady of considerable fortune, of good family, and as Heywood says in his *Lancashire Witches*, "I knew her a good woman and well bred, of an unquestion'd carriage, well reputed amongst her neighbours, reckoned with the best."

Master Potts, in his description of the trial of Alice Nutter, declared there were two types of persons who practised witchcraft: one which was in great misery and poverty, "for such the Devill allures to follow him by promising great riches and worldly commodity; others though rich yet burn in a desperate desire of revenge." This he advances as the reason for Alice Nutter, "a rich woman who had a great estate, and children of good hope: in the common opinion of the world a good temper, free from envy or malice," finding herself accused of witchcraft. The charges against her were both childish and absurd. She was accused of having killed Henry Mitton by witchcraft, because he had refused to give Old Mother Demdike a penny! The judge and jury accepted the evidence of Elizabeth and James Device that they had heard Old Demdike say she and Alice Nutter had bewitched Henry Mitton to death. The second charge was that she had taken part in the meeting at Malkin Tower on Good Friday, and here again the evidence of Elizabeth and James Device and that of the horrible child Jennet, satisfied the jury. As in the case of Catherine Hewitt, Jennet Device identified Alice Nutter in the court, and taking her by the hand accused her of being a witch, describing the place she had occupied at the feast, and the whole of the conferences which took place. It was in vain that Alice Nutter protested her innocence, but to quote Master Potts, "Nothing would serve, for Old Demdike, Old Chattox and others had charged her with innocent blood which cries out for Revenge and will be satisfied. And therefore Almightie God, in his justice hath cut her off."

There can be little doubt but that Alice Nutter was the victim of a foul conspiracy. Her children showed the greatest anxiety that she should confess; neither they nor any member of her family made any effort to save her, or to clear her from the unsubstantiated charges brought against her. They accepted the finding of the court that their mother and kinswoman was a witch simply because the Devices, who were confessed witches, had said that she was one. Who knows what bitter family quarrels lay behind this appalling passiveness? We have no record of the character of Alice Nutter. She may have been a hard woman, or, on the other hand, she may have had bad children; but whatever lies hidden, it is impossible to dismiss the conviction that, in order to secure her money, her own family were passive, if not active, agents in her destruction. Some one must have coached that child of darkness, Jennet Device, and

rewards or promises of pardon doubtless bought the ridiculous evidence of Elizabeth and James Device. Alice Nutter died maintaining her innocence. Potts says, "She died very impenitent; inasmuch as her owne children were never able to move her to confess any particular offence, or declare anything, even *in articulo mortis*, which was a very fearfull thing to all that were present."

The trial of Elizabeth Device followed that of Old Chattox. She is described as having been branded "with a preposterous mark in Nature, even from her birth, which was her left eye standing lower than the other; the one looking down, the other looking up, so strangely deformed, as the best who were present in that honourable assembly and great audience did affirm, they had not often seen the like." When Jennet Device was put up to give evidence against her mother, the latter broke out into such a storm of curses and reproaches that the child "with weeping tears cried out to my Lord the judge, and told him she was not able to speak in the presence of her mother." Nothing would silence Elizabeth Device, and the learned judge, seeing in her curses and threats nothing but an attempt to terrify the child into withdrawing the statements she had already made to Mr. Nowell, ordered her removal from the court. Jennet was then placed upon a table in the presence of the whole court, and there gave evidence that her mother was a witch, and that she had frequently seen her familiar spirit, which was called Ball, in the shape of a brown dog. James Device told practically the same story.

On August 13th, the day after their trial, Old Chattox, Anne Redfern, Elizabeth, James and Alison Device, Alice Nutter, Catherine Hewitt, John Bulrock and his mother, were taken to Gallows Hill, amidst the insults and execrations of an infuriated populace, and there they were hanged. Old Chattox and the Devices were convicted on their own confession, but the others were legally murdered on the unsupported testimony of these miserable wretches. Nothing marks more strongly the credulity of the age than the acceptance of the evidence of Jennet Device. Although she confessed to having taken part in her mother's practice of witchcraft, she was pardoned as King's evidence. What became of her after the extinction of her family, which she herself so largely helped to bring about, is not known; but in all probability she dragged out a miserable existence, an outcast, every one in Pendle Forest pointing the finger of scorn at the murderess of her mother, her brother, and her sister.

There is a tradition, which, if based on fact would show that a retributive punishment awaited her. She is supposed to have been the Jennet Davies who was condemned to death for witchcraft in 1633, together with Mother Dickinson, but was not executed.

OLD READING DESK AND CHAIR AT CHETHAM COLLEGE, MANCHESTER

STORIES OF THE COTTON FAMINE

WHEN the first shot was fired in the war between the Northern and Southern States of America on 13th April, 1861, the whole world was taken by surprise. And if any one had prophesied that the bloodless bombardment of Fort Sumter on that day was the prelude to months of want and privation and to a distress hitherto unknown in Lancashire, he would have been looked upon as a madman.

No one believed that the war between North and South would be of long duration, and no one dreamed that it would affect Lancashire. Never had the cotton trade " boomed " so strongly as in 1859. New markets had opened, with the result that new mills had sprung up in every town and township in the Lancashire cloth districts. In 1860, India alone had taken manufactures to the value of seventeen millions of money—one-third of the whole export. So high indeed had been the production in 1859 and 1860 that at the outbreak of the war the manufacturers' warehouses were filled with huge stocks which they could not dispose of, as they had already glutted the markets. This collection of stock, which was estimated to be of the value of twenty millions sterling, was the direct cause of the Cotton Famine. Mr. Arthur Arnold says of the manufacturers: " They had recklessly pushed production beyond requirement; with all the assistance of low wages, light taxation, and perfect domestic peace, manufacturers had made their spindles revolve faster, their shuttles move more quickly, than they had ever done before. They had done this in fear and trembling —they had been encouraged by the excitement which burned at the prospect of such increasing markets—they had aroused a competition which recognised no duty paramount to that of obtaining the largest share of profits; and at the moment in which they might have expected judgment and execution—in the shape of a large depreciation in the value of their commodities—almost in the very hour when the reaction to which they had given no heed was upon them, the scene shifted— the war in America assumed an aspect of determined continuance, and the blockade of the Southern ports was declared effective." The price of cotton goods rose immediately, and many manufacturers who were faced with ruin became rich men.

If there had been no war in America the overstocked markets, and the huge amount of material on the hands of the Lancashire manufacturers, would have brought " hard times " to the operatives in the winter of 1861. The war brought relief to the manufacturers, but by the time they had disposed of their stocks, the supply of raw cotton from the Southern States had ceased, and the blackest of all black times for industrial Lancashire was the result.

Many mills began to run short time in October 1861, then, as the supplies of raw material grew less, and its price went up to abnormal figures, mill after mill closed its doors, until in January 1862, south-west Lancashire was in the grip of famine. And no greater heroism was ever shown in siege or battle than that with which the Lancashire operatives faced the ordeal. Savings to the amount of two million pounds were drawn from the Post Office, furniture, clothes, little family treasures went to the pawnbrokers, before help was sought from the Guardians or from the relief funds which were started in every town, funds to which all England subscribed with sympathetic generosity. Acceptance of charity was the deepest wound to the pride of these brave people. " Many found it the sorest trial of their lives to ask for food, and it is a happy circumstance for all to remember, as it is honourable to those of whom it is recorded, that none suffered more severely than those who had a struggle to overcome their unwillingness to subsist upon food which they had not earned."

The sittings of the Board of Guardians brought to light not only the tragedies of famine, but the grit and the unselfishness of the people. The following is a record of such a sitting by an eye-witness:

"A clean, old decrepit man presented himself. 'What's brought you here, Joseph?' said the chairman.

" ' Why, aw've nought to do, nor nought to tak' to.'

" ' What's your daughter Ellen doing, Joseph?'

" ' Hoo's eawt o' wark.'

" ' And what's your wife doing?'

" ' Hoo's bin bed-fast aboon five year.'

" The old man was relieved at once, but as he walked away he looked hard at his ticket, as if it wasn't exactly the kind of thing ; and, turning round, he said ;

" ' Couldn't yo let me be a sweeper i' th' streets, istid, Mr. Eccles?'

" A clean old woman came up with a snow-white nightcap on her head.

" ' Well, Mary, what do you want?'

" ' Aw could like yo to gi' me a bit o' summat, Mr Eccles, for aw need it.'

" ' Well, but you've some lodgers, haven't you, Mary?'

" ' Yigh, aw've three.'

" ' Well, what do they pay you?'

" ' They pay'n mo nought. They'n no wark—an' one connot turn 'em eawt.'

" This was all quite true. 'Well, but you live with your son, don't you?' continued the chairman.

" ' Nay,' replied the old woman, '*he* lives wi' *me* ; an' he's eawt o' wark, too. Aw could like you to do a bit o' summat for us. We're hard put to't.'

" ' Don't you think she would be better

in the workhouse?' said one of the guardians.

" ' Oh, no,' replied another, 'don't send th' owd woman there. Let her keep her own little place together, if she can.'

Another old woman presented herself with a threadbare shawl drawn closely round her grey head.

" ' Well, Ann,' said the chairman,'there's nobody but yourself and your John, is there?'

" ' Naw.'

" ' What age are you?

" ' Aw'm seventy.'

" ' Seventy!'

" ' Aye aw am.'

" ' Well, and what age is your John?'

" ' He's gooin' i' seventy-four.'

" ' Where is he, Ann?'

" ' Well, aw left him deawn i' th' street yon, gettin' a load o' coals in.'

" There was a murmur of approbation around the board ; and the old woman was sent away relieved and thankful. There were many of all ages, clean in person, and bashful in manner, with their poor clothing put into the tidiest possible trim ; others were dirty and sluttish, and noisy of speech, as in the case of one poor woman, who, after receiving her ticket for relief, partly in money and partly in kind, whipped a pair of worn clogs from under her shawl and cried out :

" ' Aw mun ha' some clogs afore aw go, too. Look at thoose ! They're a shame to be sin!'

" Clogs were freely given, and in several cases they were all that was asked for. In three or four instances the applicants said, after receiving other relief:

" ' Aw wish yo'd gi' me a pair o' clogs, Mr. Eccles. Aw've had to borrow these to come in.' One woman pleaded hard for two pairs, saying:

" ' Yon chylt's quite bar-fut ; an' he's witchod (wet-shod) an' as ill as he con be.'

"'Who's witchod?' asked the chairman.

"'My husban' is,' replied the woman; 'an' he connot ston it just neaw, yo mun let *him* have a pair if yo con.'

"'Give her two pair,' said the chairman. Another woman took her clog off and held it up saying, 'Look at that! We're a' walkin' o' th' floor, an' smoor't wi' cowds.'"

Although sad stories such as these were disclosed in the board-room of the Guardians, cases of even deeper suffering were discovered by the relief committees. A correspondent, after visiting the secretary of one of these committees, wrote as follows to the *Manchester Examiner*:—

"He pointed to some of the cases in his books. The first was that of an old man, an overlooker of a cotton mill. His family was thirteen in number; three of the children were under ten years of age; seven of the rest were factory operatives; but the whole family had been out of work for several months. When in full employment the joint earnings of the family amounted to eighty shillings a week; but after struggling on in the hope of better times, and exhausting the savings of past labour, they had been brought down to the receipt of charity at last, and for sixteen weeks gone by, the whole thirteen had been living upon six shillings a week from the relief fund. They had no other resource. I went to see them at their own house afterwards, and it certainly was a pattern of cleanliness, with the little household gods there still. To see that house a stranger would never dream that the family were living on an average income of less than sixpence a head per week. But I knew how hard some decent folk will struggle with the deepest poverty before they will give in to it. The old man came in whilst I was there. He sat down in one corner, quietly tinkering away at something he had in his hands. His old corduroy trousers were well patched and just new washed. He had very little to say to us, except that 'He would like to get summat to do; for he 'were tired o' walkin' abeawt."

"Another case was that of a poor widow woman, with five young children. This family had been driven from house to house, by increasing necessity, till they had sunk at last into a dingy little hovel up a dark court, in one of the poorest parts of the town, where they huddled together about a fireless grate, to keep one another warm. They had nothing left of the wreck of their home but two rickety chairs and a little deal table reared against the wall, because one of the legs was gone. In this miserable hole—which I saw afterwards—her husband died of sheer starvation, as was pronounced by the jury on the inquest. The dark, damp hovel where they had crept to was scarcely four yards square; and the poor woman pointed to one corner of the floor, saying,

"'He deed i' that corner.'

"He died there with nothing to lie upon but the ground, and nothing to cover him in that fireless hovel. His wife and children crept about him, there to watch him die; and to keep him as warm as they could. When the relief committee first found this family out, the entire clothing of the family of seven persons weighed eight pounds, and sold for fivepence as rags."

The operative who had spent all his life in a mill gladly accepted the hard physical work of quarrying, set by the guardians to the able-bodied who sought relief. What the work meant to him, and how cheerfully and bravely he carried it out, is shown by this account, written at the time:—

"It was not difficult to distinguish the trained quarrymen from the rest. The latter did not seem to be working very hard at their new employment, and it can hardly be expected that they should, considering the great difference between it and their usual labour. Leaning on their spades and hammers, they watched me with a natural curiosity, as if wondering whether I was a new ganger or a contractor come to buy stone. There were men of all ages amongst them, from about eighteen years old to white-headed men past sixty. Most of them looked healthy and a little embrowned by recent exposure to weather; and here and there was a pinched face which told its own tale. I got into talk with a quiet, hardy-looking man, dressed in soil-stained corduroy. He was a kind of overlooker. He told me that there were from eighty to ninety factory hands employed in that quarry.

"'But,' said he, 'it varies a bit yo known. Some on 'em gets knocked up neaw an' then, an' they have to stop at whoam a day or two; an' some on 'em connot ston' gettin' weet through; it mays 'em ill. And here an' theer one turns up at doesn't like the job at 'o; they'd rather clem. There is 'at's both willin' an' able. Thoose are likely to get a better job somewheer. There's other some 'at's willin' enough, but connot ston' th' racket. They dun middlin', tak' 'em one wi' another, an' considerin' 'at they're noan use't to th' wark. Th' hommer fo's leet wi 'em; but we dunnot like to push 'em so mich, yo known, for what's a shillin' a day? Aw know some odd uns i' this delph at never tastes fro' mornin' till they'm done at neet —an' says nought abeawt it noather. But then they'm families. Besides, fro' wake lads sich as yon, at's bin train't to nought but leet wark, an' a warm place to wortch in, what can yo expect? We'm had a deeal o' bother wi' 'm abeawt bein' paid for weet days, when they couldn't wortch. They were no paid for weet days at th'

furst; an' they geet it into their yeds at Shorrock was to blame. Shorrock's th' paymaister, under th' guardians. But then, he nobbut went accordin' to orders, yo known. At last th' Board settle't it 'at they mun be paid for weet an' dry, an' there's bin quietness sin. They wortchen fro' eight till five; an' sometimes, when they'm done, they drill o' together i' th' road yon, just like sodgers, an' then they walken away i' procession."

The most touching feature of those two years of semi-starvation and distress is the infinite kindness of the workers one to another. Many, whose savings enabled them to fight the lack of work, shared what they had with neighbours; those who could still afford a fire called in less fortunate friends. The following story, which appeared in the *Manchester Examiner*, gives an instance of the splendid spirit that animated the few fortunate ones. The kindness of Ann, the feelings of Sarah, had their counterpart amongst thousands and thousands.

"Three young women stopped on the footpath in front of the inn where we stood, and began to talk together in a very free, open way, quite careless of being heard. One of them was a stout, handsome young woman, about twenty-three. Her dress was of light printed stuff, clean and good; her round, ruddy arms, her clear, blonde complexion, and the bright expression of her full, open countenance, all indicated health and good-nature. I guessed from her conversation, as well as from her general appearance that she was a factory operative in full employ, though that is such a rare thing in these parts now; the other two looked very poor and down-hearted. One was a short, thick-set girl, seemingly not twenty years of age; her face was sad, and she had very little to say. The other was a thin, dark-haired cadaverous woman, about thirty years of age, as I supposed. Her shrunk visage was the picture of want, and her frank, child-like talk showed great simplicity of character. The weather had been wet for some days previously and the clothing of the two looked thin and shower-stained. It had evidently been worn a good while, and the colours were faded. Each of them wore a poor, shivery bit of shawl, in which their thin hands were folded, as if to keep them warm. The handsome lass, who seemed to be in good employ, knew them both, but she showed an especial kindness towards the eldest of them. As these two stood talking to their friend, we did not take much notice of what they were saying, until two other young women came slowly from townwards, looking poor, and tired, and ill like the first. These last comers instantly recognised two of those who stood talking together in front of the inn, and one of them said to the other—

"Eh, sitho! There's Sarah an' Martha here. Eh, lasses! han yo bin' a-beggin' too?"

"Aye, lass, we han," replied the dark-complexioned woman. "Aye, lass, we han. Aw've just bin tellin' Ann here. Aw never did sich a thing i' my life afore— never! But it's th' furst time an' th' last for me—it is that. Aw'll go whoam, an' aw'll dee theer, afore aw'll go a-beggin' ony moor,—aw will, for sure. Mon, it's sich a nasty, dirty job, aw'd as soon clem. See yo, lasses! We set eawt this mornin' —Martha an' me—to go to Gorton Tank, becose we yerd that it wur such a good place. But one doesn't know wheer to go these times, an' one doesn't like to go a-beggin, mong folk as they know. Well, when we coom to Gorton, we geet two-pence hawpenny theer, an' that wur o'. Now, there's plenty moor beggin' besides us. Well, after that twopence hawpenny we geet twopence moor, an' that's o' at

we'm getten'. But eh, lasses, when aw coom to do it, aw hadn't th' heart to ax for nought, aw hadn't for sure. Martha an' me's walked aboon ten mile iv we've walked a yard; an' we geet weet through th' first thing, an' aw wur ill when we set off, an' so wur Martha too; aw know hoo wur though hoo says nought mich abeawt it. Well, we coom back through t' teawn, an' we were both on us fair stagged up. Aw never were so done o'er i' my life wi' one thing an' another. So we co'de a-seein Ann here, an' hoo made us a rare good baggin', th' lass did. See yo! aw wur fit to drop o' th' flags afore aw geet that sup o' warm tay into me—aw wur for sure. An' neaw, hoo's come'd a-gate wi' us hitherto, an' hoo would have us to hev a glass o' warm ale apiece at yon heause lower deawn a bit; an' aw dar say it'll do me good, aw getten' sich a cowd; but, eh dear, it's made me as mazy as a tup, an' neaw hoo wants us to have another afore we starten off whoam. But it's no use, we mun' be gooin' on. Aw'm noan used to it, an' aw connot ston' it; aw'm as wake as a kittlin' this minute."

Ann, who had befriended them in this manner, was the handsome young woman who seemed to be in work; and now the poor woman who had been telling the story laid her hand upon her friend's shoulder and said—

"Ann, thee's behaved very weel to us o' roads; an' neaw, lass, go thi ways whoam an' dunnot fret abeawt us, mon. Aw feel better neaw. We's be reet enough to-morn, lass. Neaw, there' awlus some way shap't. That tay's done me a deeal o' good. Go thi ways whoam, Ann, neaw do, or else aw shan't be yezzy abeawt tho'."

But Ann, who was wiping her eyes with her hand, replied—

"Naw, naw, aw'll not go yet, Sarah!" And then she began to cry, "Eh, lasses, aw dunnot like to see yo o' this shap—aw dunnot for sure! Besides, yo bin far enough to-day. Come back wi' me. Aw connot find reawm for both on yo; but thee come back wi' me, Sarah. Aw'll find thee a good bed an' thae'rt welcome to a share of what there is—as welcome as th' flowers i' May—thae knows that. Thae'rt th' owdest o' th' two, an' thae'rt noan fit to trawnce up an' deawn o' this shap. Come back to eawr heawse, an' Martha'll go forrud to Stopput (Stockport)—winnot tho', Martha? Thae knows, Martha, thae munnot think nought at me axin' Sarah, an' noan o' thee. Yo should both on yo go back iv aw'd reawm; but aw haven't. Beside, thae'rt younger and strunger than hur is."

"Eh, God bless thee, lass," replied Martha; "aw kneaw o' abeawt it. Aw'd rayther Sarah would stop, for hur'll be ill. Aw con go forrud by mysel', weel enough. It's noan so fur, neaw."

But here Sarah, the eldest of the three, laid her hand once more on the shoulder of her friend, and said in an earnest tone—

"Ann, it will no do, my lass. Go aw mun. I never wur away fro' whoam o' neet i' my life—never! Aw connot do it, mon! Beside, thae knows, aw've laft yon lad, an' never a wick soul wi' him. He'd fret hissel' to death this neet, mon, if aw didn't go whoam! Aw couldn't sleep a wink for thinkin' abeawt him! Th' child would be fit to start eawt o' th' heawse i' th' deead time o' th' neet a-seechin' mo—aw know he would! Aw mun go, mon. God bless tha, thae knows heaw it is!"

Half a million people were supported during the dread time of the Cotton Famine by subscriptions from England and the Colonies.

CURIOUS TRIPLE RAINBOW SEEN NEAR LANCASTER IN 1724

THE ROMANS IN LANCASHIRE

IT is an interesting fact, and one, perhaps, not generally known, that our modern railroads follow approximately the course of the old Roman roads, which connected London with the rest of the country. Three of these roads crossed Lancashire in directions which also have been followed, more or less closely, by the builders of railways. One of these ran from Chester through Manchester to York, another went from Manchester to Blackburn, and passing round the Forest of Bowland went to Kirby Lonsdale; the third went through Warrington, Wigan, and Lancaster to the same place, whence another road led directly to Carlisle. But when the Romans came into Lancashire towards the middle of the first century A.D. the Latin historian Tacitus tells us, " It was a land of uncleared forests, with a climate as yet not mitigated by the organised labours of mankind. The fallen timber obstructed the streams, the rivers were squandered in the reedy morasses, and only the downs and the hilltops rose above the perpetual tracts of wood." Professor Boyd Dawkins tells us that " The bottoms of the valleys were for the most part marshes, and the low-lying region of the Lancashire and Cheshire plain was covered with forest and marshes so impenetrable that even as late as the Bronze Age it was rarely traversed. This is proved by the rarity of the remains of this age in the Lancashire and Cheshire plain." The Romans reclaimed the wilderness of morass and forest. They felled the trees along the lines mapped out for their military roads, they banked the rivers and made causeways across the marshes. Tacitus tells us, too, that the native Britons who were forced into this labour complained that " their very bodies and hands were worn out in draining the fens and extending the clearings in the forest."

The three roads were built for purely military purposes, the country north of a line drawn from York through Derby and Chester being the last part to be subdued. Lancashire, together with Yorkshire, was inhabited by a fierce and warlike tribe called the Brigantes, who were only subdued after prolonged fighting. After the close of the first century archæologists tell us there was probably not a fort or a fortress to be found in the South of England, but in Lancashire all the Roman settlements were forts, built to guard the roads and the frontier, as well as to overawe and hold in check the turbulent Brigantes. And of these forts the little village of Ribchester, near Blackburn, was one of the largest in the country. There were also forts at Manchester, Wigan, Lancaster and Overborough. Excavation has shown that these Roman forts were all built practically upon the same plan, the only difference being in size. They were either oblong or square, with the corners rounded off; they had four gates, each placed in the centre of one of the four walls. A broad street connected two of these gates, on one side of which stood the Commandant's house, the headquarters buildings and the granaries; on the other side were long blocks of buildings which were clearly the barracks of soldiers.

The fort at Manchester stood close to the junction of the Medlock and the Irwell, and was built by a cohort of Frisians. Mr. Bruton points out that a fragment of the wall surrounding the fort may be seen under one of the arches of the Manchester South Junction and Altrincham Railway. Trenches cut for a railway viaduct in 1898 brought to view a portion of the northern wall; and in 1907 forty feet of the western wall was discovered, by excavations made especially for the purpose. Mr. Bruton gives us a clear indication of the position occupied by this Roman fort, which was the earliest beginning of Manchester. "For those who would like to trace the outlines of the Roman fort," he says, "among the streets and yards of the modern city, the following itinerary may be recommended. Turn along Castle Street (which opens out of Deansgate immediately opposite Knot Mill Station), and follow its windings till it crosses the Rochdale Canal and leads into the open space still known (and marked) as Castlefield. If the pedestrian will cross this space and halt for a moment at the junction of the railway arches numbered seven and eight, he will probably be standing on the south-west corner of the fort, though much lower than the original level. The southern wall (part of which was visible in 1850) ran from this point in a line crossing the canal some forty or fifty feet beyond the little lock, and by crossing the bridge again and following the tow-path for a little distance it must be possible to approach very near to the position of the southern gate. This is perhaps the best spot from which to obtain a general idea of the lie of the Roman station."

Ribchester, however, appears to have been something more than a mere fort or military station, and was not only a place of considerable size but also of wealth. There is an old saying "'Twas written on a wall in Rome that Ribchester was the second richest city in the world," which in all probability is the echo of tradition of the prosperity of the place in Roman times. That Ribchester was a town as well as a fortress is shown by the gravestones discovered at a place on the river bank about a quarter of a mile away. The Roman officers would not have taken their wives and families to live in a fort. One gravestone records, "In this earth is held the last of Aelia Matrona, she lived 28 years, 2 months and 8 days, and Marcus Julius Maximus, her son, he lived 6 years, 3 months and 20 days, and Campania Dubitata, her mother, she lived 50 years. Julius Maximus, a 'singularis consularis' of the wing of Sarmatian cavalry, the husband, placed this monument to an incomparable wife, to a son most dutiful to his father, and to a mother-in-law very dear." Here, after all these centuries, we have the story of a tragedy in the life of a Roman cavalry officer. One wonders if some pestilence carried off the young wife, her mother and the little child, or if the unhappy husband and father saw them perish one by one in that far away post on the confines of the great Roman Empire. An altar, now kept in the library of St. John's College, Cambridge, which was found at Ribchester, gives us the approximate date of this tragedy. It is recorded upon this altar that a troop of Sarmatian cavalry was stationed at Ribchester during the first half of the third century.

Ribchester under the Romans had a large manufactory of brass, which is shown by the quantity of fragments of various utensils and ornaments wrought in that metal, that have been found, and above all by the innumerable fragments of brass, believed by antiquarians to have been the sweepings of shops, which used to be picked up on the banks of the Ribble.

The river has undermined and probably buried a large portion of Roman Ribchester; a considerable portion also lies beneath the church and the churchyard. Nevertheless the "finds" at Ribchester are amongst the most important in the country. Columns of temples have been found in Roman wells, as well as a large number of coins ranging in date from A.D. 50 to A.D. 380. Pottery, too, has been found, belonging to the first century. But the two most important objects are a bronze helmet with a mask, and a

THE BRONZE HELMET FOUND AT RIBCHESTER

gold fibula, both of exquisite workmanship and pointing to a high state of civilisation.

The bronze helmet was found in the river bank in 1796 by a boy at play, at a spot just opposite the Rectory gate, and buried some nine feet beneath the surface of the earth. It is carefully preserved in the British Museum and no more beautiful relic of the Roman occupation has ever been found in Britain. The helmet and mask, which fit exactly, were fastened together with rings and studs, some of which remain. On the front of the helmet is a diadem representing a bastioned wall with figures upon it. The back part of the helmet is decorated with six Roman soldiers on horseback, and eleven on foot, all in fighting attitudes. The use of these decorated helmets with masks, is unknown. They are extremely rare, and from a passage in a Latin author it is conjectured

they were worn at the exercises of the cavalry, the men wearing them acting as leaders in evolutions.

The fibula, or brooch, was found in 1884 outside the northern gateway of the fort. It is harp-shaped, and is attributed to the second half of the second century. The fibula was used for fastening the toga upon the shoulder, and this one being of gold probably belonged to a person of high rank. This fine example is kept in the museum at Blackburn.

During the eighteenth century, when it became the fashion to admire and collect relics of the classical period, many of the Lancashire gentlemen paid visits to Ribchester, "curiosity" hunting. The beautiful helmet as well as a pierced bronze basket, were in the collection of Charles Townley, the most famous of all Lancashire art-lovers; whilst at Browsholme the Parkers possessed one of the stones which were placed by a legion to mark its work

THE BACK OF THE HELMET

upon a fort. It is by these legionary stones, as they were called, that much of the history of the Roman occupation of Britain has been traced.

Ribchester appears to have been destroyed by fire. Corn found in the granaries was scorched and charred, whilst everywhere amongst the ruins were soot and charcoal, and other evidences of fierce burning. Unlike the other Roman stations in Lancashire, Ribchester did not become the site of a Saxon town. It fell into decay. " Even in the reign of the Conqueror," says Whitaker, " remaining in

in which the remains of private houses have so nearly perished, and the religious edifices are so entire, that a traveller is inclined to ask whether they were intended only for habitations of the gods."

More than four centuries after the Conquest, Ribchester was visited by Leland the chronicler. " But Ribchester," he says, " is nowe a poore thing : it hath been auncient towne. Great squarid (squared) stones, voultes (arches) and antique coins be found ther, and ther is a place wher that the people fable that the Jues had a temple."

ROMAN LEGIONARY STONE FROM RIBCHESTER

a state approaching to desolation, its firm and durable walls must long have defied the ravages of time, and long have presented a noble monument of Roman greatness. Something, perhaps, like the state of Silchester and Caergwent at present, might have been its appearance at the last of these periods ; that is, a spacious parallelogram, surrounded with vast walls of excellent masonry, strengthened with herring-bone work within, and laced at intervals with courses of different dimensions, or variegated by lozenge and chequer-work without. Within must have appeared the slender remains of Roman habitations in their last period of decay ; while the massy temple might still have all its columns erect and vast vaults unbroken, its dedication legible, and even its altars on their bases. So at this day appear some of the cities of *Magna Græcia*,

This tradition of the existence of a Jewish temple at Ribchester continued through eleven or twelve centuries. The only idea the peasant-folk, round about, had of a temple was based upon the description of the Temple of Solomon in the Bible ; hence the belief that the temple at Ribchester belonged to the Jews. The temple was actually dedicated to the worship of the goddess Minerva, and in 1811 an inscription was found which led to its discovery. Few stories of antiquarian discovery are more interesting.

In July 1811, some workmen, who were employed to stop an encroachment of the Ribble upon the bank almost opposite to the parish church, came upon the foundations of two parallel walls, strongly cemented, and standing about seventy feet from one another. Between the walls—

that on the south side appeared to have been carried away by the river—lay a flagged floor, near one end of which were the remains of a large flat stone. In removing this stone, the workmen broke it into many pieces before they discovered that upon its underside was an inscription. The illustration shows the appearance of this stone after the fragments had been collected and carefully pieced together. From this apparently hopeless puzzle the learned Dr. Whitaker gathered the history and the date of the temple! In the broken fragments of the first line he found that Julia Mammæa, the mother of the Emperor Severus, was mentioned, and after many months of labour reproduced the inscription as it originally appeared. A comparison between the inscription as it was found, and its restoration by Dr. Whitaker, given below, will show the skill and ingenuity he displayed :—

DEAE MINERVA PRO SALVTE IMP ALEXANDRI AVG ETE IVLI MAM-MEAE MATRIS DNET CASTR SVOR ET VAL CRESCENTIS FVLVIANI LEG EIVS PP. PR. PR. T. FLORIDVS NATALIS LEG PRAEP Ñ ET REGINAE TEMPLVM A SOLO EX RESPONSU RESTITVIT ET DEDICAVIT.

This, with all its contractions put into words runs: " Deae Minervae—Pro salute Imperatoris Alexandri Augusti et Juliae Mammeae matris Domini nostri et Castrorum suorum, et Valerii Crescentis Fulviani Legati provinciae praesidis, pro-praetore, Titus Floridus Natalis Legatus praepositi numini et reginae templum restituit et dedicavit."

The Emperor Alexander Severus reigned from A.D. 222 to A.D. 235 ; it is to the later part of this period that Dr. Whitaker assigned the date of this inscription, which tells that the Legate, Titus Floridus Natalis, restored and dedicated the Temple

to Minerva, the Queen of the Clouds, in honour of the Emperor, his mother Julia Mammæa, and of the Imperial Legate, Valerius Crescentius Fulvianus, who had preceded him.

An inscription found in Cumberland united the names of the Emperor Severus and his mother Julia Mammæa in precisely the same manner.

The discovery of the stone led to the discovery of the site of the temple itself. Dr. Whitaker was one of the exploring party. "The distinct mention of a Temple, from which the stone could not have been far removed," he says, " excited curiosity ; and accordingly the Author, with some friends, having obtained leave in July 1813, to explore the adjoining ground, proceeded to dig in the gardens which intervened between the brink of the stream and the churchyard. Their search was instantly rewarded ; for immediately beneath the vegetable mould, the walls were distinctly traceable by the remains of mortar and rubbish. Within these lay almost a continued structure of charcoal, formed of the timbers of the roof, which had been evidently consumed by fire, and, nearly in the centre, a cavity had been formed by the falling-in of the beams, so that the ends had sustained each other, four or five feet wide, and from three to four in height. Beneath this fallen roof lay several human skeletons (apparently those of very tall and robust men) in every direction, and innumerable fragments of large amphoræ, besides one which we had nearly retrieved entire, together with great quantities of the red or Samian ware, beautifully stamped ; part of the beam of a stag, nearly eight inches in circumference; and a perfect steel yard of copper, very nicely and exactly graduated . . . . From these appearances it was impossible to deduce any other conclusion than this—that the Temple had been stormed and burnt, and that several of its defenders had been overwhelmed, and perished by the fall of the roof."

Dr. Stukeley, a learned antiquarian and a friend of Sir Isaac Newton, gave a vivid account of Ribchester, or Ribblechester as he called it, in a book, *Itinerarium Curiosum*, published in 1724, and its appearance in his day. "The Ribble," he says, "is very broad at this place, rapid and sonorous, and Viewing the breach of the bank exposed thereby, I saw the joists and boards of a floor of oak four feet beneath the present surface, with many bits of Roman brick, potsherds and the like, and such floors are to be seen along the whole bank, whence most antiquities are found in the river." Mr. Ogden, the minister at Ribchester, Stukeley tells us, was a great collector of all the Roman antiquities, but

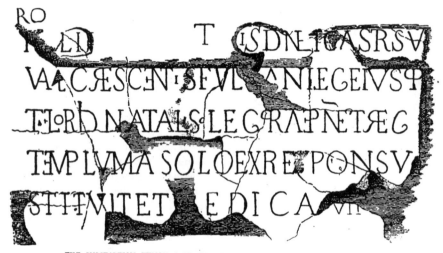

THE INSCRIPTION WHICH GAVE THE DATE OF THE TEMPLE AT RIBCHESTER

what is much to be lamented runs over innumerable Roman antiquities; for in this long tract of time it has eaten away a third part of the city." At the door of the Red Lion he saw the base of a pillar and a column which had been "fished out of the river." One corner of the house was a Roman partition wall, built of pebbles and hard mortar. "This house," he continues, "now is by the brink of the river, leaving only a scanty road between; but within memory, a great many houses opposite, and among them the chief inn of the town, were washed away. Farther on, down the stream, a great part of an orchard fell down last year, and the apple-trees still grow in their own soil at bottom.

he had died before the writer's visit took place, and his widow had disposed of his coins, intaglios, etc., to a Mr. Prescot at Chester. "Many urns have been found hereabouts, but all lost and disregarded since Mr. Ogden's death, who collected such things. They know the track of the Roman road all over the hills. In a garden of the Unicorn's head, a gold finger was found, and a brass finger as large as a man's; two intaglios of Mercury, found at Anchor Hill; much ashes and bones found near the city."

The north-west angle of the city could still be seen in 1724, and "where the northern wall turned down the north side of the church, a little way down a lane at that angle, a great bank runs westward, made of stone, like a Roman road. There is a lane goes down north of the city to the brook, called the Strand, which confirms there having been some sort of navigation here. At the end of this lane is the street, which is the Roman Road, running directly northward up the Fell, called the Green Gate, it passes over Langridge, a great mountain so named from it, so through Bowland Forest; it appears green to the eye."

The eastern wall of the Roman city then stood on a sort of precipice, and amongst other information Stukeley gathered was that "horses and carriages frequently fall down the steep from the street, because it is narrow, and but factitious ground."

In the time of the Romans the Ribble must have been navigable, for at a place called Anchor Hill, ships' anchors have been dug up, as well as iron pins, of all sizes, for barges and ships.

PIERCED BRONZE BASKET FOUND AT RIBCHESTER

AN OLD=TIME WEDDING CUSTOM

THIS old-time custom is still prevalent at marriages in the districts round Burnley. A wedding-ring is put in the posset, and after serving it out the unmarried person whose cup contains the ring will be the first of the company to be married. An ordinary flat cake of flour, water and currants is also made. In this are placed a wedding-ring and a sixpence. When the company is about to retire after the marriage festivities the cake is broken and distributed amongst the unmarried women.

She who gets the ring in her portion of the cake will shortly be married; and the one who gets the sixpence will die an old maid.

THE DANES IN LANCASHIRE

NO race, which in the early days conquered and occupied Lancashire, has left so many traces of its occupation as the Danes. When the Romans had withdrawn from Britain, the half-civilized natives were no match for the hardy Saxons who poured into the country and speedily made it their own. For over three hundred years England was ruled by the Heptarchy—the seven Saxon kings who divided the country among them. Then came the first attack upon their power in the landing of the Danes on the east coast. During the next one hundred years these descents were repeated, the fierce Norsemen plundering the east coasts and slaughtering the inhabitants. Gradually, in the next hundred years, they conquered and settled in various parts of the east and southern sea-boards; but it was not until 894 that their great leader, Hastings, who had been driven by Alfred the Great from Wessex, sailed up the western coast and took the city of Chester, and from this point they spread over a considerable part of Lancashire, chiefly in the region of the sea-coast, as is shown in the names of the hundreds into which the shire was divided.

The Anglo-Saxons kept inland, and, as Mr. Partington observes, "the broad Anglo-Saxon frame is seen to perfection in the eastern districts and the light ruddy complexion." Of the five hundreds into which Lancashire was divided, three were under Danish domination, and all three bordered the sea. Thus, the first hundred of the shire was called Lonsdale, which really meant Lunesdale; the second hundred was Amoundering, so called from Amounder, the first Dane who settled there. Blackburn—or, as it was called

in those days, Blagbournshire—the third hundred, is purely an Anglo-Saxon name, as is also the name of the fourth hundred—Salford. The West Derby hundred, on the other hand, is entirely Danish; the word Derby (or Deorby) meaning, in Danish, a spot where deer abounded. Everywhere we find interesting traces of these hardy conquerors, especially in the names of places. The letters "bi" at the end of a word in Danish meant that it was a place of residence, and when the Danes became converted to Christianity, after their conquest of Lancashire, it is easy to tell where they built their churches. The Danish word for church was "kirkja"; so wherever the word "kirk" occurs, such as in Kirkby, Ormskirk, and Kirkdale, it is a sign that a church was built there by the Danes.

Many Danish words, especially those dealing with the sea, have become part of the English language: such as "flaade," a fleet; "weinde," windlass; "skibsbord," shipboard; "mast," mast; "vrag," a rock; "asseile," sails; "styrmand," steersman. In Lancashire that curious custom of "long weight" and "long hundred" has come down directly from the Danes. Cheese is still being sold at one hundred and twenty pounds to the hundredweight, and eggs one hundred and twenty to the hundred. In the timber trade one hundred and twenty deals are counted to the hundred; in Westmorland six score to the hundred is still the measure of crops and timber. This mode of counting by the Danes was taken from the Icelandic term "hundred," which meant one hundred and twenty.

By some great authorities the Danes have been accused of teaching the Anglo-Saxons drunkenness, a vice from which they had hitherto been free. Lord Coke says that it was the Danes who made ale the national beverage of England; the word itself coming from the Danish word "ol." The Danes—according to the old chronicler, John Wallingford—if they set the Saxons a bad example in drinking, certainly set them a good one in the way of cleanliness. "They were wont," he says, "after the fashion of their country, to comb their hair every day, to bathe every Saturday — 'langardag' which means 'bath-day'—and to change their garments often and to set off their persons with many such frivolous devices";

those of Saxon and Danish origin thus: the addition of "son" and "sen" was very common among the Danes but unknown to the Anglo-Saxons. The capital of Denmark, Copenhagen, which means the harbour of merchants, has given England many place-names and surnames: thus, the Danish word "copeman," a merchant or a dealer, in English gradually became "chapman," from which came the word "cheap" and "Cheapside," which meant the place where the merchants met to sell and buy. The expression "chop and change" comes from this word. The word "copeman"

DANISH BOAT DISCOVERED AT PRESTON

and, being an Anglo-Saxon and cordially disliking a conquering race, he somewhat spitefully adds, "and in this manner laid siege to the virtue of the women."

Another word which is found in many towns in Lancashire is "gate." This is generally taken for granted as meaning that it was a street leading from some ancient gateway into the town, long since demolished. But the word is of purely Danish origin; they had no word in their language which described a street of houses, and they called it "gata."

In this derivation of names it is interesting to note that the great Lord Nelson bore a Danish name which originally was Nielsen, and was born in one of the parts of Norfolk which were amongst the first to be colonized by the Danes. In names we can easily distinguish between

or "copemaster" survived many hundreds of years, for Calvin in 1579 in one of his sermons said, "they play the copemaister and make merchandise of the doctrine of the gospel."

The Danes have left a strong mark upon the physical attributes of their descendants in the districts in which they settled in Lancashire. As Mr. Partington says: "Their Scandinavian descent, their constant exposure to a highly oxygenized atmosphere, their hereditary passion for athletic sports and exercises, their happy temperament, their exemption from privation, and many other causes have contributed to develop and maintain their physical pre-eminence, and to enable them to enjoy as pastime an amount of exposure and fatigue that few but them would willingly encounter."

Thomas de Quincy, who was a Lancashire man himself, and had studied his fellow-countrymen very closely, declared that "it is the lower classes that in every nation form the *fundus* in which lies the national face as well as the national character. Each exists here in racy purity and integrity not disturbed by alien intermarriages nor in the other by novelties of opinion or other casual effects derived from education and reading." He also says: "There you saw old men whose heads would have been studies for Guido; there you saw the most colossal and stately figures among the young men that England has to show; there the most beautiful young women; there it was that sometimes I saw a lovelier face than ever I shall see again."

Mr. Partington tells two very amusing stories, which not only show that old words derived from the Danish are still in use in the northern Lancashire dales, but, that there, they still maintain the old Danish independence. In a northern village Mr. Partington once stopped to speak to an old lady at her door, and began by remarking that the river was much swollen. "We call it a beck," said the old lady, turning her back and telling her grand-daughter to bring out the "scrapple." "Whatever may a 'scrapple' be?" asked Mr. Partington. "Why, that is what a scrapple may be," she said, pointing to a coal-rake in the girl's hand. As Mr. Partington moved away he heard her say to a neighbour: "I don't know where he has been brought up. He calls the beck a river, and does not know what a scrapple is." These northern folk have a strong sense of humour, and Mr. Partington records this answer to a tourist who inquired, somewhat stupidly, if it ever rained in a particular village: "Why it donks and it dozzles, and sometimes gives a bit of a snifter, but it ne'er comes in any girt pell."

Our illustration shows a Danish trough, or trow, which was discovered deeply sunk in the river bank at Preston, and is now carefully preserved in the Harris Library; it is hewn out of the trunk of a tree. As a rule, there were two of these boats held together by a cross-pole, and they were originally used by shepherds for crossing rivers—hence our word for the feeding-troughs for cattle and sheep. The shepherd placed a foot in each trough and rowed himself across the river with the help of an oar. According to tradition, when the Danish king, Canute, conquered the Anglo-Saxon king, Edmund Ironsides, and concluded an agreement to divide the country between them, he crossed over the Severn to meet his defeated rival in this manner.

SOME STORIES OF WINWICK

WINWICK was the favourite residence of Oswald, King of Northumbria, and it was near this place that he was killed, in A.D. 642, at the Battle of Makerfield. Oswald was a Christian, and he fell not only fighting for his kingdom, but for his religion, against the pagan king and army of Mercia. The Venerable Bede, the Anglo-Saxon chronicler to whom we owe so much of our knowledge of the Saxon Heptarchy, tells us that the spot upon which King Oswald's body lay after he was slain became holy ground. Man or beast touching the place where he had lain if they were sick were instantly restored to health. He also says that so many people carried away the earth in order to bestow its miraculous powers upon their friends and relations, that in the course of time a hole, or a fosse as Bede calls it, was formed as large as a man's body.

King Oswald was canonised for his valour against the pagans and for the miracles wrought by the earth. Half a mile from Winwick Church—which is dedicated to the King as St. Oswald—is St. Oswald's Well which, from time immemorial, has been reputed to be holy and health giving. Legend says that this well was formed by the excavation of the earth consecrated by the Saint's blood, mentioned by Bede. Time, instead of lessening the belief in the efficacy of the water of the well and the earth surrounding it, increased it, and all the neighbouring Roman Catholic Chapels took their holy water thence; and on into the nineteenth century a man was paid a small annual sum to keep the well clear of weeds in order that the water should not be contaminated.

There are some historians who claim Shropshire as the scene of St. Oswald's defeat and death. In that county there was a place called Muserfeld, now Oswestry, and here it is said the great battle took place, and that the head and quarters of the slaughtered king were hung upon a tree on the battlefield—hence the name Oswestry—Oswald's Tree. Further colour is given to this theory by the existence of St. Oswald's Well near Oswestry. But this well comes from a spring, and is not a hole or fosse so distinctly described by Bede. Also the name of Makerfield in Lancashire goes back to the very earliest times. There is further proof of the battle having taken place at Makerfield in the fact that the church, whose foundation is one of the oldest in the kingdom, was dedicated to St. Oswald, the first Christian king amongst the Saxons. In addition there is a Latin inscription on the south wall of the church, which being translated runs :—

This place, O Oswald formerly delighted you much.
You were king of the Northumbrians, now in heaven
You possess a Heaven, having fallen in the field of Marcefield.
We beseech thee Blessed Saint to remember us.

Then comes a line which has been obliterated, and below three Latin lines which say :—

In the year fifteen hundred and thirty
Sclater restored and built this wall again,
Henry Johnson at that time was curate here.

A suggestion accounting for the existence of the St. Oswald legend both at Winwick and Oswestry was put forward by the late Dean Howson in an address he gave at Chester in 1873. He was not going to decide between the claims of the two places, he said, but he was inclined to think both views might be reconciled. "Oswald had a palace at Winwick, and there was a well there that bore his name and an inscription that recorded his attachment to the locality. Oswestry is said to mean Oswald's Tree. There was no reason why they should not believe that he was killed at Winwick and that his head and arms were taken away and put on a stump of wood at Oswestry. The conflicting statements would then be reconciled." It is suggested that this opinion was in no way inconsistent with the character of the King of the Mercians, whose fierce and revengeful nature would not improbably lead him to send the mangled remains of Oswald to his Welsh allies as a proof of his victory over the Northumbrians.

James Stanley, one of the sons of Thomas Stanley, the first Earl of Derby, by his first wife, was rector of Winwick in 1493, and when Henry VII. made his "progresse into Lancashire there to make merrie with his mother the Countess of

PIERS GERARD

Derbie which then laie at Lathom," the Rector of Winwick entertained him and his Queen and all their Court for one night. Owing to the paramount influence of his step-mother, Margaret, Countess of Richmond and Derby, James Stanley was made Bishop of Ely. He was singularly tall and handsome.

"A goodly tall man he was as any in England. He did end his life in merry Manchester, And right honourably he lies buried there."

But James Stanley was ill-suited for an ecclesiastic. He paid scant attention to his vows of celibacy as a priest of the Roman Catholic Church, and openly acknowledged an illegitimate son who went by the name of John Stanley. Cock-fighting was then a popular pastime, and one to which James Stanley was par-

SIR PETER LEGH

177

ticularly devoted. It is recorded that he agreed with his neighbour, Thomas Butler of Bewsey, and other friends, to have a cock-fight every Saturday at Winwick. He died in 1515, and was buried at Manchester, where his tomb with his effigy in brass, may still be seen.

The ancient families of Legh and Gerard of Bryn both had their chapels in Winwick Church. In the Gerard chapel is a tombstone over four hundred years old. At the bottom, engraved in the quaint old Church text, is the epitaph :—

" Here lieth Peers Gerard Esquyer, son and heire of Thomas Gerard knyght of the Byrne, which married Margaret daughter to William Stanley of Hoton, knyghte, and one of the heires of John Bromley knyghte, which died the 19th of June 1492, on whose sowle God have mercy. Amen."

A full-length brass figure in plate armour, with sword and dagger and wearing a surcoat upon which are lions— the crest of the Gerards—stands upon another lion, which is lying on a rock. This is one of the most perfect monumental brasses in England, and shows the appearance of an esquire in the reign of Henry VII.

The Legh chapel contains a monumental brass which tells its own story. Upon one side is the figure of Sir Peter Legh clad in armour and wearing the spurs of knighthood, but over this garb of the soldier the chasuble of the priest is engraved. His head is bare and shows the tonsure of the eccclesiastic. On the other side is the effigy of his wife, dressed in a long robe, and wearing the head-dress of the time of Henry VII., with long lappets. Between them is a coat-of-arms, which is also engraved on the front of Sir Peter's chasuble. The inscription reads :—

" Pray for the soul of the excellent man, Sir Peter Legh, knight, here buried, and of the Lady
Elene his wife, daughter of John Savage, knight, the body of which Elene was deposited at Bellingisett 17th May A.D. 1491. The same Peter after the death of this Elene, having been consecrated to the priesthood, died at Lyme, in Hanley, 11th August 1527 "

In these bald words, " after the death of this said Elene, having been consecrated to the priesthood," lies the tragedy of a life. They loved as devotedly in those far off days as we do now, and when Death took his beloved wife from his side, Sir Peter Legh, the armoured knight, could find no consolation. His position, his possessions were as nothing; his world was empty. He sought refuge in his Church and became a priest, and for thirty-six years out of the desolation of his own heart ministered to others.

THE STORY OF LYDIATE

LYDIATE CHAPEL

LYDIATE HALL, a fine old timbered house which has been much altered and spoilt, was always in the hands of Catholic families, passing from the Irelands of Hale to the Andertons by the marriage of an Ireland heiress with the second Anderton baronet. At the death of the sixth baronet, Sir Francis, in 1759, the property passed to the Blundells of Ince-Blundell. Near by are the ruins of a church which the country-folk used to call Lydiate Abbey, but which was actually the private chapel of the Hall built by Laurence Ireland and his wife Catherine, towards the close of the reign of Henry VI.

At the Reformation this chapel was practically gutted, in common with all other Roman Catholic places of worship. The Irelands doubtless received a warning of the impending spoliation, for four elaborate panels, representing the martyrdom and burial of St. Catherine of Alexandria, were found carefully hidden away in Lydiate Hall. From the marks of violence upon them they must have been torn in haste from their places in the reredos above the altar. But for three hundred years these panels were carefully treasured at the Hall, at first in secret, and then, as religious intolerance decreased, more openly. With them was an elaborate figure of a seated bishop, wearing his mitre. This is supposed to represent St. Cuthbert, to whom the parish church at Halsall was dedicated, which was saved from destruction at the same time. This statue and the four panels are now in the church of Our Lady at Lydiate which was built in 1854. Until that time the upper part of the Hall was used as a chapel.

As in most of the houses of the Catholic gentry, there was a priest's hiding-place at Lydiate. This was a little dark chamber in the right wing, where the roof dips, and is only accessible through the rafters. It would hold about six people, and was brought to light in 1863 during the re-slating of the house. A pewter chalice and some fowl bones were found in it, nothing else.

The last Sir Francis Anderton was singularly unfortunate. He joined the Pretender's army at Preston in 1715, and was taken prisoner the very next day. He narrowly escaped with his life, and had to pay an enormous fine. At his death Lydiate nearly passed into alien hands by fraud. We are told that :—

" Sir Francis Anderton on his fortunate escape from the scaffold after his day's ' out with the rebels' in 1715, resided altogether at Lydiate Hall, and his relative, Mr. Blundell of Ince, is said to have been surety for him that he would not go beyond six miles from its walls. He lived the life of a country gentleman and was much addicted to the sports of the field. Like most of the Lancashire Catholic gentry, he kept aloof from the Rebellion of 1745, and was better employed in adding a wing to the Hall, and erecting some farm buildings (which bear the above date) for the accommodation of a favourite servant, to whom he then relinquished the care of his land. This man, Henry Rimmer, had been sent up to him while in prison in London by his kinsman Lord Molyneux, to whom he had applied for a servant, stipulating only that he should be a Lancashire man, and his descendants continued to occupy a portion of the Hall and to manage the farm till within the last few years, when the late Mr. C. Rimmer retired to a smaller farm in the vicinity. Sir Francis Anderton died at Lydiate in 1759, and a somewhat curious contest followed his death. Lady Anderton, in the minority of her son, in order to secure the estate from forfeiture, had made a deed of gift of it to her lawyer (a Protestant), in whom she reposed great confidence. She died without revoking the grant, and the lawyer also having died, his son, finding the deed amongst his father's papers, laid claim to the property on the death of Sir Francis. Mr. Blundell of Ince, the heir-at-law, naturally resisted the claim, but on the production of the deed, considering the insecurity of his position as a Catholic recusant, judged it best to compromise the matter by the payment of a large sum of money. This is an instance of injustice which was fortunately rare in those times, for though much Catholic property was confided from time to time to Protestant neighbours for purposes of safety, it was seldom that the confidence was found to have been misplaced."

In Aughton Church, near by, is this curious inscription by a member of the Mossock family :—

" My Ancestors Have Been Interred Here Above 380 Yeares,
This TO Me by Auncient Evidence Appeares ;
Which That All May Know, And None Doe Offer Wrong,
It Is Ten Foot and One Inch Broad. and Foure Yards and Half Long
Richard Mossock 1686   Amen.
God Save The King To The Greate Glorye of God."

"POTS AND PANS"

MANY old legends cling round the rugged district where the spurs of the Pennines run out into the lowlands of Lancashire and Cheshire, but none of the many peaks have a richer store of romance than that near Saddleworth, which locally is called by the curious name of "Pots and Pans."

In the far away legendary days when giants and fairies dwelt in the land, two giants named Alder and Alphin dwelt upon two neighbouring hill-tops, Alder upon "Pots and Pans," Alphin upon the height of Greenfield. These colossal creatures were great friends and used to amuse themselves by throwing great fragments of rock across the valley as small boys would throw stones into a pond. One of these great boulders, weighing many tons, and with the marks of giant fingers upon its hard surface, was said to have been thrown as far as Ashton-under-Lyne. But at length there came a shadow across their friendship in the shape of a woman. A beautiful maiden named Rimmon lived near by, in a charming dell still known as Rimmon Pits—

"Near Greenfield's utmost bounds
A circling rock a crystal fount surrounds
Where beauteous Rimmon oft concealed did lave
Her flowing tresses in the silvery wave."

Both giants fell in love with the lady, but her choice fell upon Alphin, whom she married. Whereupon Alder, in rage and mortification at his rejection, challenged his former friend to mortal combat. From the topmost peak of their lofty hills the giants hurled great rocks at one another across the valley, until Alphin was struck down and died. The unhappy Rimmon, rather than fall into the hands of the victorious Alder, leapt over a precipice and was killed. Nymphs which dwelt in the fountain tenderly lifted her corpse and placed it in the same grave with Alphin, at the foot of the hill of Greenfield.

On the summit of "Pots and Pans" there are some of the most interesting Druidical remains in the country, a fine stone altar, with massive-shaped stones which probably formed the walls of a Druid temple lying round it. This altar is shaped like a rough stone font, with a slight depression on its flattened top. Amongst antiquarians there has been a considerable difference of opinion as to the uses to which this altar was put. Some consider it to have been a sacrificial stone, whilst others connect it with the old Pagan superstition of healing by water. Local tradition certainly bears out the latter supposition, for down to quite recent times it was believed that sore eyes could be cured by washing them in water taken from the altar on "Pots and Pans." Many of these basins were set up on the highest hills to catch the rain and keep it from pollution. Close by the altar on "Pots and Pans" is a long, uneven hole, which it is supposed was made so that persons suffering from disease could immerse their whole body, in the belief that the god of the rock would heal them through the magic virtues of the pure water.

"Pots and Pans" narrowly escaped destruction at the time the canal in the vicinity was in the course of being made, and during the last half century many of the caves on the hill-side which were known as "fairy holes" have disappeared under the pick of the quarryman. Other rocks in this romantically beautiful region have disappeared, and amongst them the Giant's Rock, so called because it bore the exact impression of a giant's hand.

A short distance from the foot of "Pots and Pans," a portion of the old Roman road which ran from Manchester to York can still be traced. And near by, too, is the old "Bill o' Jack's" public-house, now called the Moorcock Inn, the scene of a brutal murder of a father and son—Bill o' Jack's and Tom o' Bill's—by poachers. Bill o' Jack's stands for Bill the son of Jack. The story of the crime is recorded upon a gravestone in Saddleworth Churchyard :—

IN REMEMBRANCE OF WILLIAM BRADBURY AND THOMAS HIS SON,

of Greenfield, who were together savagely murdered, in an unusually horrid manner, on Monday night, April 2nd, 1832 ; William being 84, and Thomas 46 years old.

BILL O' JACK'S

Throughout the land, wherever news is read,
Intelligence of their sad death has spread ;
Those who now talk of far-famed Greenfield Hills
Will think of Bill o' Jack's and Tom o' Bill's.

Such interest aid their tragic fate excite
That, ere they were removed from human sight,
Thousands on thousands daily came to see
The bloody scene of the catastrophe.

One house, one business, and one bed,
And one most shocking death they had ;
One funeral came, one inquest passed,
And now one grave they have at last.

BILL O' JACK'S

THE WINWICK BROAD OAK

THERE formerly stood at Winwick an old oak of so unusual a size that its branches once served as a canopy for a dinner of one hundred and twenty-four persons, a company "never exceeded in respectability upon any public occasion in the city of Lancaster." The dinner was given to Captain Phipps Hornby, who had commanded the *Volage* at the Battle of Lissa, and captured a

French flag. The young captain, whose father, the Rector of Winwick, lived at Winwick Cottage, had returned to the village early in August 1811 after five years' absence, and his friends and neighbours, anxious to honour one who had so honoured his native place by his bravery and his services to his country, arranged a princely banquet for him on the 26th. The interior of the great tree was covered with fine white cloth, giving it the appearance of a huge tent, the tables being ranged in a semicircle round the trunk, as shown in the illustration.

The gentry and yeomen for miles around assembled at this dinner in honour of the local hero. Never was there such a feasting in Winwick. There was music, speeches, and finally a song, composed especially for the occasion.

Song sung at the Dinner to Captain Phipps Hornby.

Ye Britons, venerate this tree
Which forms our verdant canopy,
    Fam'd in historic page;
Beneath its shade the Druid rose,
And wak'd the British youth from woes
    To true heroic rage.

Forth from their woods they rush'd like flame,
What time Rome's hostile legions came
    They met them at the wave.
And who shall call the conflict vain?
They perish'd on their native plain,
    Nor liv'd a race of slaves.

And still the oak, our island's boast,
From hostile foes protects our coast,
    Hence are our terrors hurl'd.
Ye Britons, venerate the oak!
Nelson from this in Vengeance spoke
    And shook th' astonish'd world.

Nelson's no more! Hoste, Whitby live,
Gordon and Hornby too survive,
    Enrob'd in Nelson's vest.
"Remember Him!" on Lissa's coast
Said he, who was himself a Hoste,
    And thunder spoke the rest.

While th' oak shall flourish in the glade,
What foe shall dare our shores invade?
    O lovely tree, increase!
Still spread thy verdant Branches far,
Protect us in the time of War
    And shelter us in peace.

Captain Hoste, who is referred to in this song, commanded the small English squadron of ships at the Battle of Lissa in the Adriatic, on March 13, 1811, a battle which "was considered one of the most brilliant achievements" during the long war with France. Three years later he was made a baronet. He entered the Navy in 1793, and was placed under the personal care of the great Nelson. The "Remember Him," in the song, was the poetical version of Hoste's signal at Lissa as the French and English squadrons went into action, "Remember Nelson!" It was said of him "His constant endeavour was to act as became a pupil of Nelson."

Captain Phipps Hornby, whose mother was Lady Lucy Stanley, a daughter of the twelfth Earl of Derby, entered the Navy in 1797. He had a most distinguished career, holding many high posts, amongst them that of a Lord of the Admiralty. He was knighted in 1852, and lived to the age of eighty-two. His elder son, Admiral Sir Geoffrey Phipps Hornby, achieved an equally distinguished position in the Navy.

At the time of the famous dinner under the Winwick Broad Oak, the hero of the festival was only twenty-six.

In those days Winwick had many charities, one of which was the granting of one year's rent of their cottages to six "poor labouring people of exemplary piety, industry, and good behaviour." A painted board announcing the fact used to be placed outside the cottages of those who had gained the charity, and was regarded, most justly, as a mark of honourable distinction. But in the year 1824 for some unrecorded reason the practice was discontinued. Writing in 1844, the author of the *Pictorial History of the County of Lancaster*" says : " Few parishes in England have so large a number of It covered an area of ground 100 yards in circumference, the lower branches extending 99 feet from north to south, and 87 feet from east to west. The girth

THE DINNER UNDER THE WINWICK OAK

endowed charities as Winwick. There are no less than thirty-seven enumerated in the Report of the Charitable Companies."

The Winwick Oak stood in a field a little distance to the south of the church.

of the trunk at the base was 14 feet ; and 11½ feet at a height of 5 feet. The first branch was 7½ feet from the ground. This wonderful old tree was blown down in a gale of wind on the 4th of February 1850.

A ROYAL VISIT TO HOGHTON TOWER

HOGHTON TOWER

IN August 1617, Hoghton Tower for three days was the scene of great feasting and entertainment in honour of King James I., who was visiting Sir Richard Hoghton.

King James, on his way back to the South on his return from Scotland, made a progress through Lancashire, and was most royally entertained first by Lord Gerard at Hornby Castle, next by Edward Tyldesley at Meyerscough Lodge, and then by Sir Richard Hoghton, honouring Preston with a brief visit on his way from Garstang to Hoghton. But of all these entertainings that of Hoghton Tower was the most lavish and magnificent. Nor was this visit memorable only for the profusion and display with which Sir Richard delighted his royal guest. It left a deep mark on the history of the country; for it was at Hoghton, as we shall see, that James conceived the idea of his famous *Book of Sports* which gave the royal authority to the playing of games on Sundays. The publication of this book laid the foundations of that bitter feeling against the throne which culminated in the Great Rebellion and the execution of his son, Charles I., on the scaffold at Whitehall.

When the civic banquet at Preston was ended, James and his immense following of courtiers and servants, together with a large number of Lancashire gentlemen who had come to do homage, set out for Hoghton, the town dignitaries dressed in mulberry-coloured taffeta gowns, and bearing white staves, accompanying him as far as Walton. The King drove in a great unwieldy carriage, the elaborate gilding of which had suffered not a little during the journey into Scotland, followed by his court in other carriages or on horseback, the end of the procession being occupied by the baggage-wagons and pack-horses. The road was full of ruts, and the great carriage, therefore, made only slow progress, swaying from side to side under successive bumps like a boat in a rough sea; the head of the procession raised clouds of dust, but even royalty in those days was accustomed to the discomforts of ill-made roads. After passing over the Ribble at Walton Bridge the royal procession went along the old road to Blackburn, whence James had for the greater part of his journey a full view of the house he was about to visit, standing proudly upon the summit of a hill. At length the foot of Hoghton Hill was reached, and, as the carriage could not be drawn up the steep ascent, the King and his courtiers descended.

Sir Richard Hoghton had accompanied the King from Preston; his son Gilbert, therefore, received the monarch at the bottom of the great avenue, kneeling and kissing his hand. Gilbert Hoghton was gorgeously attired. " His cloak and hose were all glistening and spangled with embroidery; his vest was cloth of gold, enriched with rare and costly stones; his shirt-bands and ruffles were worked in silver; and his gloves, Spanish, breathing out the choicest perfume; his hat was of French murrey, the brims thick set with gold twist and spangles; round it was a band of goldsmith's work, looped with a crystal button."

The whole length of the avenue was covered with purple velvet, and over this the King rode to the Tower escorted by Sir Richard and his son, and followed by the Duke of Buckingham, the Earls of Richmond, Pembroke, Nottingham and Bridgewater, Lords Zouch, Knollys, Mordaunt, Grey, Stanhope and Compton, the Bishop of Chester and many baronets and knights, and over a hundred Lancashire gentlemen, amongst whom were Sir Edward Mosley, Sir Edmund Trafford (Sheriff for the county that year), Cecil Trafford (he was knighted at Hoghton by King James), Richard Townley of Townley, Ralph Assheton of Whalley, Richard Sherburne of Stonyhurst, Richard Shuttleworth of Gawthorpe, Nicholas Girlington of Thurland Castle, and William Anderton of Anderton. All the Lancashire gentlemen wore the Hoghton livery to do the greater honour to their host. These liveries were sent round to his neighbours by Sir Richard Hoghton, as we learn from the diary of Nicholas Assheton, they having been approached on the subject as early as June.

" June 1. Sunday.—Mr. P. C. moved my brother (-in-law) Sherborne from Sir Richard Hoghton to do him such favour, countenance, grace and courtesie, as to wear his clothe, and attend him at Hoghton, at the King's coming in August, as divers other gentlemen were moved, and would. He likewise moved mee. I answered I would bee willing to doe Sir Richard anie service." The livery cloaks were sent out four days before the King arrived. " August 11.—My brother Sherborne his taylor brought him a suitt of apparel, and us two others and a livery cloake from Sir Richard Hoghton, that we should attend him at the King's coming, rather for his grace and reputation, showing his neighbors' love than any exacting of mean service."

In front of the Tower the tenantry of the Hoghtons and those of neighbouring families, all wearing " livery cloaks," were assembled. Loud and enthusiastic cheers greeted the appearance of the sovereign at the head of the imposing cavalcade, then suddenly two men appeared through the centre gateway. After the quaint conceits of the time they were supposed to represent the Household Gods of Hoghton, coming to welcome the sovereign. The first, according to the archives of the Hoghton family, wore a purple taffeta mantle, in one hand he carried a palm-tree branch, and in the other a dog; he wore a garland of palms on his head. The dress of the second is not given in the account of "A Speech made to King James at his coming to Hoghton Tower, by two conceaved to be the Household Gods," but the "speech" in its entirety has been preserved. Fulsome adulation and flattery could not go to greater lengths, but James accepted it with pleasure.

This day, great kinge for government admired!
Which these thy subjects have so much desir'd,
Shall be kept holy in their heart's best treasure
And vow'd to James as is this month to Cæsar.
And now the Landlord of this ancient Tower,
Thrice fortunate to see this happy hower
Whose tremblinge heart thy presence setts on fire,
Unto this house (the heart of all the shire)
Does bid thee hearty welcome, and would speak it
In higher notes, but extreme joy doth breake it.
He makes his Guest most welcome, in whose eyes
Love-teares do sitt, not he that shouts and cryes,
And we the gods and guardians of the place—
I of this house, he of the fruitful chace—
(E'er) since the Hoghtons from this hill took name
Who with the stiffe, unbridled Saxon came,
And soe have flourish't in this fairer clyme,
Successively from that to this our tyme,
Still offering upp to our Immortall Powers
Sweet incense, wyne, and odoriferous flowers;
While sacred Vesta in her virgin 'tyre
With vowes and wishes tend the hallowed fyre—
Now seeing that thy Majestye we see
Greater than country gods, more good than we;
We render upp to thy more powerfull guard

This house; this Knight is thine, he is thy Ward,
For by thy helpinge and auspicious hand
He and his home shall ever, ever stand
And flourish in despite of envious fate;
And then live, like Augustus, fortunate,
And longe, longe may'st thou live! to which both men,
Gods, saints and angells, say "Amen, Amen!"

The second Tutelar God begins.

Thou greatest of mortals—
(He's nonplust).
The first God begins again.
Dread Lord! the splendor and the glorious raye
Of thy high majestye hath stricken dumbe
His weaker god-head; if t' himselfe he come
Unto thy service straight he will commend
These Foresters, and charge them to attend
Thy pleasure in this park, and show such sport
To the Chief Huntsman and thy princely court,
As the small circuit of this round affords,
And be more ready than he was in 's words.

The second god being stricken to silence by "the splendor and the glorious raye" of James's majesty was the most flattering touch of all, and was cleverly calculated to appeal to the Stuart king's overweening vanity.

Although it was somewhat late in the day and James had been bumped and jolted in his great carriage from Myerscough to Preston, and from Preston to Hoghton, he insisted on going hunting before supper was served. The following morning he went hunting again, and in the afternoon paid a visit to the Alum Mine at Alum Scar, about a mile north of Hoghton, and on the Blackburn side of the River Darwen. We have the diary of the day from Nicholas Assheton. "Aug. 16, Houghton. The King hunting: a great companie, killed affore dinner a brace of staggs. Verie hott: soe hee (the king) went in to dinner. Wee attend the lords' table: and about 4 o'clock the king went downe to the Allome mynes, and was there an hower, and viewed them preciselie, and then went and shott at a stagg and missed. Then my Lord Compton had lodged two brace. The King shott again, and brake the thigh-bone. A dogg long in coming, and my Lord Compton shott again and killed him (the stagg). Late in to supper."

James was passionately fond of hunting, but he was both a bad shot and a bad rider. His lack of personal courage was nowhere more apparent than when out hunting, but his love of the sport was greater than his fears, and he never lost an opportunity of indulging it.

JAMES I.
(From a contemporary engraving)

sermon, he says, " Wee served the lords with bisket, wyne and jelly."

The afternoon and evening were given up to amusement. In the afternoon the Lancashire custom of rushbearing was represented to the King in the middle courtyard of the Tower.

After this "rushbearing" was over, it is said that a petition was presented to the King by a great number of Lancashire peasants, bedesmen and servants complaining of the prohibition by Queen Elizabeth's Commissioners in 1579 of all the old games on Sundays and holidays, such as dancing, archery, leaping, vaulting, May-games, Whitsun ales, morris dancing and the setting up of Maypoles, etc., and praying

The third day of the royal visit being Sunday, the King and his court, with all the large company staying in the house, assembled in the great hall in the morning and heard a sermon from the Bishop of Chester. Nicholas Assheton and the other neighbours of Sir Richard appear to have given their services in waiting on the higher members of the Court, for before mentioning the preaching of the

that they might be allowed to indulge in these games, as they did formerly, after divine service on Sundays. James received the petitioners very graciously and acknowledged the justice of their complaint against the prohibition of the "lawful recreations and honest exercises" of the "good people" of Lancashire.

Although tradition ascribes the scene of the presentation of this petition to

Hoghton, it would appear to have taken place at Myerscough Lodge, for Nicholas Assheton says under the date of August 13, " To Mirescough, the Court . . . The King killed five bucks. The King's speech about libertie to pipeing and honest recreation." But whether Hoghton or Myerscough was the scene of James's openly expressed sympathy with the petitioners it brought about momentous happenings. James detested the Puritans, and being persuaded that it was only Puritans who forbade Sunday amusements, and that they, too, were Jewishly inclined because they called the seventh day the Sabbath, he wrote the *Book of Sports*, recommending that diverting exercises should be used after evening prayer on Sundays, and ordered that it should be read in all the churches. " This legal violation of the day which is unequivocally the Christian Sabbath roused at the time the indignation of the seriously disposed," says Nicholas in his *Royal Progresses of James the First.* In the minds of the more bigoted the old public amusements were still associated with the Roman Catholic religion, and as England at that time was becoming more and more Puritanical in sentiment, a storm of indignation broke out against both the *Book of Sports* and its royal writer. The bitter invective of many historians has fallen upon James; his point of view in the matter has only been set forth in more modern times, and by the father of the late Lord Beaconsfield, Mr. D'Israeli, who put the question very clearly. " The King," he says, " found the people in Lancashire discontented, from the unusual deprivation of their popular recreations on Sundays and holidays after the church service : ' With our own ears we heard the complaint of our people.' The Catholic priests were insinuating among the lower orders that the Reformed religion was a sullen deprivation of all mirth and social amusement, and thus were ' turning the people's hearts.' But while they denied what the King terms ' lawful recreations,' . . . they had substituted some vicious ones. Alehouses were more frequented, drunkenness more general, tale-mongering and sedition, the vices of sedentary idleness prevailed, while a fanatical gloom was spreading over the country. The King, whose gaiety of temper instantly sympathised with the multitude, being perhaps alarmed at this new shape which Puritanism was assuming, published the *Book of Sports*, which soon obtained the contemptuous name of *The Dancing Book.*"

Charles I. re-published the *Book of Sports*, but public opinion had moved quickly in the intervening years, and he was held up as wishing his people to desecrate the Sabbath. This re-appearance of *The Book of Sports*, when the day of struggle came, gave the Parliament more adherents than any of Charles's tyrannies.

To return to Hoghton. James certainly carried out his opinion as to merrymaking on Sunday. After the rushbearing was over, the party went to supper, and supper ended, " at about ten or eleven o'clock," Nicholas Assheton tells us, there was a grand masque of " noblemen, knights, gentlemen, and courtiers, afore the king, in the middle round in the garden. Some speeches : of the rest dancing the Huckler, Tom Badlo, and the Cowp Justice of the Peace." In these bare words Assheton describes one of those magnificent spectacles in which James delighted, half play, half pageant, in which the actors wore dresses of every variety and country, and most of the company wore masks. Great pains and care had been taken over the Masque at Hoghton, but unfortunately no actual details have come down to us; all we know is that the leading members of the King's suite, including the Duke of Buckingham, took part in it, and that James himself was hugely delighted with the spectacle.

On the following morning, Monday, August 1, the King was not early astir, for it was twelve o'clock when his gilded coach carried him away to Lathom. But, as will be seen from the list of menus, the royal party consumed a prodigious breakfast before it set off for the Earl of Derby's house. Sir Richard Hoghton and his train of neighbours in their "livery cloakes" escorted the King some little way on his journey and then returned to Hoghton, where they all repaired to the cellar. "Wee back with Sir Richard," says Assheton in his journal. "He to seller, and drunk with us kindlie in all manner of friendlie speche." Then the neighbours went off to Preston, where they were "as merrie as Robin Hood and all his fellows," keeping up the festivity upon the next day, for on August 19 we have this significant entry, "All this morning we plaid the Bacchanalians."

James stayed two days at Lathom and finished his Lancashire progress at Bewsey Hall, whose owner, Thomas Ireland, he knighted.

But the entertainment at Hoghton Tower outshone all the others. The expense of entertaining James and his Court must have been enormous, seeing that the bills of fare given below are for one day and a breakfast only, and do not include the food for the large retinue of servants.

Notes of the Diet at Hoghton Tower, at the King's Coming There.

Sunday's Dinner the 17th August.
For the Lords' Table.

First Course.—Pullets, boiled capon, mutton boiled, boiled chicken, shoulder of mutton roast, ducks boiled, loin of veal roast, pullets, haunch of venison roast, burred capon, pasty of venison hot, roast turkey, veal burred, swan roast, one, and one for to-morrow, chicken pye hot, goose roasted, rabbits cold, jiggits of mutton boiled, snipe pie, breast of veal boiled, capons roast, pullets, beef roast, tongue pye cold, sprod boiled, herons roast cold, curlew pye cold, mince pye hot, custards, pig roast.

Second Course.—Hot pheasant, one and one for the King, quails, six for the King, partridge, poults, artichoke pye, chickens, curlews roast, peas buttered, rabbits, ducks, plovers, red-deer pye, pig burred, hot herons roast, three of a dish, lamb roast, gammon of bacon, pigeons roast, made dish, chicken burred, pear tart, pullets and grease, dryed tongues, turkey pie, pheasant tart, hog's cheeks dryed, turkey chicks cold.

Sunday Night's Supper.

First Course.—Pullet, boiled capon, cold mutton, shoulder of mutton roasted, chicken boiled, cold capon, roast veal, rabbits boiled, pullet, turkey roast, pasty of venison hot, shoulder of venison roast, herons cold, sliced beef, umble pie, ducks boiled, chickens baked, pullet, cold meats, tongue pye, neat's tongues roast, sprod boiled, curlews baked, turkeys baked cold, neat's feet, boiled rabbit, rabbits fried.

Second Course.—Quails, poults, herons, plovers, chickens, pear-tart, rabbits, pease buttered, made dish, ducks, gammon of bacon, red-deer pye, pigeons, wild-boar pie, curlew, dry neat's tongue, neat's tongue tart, dried hog's cheek, red-deer pye.

Monday Morning's Breakfast, the 18th of August.

Pullets, boiled capon, shoulder of mutton, veal roast, boiled chickens, rabbits roast, shoulder of mutton roast, chine of beef roast, pasty of venison, turkey roast, pig roast, venison roast, ducks boiled, pullets, red-deer pye cold, four capons roast, poults roast, pheasants, herons, mutton boiled, wild boar pye, jiggits of mutton boiled, jiggits of mutton burred, gammon of bacon, chicken pye, burred capon, dried hog's cheeks, umble pie, tart, made dish.

There were two chief cooks, who had the assistance of four labourers for the pastries, four for the ranges, two for boiling, and two for the cooking of the pullets.

A FAIRY VISITOR TO BLACKBURN

Under the Patronage of her Royal Highness the Duchess of York,

Who, with a Party of Nobility and Gentry, honoured LADY MORGAN with a Visit, on Monday, December 27, 1802.

The Author of Nature is Wonderful, even in the least of his Works!

JUST ARRIVED IN THIS TOWN,

And to be seen in a Commodious CARAVAN,

THE CELEBRATED WINDSOR FAIRY,

Known in London and Windsor by the Appellation of

LADY MORGAN,

A Title which his present Majesty was pleased to confer upon her;

Who had the Honour of being visited by the DUKE OF YORK and the DUKE OF CLARENCE, at the Lyceum, in the Strand, London, previous to their embarking for Holland; and the principal Nobility and Gentry in the Metropolis; at Ascot Heath Races, on the 19th of June, 1798, was visited by the PRINCE OF WALES and the PRINCE OF ORANGE.

And at the Particular request of HER ROYAL HIGHNESS THE PRINCESS CHARLOTTE OF WALES, was introduced into Her Royal Presence at Warwick house, Worthing, Sussex, on Wednesday, August 5th, 1807.

This unparalleled Woman is in the 58th Year of her age, and only 18lb. weight. Her form affords a pleasing surprise, and her admirable symmetry engages attention. She was introduced to their MAJESTIES, at the Queen's Lodge, Windsor, on the 4th of August, 1781, by the recommendation of the late Dr. Hunter, when they were pleased to pronounce her the finest Display of Human Nature in Miniature that they ever saw. But we shall say no more of these great Wonders of Nature;—let those who honour her with their visits, judge for themselves.

Let others boast of Stature or of Birth,
This glorious Truth shall fill my Soul with Mirth,
That I am now, and hope for Years to sing,
The SMALLEST SUBJECT of the GREATEST KING!

Admitance, ONE SHILLING—CHILDREN and SERVANTS, SIXPENCE.

—oo—

J. Hanby, Printer, Blackburn.

TATTERSALL'S AT HURSTWOOD

BURNLEY, with its cotton spinning and weaving and its prosperous woollen trade, does not suggest either poetry or romance, but tradition tells us it was the site of one of the most decisive battles in early English history, the famous fight of Brunenburk—the old name of Burnley—in 937, when the Anglo-Saxon king Athelstane defeated the combined forces of the Danes, Scots and Irish, barians, were all overthrown by Athelstane and his brother Edmund in the glorious fight of Brunenburk. That fight, looked on at the time as the hardest victory that Angles and Saxons ever won, still lives in the earliest and noblest of those national lays with which chroniclers relieve the direct course of their pure narrative." Indeed, there is nothing more stirring in the *Anglo-Saxon Chronicle* than the "Song

THE SPENSER HOUSE, HURSTWOOD

and became the first king to rule over the whole of England. Freeman, the historian, calls it the "glorious fight of Brunenburk." He says: "At last the rebellious Danes and their kinsmen from Ireland who came to their help, together with the Constantine of Scotland—Owen of Strathclyde—who did not scruple to league themselves with the heathen bar- of Brunenburk." The exact site of the battle cannot be determined, but there is a huge block of hard rock on a hill near Hurstwood, the base of which is washed by the river Brun, that has been called the Battle Stone from time immemorial, which would point to this pretty village, some three or four miles from Burnley, as being the place of the historic victory.

Hurstwood, too, has a claim to a position of honour in the annals of English literature and of English sport. The little village, seen from the entrance of the street, presents exactly the same appearance to-day as it did in the reign of Queen Elizabeth, the chapel, the school and some modern cottages being hidden at this point of view. In front, stands Hurstwood Hall, and on the left the two houses which give the little place its literary and sporting traditions — the Spenser House and Tattersall's Tenements. In the Spenser House, Edmund Spenser, the "poet of poets" and the author of *The Faerie Queene*, is said to have lived. The house belonged to a branch of the Spenser family long before and long after the reign of Queen Elizabeth, and it is said that whilst on a visit to a kinsman who owned it, the poet wrote his *Shepherd's Kalendar*. Traditions handed down in local families assert that Spenser House was actually the home of the great Elizabethan poet, and there are many, the late Mr. P. G. Hamerton amongst them, who have traced resemblance to the scenery around Hurstwood in some of the descriptions in Spenser's poems. Mr. Hamerton in one of his own poems, "A Dream of Nature," which describes a scene on the Brun, introduces it with this quotation from *The Faerie Queene*—

"And just beside these trickled softly downe
    A gentle streme, whose murmuring wave did play
Amongst the punny stones, and made a sowne
    To lull him soft asleep that by it lay."

These lines might apply to any stream, but Mr. Hamerton in describing "A Dream of Nature," voices his belief that Spenser too had been inspired by the beauties of Hurstwood.

"This poem breathes the spirit of the scene
    Wherein I spent the springtime of my youth ;
    When I first worshipped Nature and her truth,
And where in elder time one may have been
    Whose perfect manhood bore a riper fruit
Than I dare hope for my maturer age,
Yet still in toils like his I would engage
Although my sole reward be pleasure in pursuit."

There are others who do not accept the

Februarie.

A CUT FROM THE RARE FIRST EDITION OF SPENSER'S "SHEPHERD'S CALENDAR"

TATTERSALL'S TENEMENT

"may have been" of Spenser's presence at Hurstwood, and in the house itself, Mr. T. T. Wilkinson's opinion that the *Shepherd's Kalendar* bears internal evidence of having been written at Hurstwood, not only because of its descriptions, but by the use of archaic words which may still be heard in the district, is shown to all visitors. Spenser himself in a dedicatory letter addressed to Gabriel Harvey with the *Shepherd's Kalendar*, wrote that he had adopted rustic words and phrases in his poem, " But whether he useth them of set purpose and choise, as thinking them fittest for such rusticall rudenesse of shepheards, either for that their rough sound could make his rhymes more rugged and rusticall, or else because such old and obsolete words are used of country folke, sure I thinke, and thinke

I thinke not amisse, that they bring great grace, and, as one would say, authoritie to the verse."

There are no known facts that discount the claim of Hurstwood to be associated with the life of one of the greatest of English poets, or that the quaint old house, with its three gables, and its square stone porch was not his resting-place, or even his home for a considerable period. A room on the right of the entrance was formerly a central hall occupying the whole height of the building, but this is now divided into two rooms by a floor, and in order to see the fine oak rafters of the timbered roof, which was once the ceiling of the hall, it is necessary to climb to the second floor.

Of Hurstwood's claim to a place in the annals of English sport there is no doubt.

A FAMOUS LANCASHIRE RUNNER

LANCASHIRE has always been renowned for its athletes, and during the first twenty years of the nineteenth century one of her sons, Abraham Wood, was the most famous runner in England. He was born at Milnrow about the time of the death of Tim Bobbin, his marvellous running powers, the strength and elasticity of his limbs, being first proved in a four-mile race over Knavesmire in May 1802, against John Brown—a noted runner of his day. The race was for a hundred guineas. Wood's reputation steadily rose until 1806, when beating another famous runner, Jonathan Pollitt, in a ten-mile race over the race-course at Doncaster in fifty-two minutes and one second, he established his record. During the same year he was matched to run a quarter of a mile in a minute for forty guineas, and this he won with the greatest ease. Another race also against time was infinitely more formidable, but he beat the clock, running forty miles in four hours and fifty-seven minutes.

In a walking match against Captain Barclay at Newmarket in October 1808, Wood covered eight miles in the first hour, and fourteen miles in the second and third hours, but was ultimately beaten by Barclay, who maintained a steady six miles an hour all through—repeating the story of the hare and the tortoise. The betting on Wood had been very heavy, and when he was beaten there was a considerable disturbance, many of the losers declining to pay their bets on the suspicion that "he had taken too much physic." Shortly after this, Wood's death was reported in the London newspapers, probably from the fact of his having arrived at Manchester on his way to Milnrow in a coffin. The coffin had holes bored in it so that he could breathe, and this curious means of journeying from Newmarket to Lancashire is supposed to have been either to win a bet, or escape the violence of those who had backed him in the walking match and had lost their money. Once, in a quarter of a mile sprint with Shipley, seven to four being laid on the latter, Wood cleverly managed to leave the issue doubtful until within a yard of the goal, when he suddenly dashed forward and won the hundred guineas.

Thrice in 1812, Wood was badly beaten and his supporters believed that he was losing his position—once in a four-mile race on Knavesmire, and the second time in a two-mile race in which he had given his opponent a hundred and fifty yards' start. But in the following year Wood proved the prophets of evil to be wrong. In nine months he won each of the six races he ran, five of which were against time. In one of these races, a hundred guineas being the prize, he covered ten miles and a half within a few seconds of the hour. On the Heath near Wakefield he ran twenty miles in two hours eleven minutes and a half, "appearing quite fresh when he came in" acclaimed by the cheers of an enormous crowd.

Abraham Wood died in 1824, after having achieved the reputation of being the swiftest runner in the North of England.

THE CONFESSION OF A WITCH

ONE of the most astonishing incidents in the trials for witchcraft which took place at Lancaster during the earlier part of the seventeenth century, was the confession of some of the accused women. By making these confessions they were literally swearing away their lives, for unquestionably their wild statements were absolutely false. A student of witchcraft asks, "By what impulse of morbid vanity, or diseased craving for notoriety, or strange mental delusion were they inspired? And whence came the wild and even foul ideas which formed the staple of their delirious narratives? How did these quiet, stolid, unlettered Lancashire peasant women become possessed of inventions worthy of the grimmest German tales of *diablerie*?' The questions are not difficult to answer. When the unfortunate women were accused of being witches and thrown into Lancaster Castle, they were frequently tortured. Under the stress of pain they answered any questions put to them by their tormentors in the affirmative; or, if they were not put to the rack or thumbscrew, they were interrogated severely, and bullied and frightened into making damaging admissions. These "confessions," therefore, with all their amazing details of intercourse with evil spirits were practically supplied by the questions of their accusers.

Such was the confession of Margaret Johnson, who was one of the Salmesbury witches tried in March 1613.[1] It was written down, and signed by the unfortunate woman, and remains as a perpetual evidence of the blind ignorance and cruel superstition of the time. The spelling is here modernised.

"Between seven and eight years since, she being in her house at Marsden in great passion and anger and discontented and withal oppressed with some want,

[1] See *The Loynd Wife*.

there appeared unto her a spirit or devil in the similitude and proportion of a man, apparelled in a suit of black, tied about with silk points, who offered her, if she would give him her soul, he would supply all her wants, and bring to her whatsoever she wanted or needed, and at her appointment would help her to kill and revenge her either of man or beast, or what she desired, and after a solicitation or two, she contracted and conditioned with the said devil or spirit for her soul. And the said devil bade her call him by the name of Memillion, and when she called he would be ready to do her will. And she saith that in all her talk and conference she called the said Memillion her god.

"And she further saith that she was not at the great meeting of the witches at Hare-stone in the Forest of Pendle on All Saints' Day last past, but saith she was at a second meeting the Sunday after All Saints' Day at the place aforesaid, where there was at that time between thirty and forty witches, which all did ride to the same meeting. And thead (*sic*) of the said meeting was to consult for the killing and hunting of man and beast; and that there was one devil or spirit that was more great and grand devil than the rest, and if any witch desired to have such an one, they might have such an one to kill or hurt anybody. And she further saith that such witches as have sharp bones are generally for the devil to prick them with which have no paps or dugs, but raiseth blood from the place pricked with the bone, which witches are more great and grand witches than they which have paps or dugs. And she being further asked what persons were at their last meeting, she named one Carpnell and his wife, Rason and his wife, Pickhamer and his wife, and one Jane Carbonell, whereof Pickhamer's wife is the most great, grand, and anorcient witch; and that one witch alone can kill a beast, and if they bid their spirit or devil to go and prick or hurt any man in any particular place, he presently will do it. And she further saith that men witches have women spirits, and women witches have men spirits; that Good Friday is one of their constant days of their general meeting, and that on Good Friday last they had a meeting near Pendle water-side; and saith that their spirit doth tell them where their meetings must be, and in what place; and saith that if a witch desire to be in any place upon a sudden, that, on a dog, or a toad, or a cat, their spirit will presently convey them thither, or into any room in any man's house.

" But she saith it is not the substance of their bodies that doth go into any such rooms, but their spirits that assume such shape and form. And she further saith that the devil after he begins to suck, will make a pap or a dug in a short time, and the matter he sucketh is blood. And further saith that the devil can raise foul weather and storms, and so he did at their meetings. And she further saith that when the devil came to suck her paps, he came to her in the likeness of a cat, sometimes of one colour, sometimes of another. And since this trouble befell her (the accusation of witchcraft and imprisonment before the trial) her spirit hath left her, and she never saw him since."

The sucking of blood by the evil spirit from the body of the person who had given his or her soul in exchange for the help of demons, was a generally accepted belief and was gravely set forth in various treatises upon magic and witchcraft. A medical examination proved that Margaret Johnson bore no mark or sign upon her body, as she declared, that her blood had been sucked by Memillion. So firmly was this horrible idea rooted in the minds of lawyers and laity alike, that the only proof brought against a woman in the Pendle district in 1636, was a fleshy excrescence on her right ear, the end of which being bloody, was declared to have been sucked by a familiar spirit.

TURTON FAIR

THE old fairs, which were the only opportunity for amusement and the gathering together of the country people, roused much indignation amongst those of a serious turn of mind. The Fair at the village of Turton, in particular, roused the indignation of a Mr. William Sheldrake to such a pitch that he wrote a long poem upon the subject, and had it printed in London. The title is:

"A Picturesque Description of Turton Fair, and its Pernicious Consequences. A Poem. By William Sheldrake.

Unhappy men! the path in which you go,
Will doubtless terminate in endless woe.

London: Printed for the Author, and sold by B. Jackson, Bolton, 1789."

It is dedicated to William Cross, Esq., Collector of Excise, Manchester, who, we gather, shared Mr. Sheldrake's opinion as to the evil influence and consequences of the Fair. Mr. Sheldrake's mastery of verse was not equal to his pious wrath and indignation, for he never rises beyond a halting doggerel. The people, he says, gain their living by weaving and agriculture, and although generally sluggards they work hard for weeks before the Fair in order that they may have money to waste. The roads "be narrow and knee deep in mud." Turton Fair was in reality a cattle-fair, but Mr. Sheldrake dismisses this as merely a pretext. Of the cattle he says—

"So quick they're driven to their destined field,
Poor injur'd innocents compell'd to yield;
Most cruel treatment they must needs endure,
Yet no submission makes their lashes few'r;
And still to make these creatures smart the more,
With sharpest goads their painful flesh is tore,
Till their lank sides are mantled round with gore"

There was a service in the chapel before the Fair opened, during which—

"The pedlars cautiously prepare
Their crazy stalls on which t' expose their ware."

The Fair proper began at mid-day, but its merriment and gaiety were not at all to the liking of Mr. Sheldrake; nor would any of these gatherings of the country-folk seem to have met with his approval. In the following lines he runs a tilt at the rush-bearing at Holcombe. Turton Fair, he says—

"'Tis doubtless bad beyond comparing,
Unless to sottish Holcombe curst rush-bearing;
But, as 'twas satirised by an abler pen,
I'll say but little on that theme again.
Yet if reports are true, as prudence tells,
The last 's unrivalled, and bears off the bells,
Because their interludes and tragic play
Are chiefly acted on the Sabbath day.
Poor souls! how eagerly they ply their lore,
And to their tawdry garlands add one number more."

It does not seem to have occurred to Mr. Sheldrake that the "interludes and tragic play" were less harmful to the people than the bull-baiting, cock-fighting and other brutal sports then in vogue.

As the day passes the writer gives a vivid picture of a free fight amongst the merry-makers—

"To these base men commence the dreadful fight,
Kicking amain and trembling with delight;
Nor will desist till the red current flows
From the burst mouth and from the flattened nose." ·

Mr. Sheldrake concludes the account with an appeal to the "zealous few" to help him in his crusade against the Fair—

"Then we'll to the lady of this place bequest
To ease our minds and rid us of this pest."

Whether he was successful or not, history has left no record.

THE LANCASHIRE DEMONIAC

SUCH was the name given to Richard Dugdale, a young gardener, who lived with his parents at Surey in the parish of Whalley, towards the end of the seventeenth century.

When he was about nineteen he was seized with a strange illness accompanied by the most violent fits, which led those about him to believe he was possessed of a devil. " When the fits were on him, he showed great despite against the ordinary God, and raged, as if he had been nothing but a devil in Richard's bodily shape; though when he was not in his fits, he manifested great inclination to the word of God and prayer ; for the exercise of which in his behalf, he desired that a day of fasting might be set apart, as the only means from which he could expect help, seeing that he had tried all other means, lawful and unlawful." Six dissenting ministers thereupon attended the youth, and meetings were arranged. The first one was held on May 8, 1689, and they were continued twice a month until the following February, vast numbers of people being present to see the exorcism of the Evil One by the worthy divines.

At the first meeting Dugdale's parents were examined. They related, " That at Whalley rush-burying (or wake) on the James's-tide, in July 1688, there was a great dancing and drinking ; when Richard offered himself to the devil on condition that he would make him the best dancer in Lancashire." Richard got extremely drunk, and after his return home he saw several apparitions—by no means an unusual occurrence to those in his condition —which offered him all kinds of delicate food and fine clothing, together with gold and precious things, inviting him to " take his fill of pleasure." During the following day, they declared, some compact or bond was entered into between Richard and the Devil, and after that his strange illness and the violent fits began.

The six ministers signed, " An Account of Satan's acting in and about the body of Richard Dugdale, and of Satan's removal thence through the Lord's blessing of the within-mentioned Ministers and People." From this we learn that, " whilst the fits were upon him his body was often hurled about very desperately," that he abused the ministers and blasphemed his Maker ; also that he talked Greek and Latin, although entirely ignorant of those languages. Sometimes his voice was small and shrill, at others "hollow and hideous." Some days he was as light as a bag of feathers, at others as heavy as lead. One day he would upbraid the ministers for their neglect of him, the next he would declare they alone had saved him from hell. He could also tell when there would be rain, and when he should receive presents. At times he vomited stones an inch and a half square, and in some of his trances there was a noise in his throat " as if he were singing psalms inwardly." At the beginning of his fits he opened his mouth so frequently that it was believed spirits went in and out of him.

But the most amazing thing of all, and one which was taken as the strongest proof of demoniacal possession, was a lump which " rose from the thick of his leg, about the size of a mole and did work up like such a creature towards the chest of his body, till it reached his breast, when it was as big as a man's fist, and uttered strange voices." His agility during these fits was phenomenal, " especially in dancing, wherein he excelled all that the spectators had seen, and all that mere mortals could perform ; the Demoniac would for six or seven times leap up, so as that part of his Legs might be seen shaking and quivering above the heads of the People, from which heights he oft fell down on his knees, which he long shivered and traverst on the ground, at least as nimbly as other men can twinckle and sparkle their Fingers, thence springing up in to 's leaps again, and then falling on his Feet, which seem'd to reach the Earth, but by the gentlest and scarce perceivable touches, when he made his highest leaps."

Notwithstanding this visible proof of power, the attending divines rated the Devil for his pupil's lack of skill. The Rev. John Carrington, one of the signatories of " the account," addressed these reproaches to His Satanic Majesty :—

" Cease, Dancing Satan and be gone from him ! Canst thou dance no better, Satan ? Ransack the old Records of all past times and places in thy Memory ! Canst thou not there find out some other way of finer trampling ? Pump thine invention dry ! Cannot that universal Seed-plot of subtle Wiles and Stratagems spring up one new method of cutting capers ? Is this the top of skill and pride to shuffle feet and brandish knees thus, and to trip like a Doe, and skip like a Squirrel ; and wherein differs thy leapings from the hoppings of a Frog, or bounces of a Goat, and friskings of a Dog, or gesticulations of a Monkey ? And cannot a Palsy shake such a loose Leg as that ? Dost not thou twirle like a Calf that has the turn, and twitch up thy houghs just like a spring-hault tit ? "

The Rev. Mr. Carrington was apparently bent upon annoying Satan by this sweeping criticism.

During his last fits Dugdale announced that he must either be killed or cured before the 25th of March. According to the depositions of his father and mother, and two sisters, this proved to be true, for on the 24th of that month he had his last fit. The diviners took the credit to their perseverance in wrestling with the Evil One for so many months, but the actual cause of " The Lancashire Demoniac's " recovery was a bolus administered by Dr. Chew.

The truth of the matter was that Richard Dugdale was an impostor. At school he was noted as a " posture-master," and for his skill in ventriloquy, and, above all, for his vanity. The Rev. Zachariah Taylor, the Bishop of Chester's curate at Wigan, exposed the deception, insisting that it was a trick of the Nonconformist ministers in order to gain credit for themselves of having performed a miracle. Some of the names of the signatories of " the account," especially those of Oliver Heywood and Thomas Jolly, deprive this contention of any value ; and it is more than probable that the ministers were themselves deceived by the " demoniac " and his family, who made a pretty penny by exhibiting him in his so-called fits and trances, and from the charity of those who sympathised with them in what appeared to be a terrible affliction.

Even after the fits departed, some trace of the Evil Spirit remained in the youth, according to an attestation signed by eight ministers and twenty respectable inhabitants in the presence of three magistrates of the district, Lord Willoughby, Ralph Egerton, and Thomas Braddill. " When he got too much drink he was after another manner than drunken persons usually are," which may be taken as showing that Richard Dugdale carried out his imposture under the influence of drink. For miles around he was firmly believed to be " possessed," in spite of the exposure of the Rev. Zachariah Taylor. There is little doubt that Dugdale began his antics in order to attract attention to himself, and that his family finding it so profitable a matter, aided and abetted him with wonderful tales and with tricks which entirely deceived the simple-minded ministers.

LOVE LAUGHS AT LOCKSMITHS

MORLEYS HALL

MORLEYS HALL, near Leigh, was in 1536 the property of Sir William Leyland, and early in the reign of Elizabeth was the scene of the romantic elopement of one of his granddaughters. Leland, the sixteenth century chronicler to whom we owe much of our knowledge of the buildings and the manner of life at that time, believed himself to be a member of the same family and wrote enthusiastically of the old Hall. With the archaic spelling—the account begins, "Morle in Darbyshire" —put into modern English, this is his description of Morleys during the Tudor period :—

"Morley in Derbyshire (West Derby) Mr. Leland's Place is builded saving the Foundation of Stone, squared, that riseth within a great Moat a VI Foot above the water, all of Timber after the common sort of building of Houses of the Gentlemen for most of Lancastershire. There is much Pleasure of Orchards of great Variety of Fruit, and fair made Walls and Gardens as there is in any Place of Lancastershire. He bringeth all Turfs and Peats for the Commodity of Mosses and Moors at hand. For Chateley Moss (Chat Moss) that with breaking up of Abundance of Water in it did much hurt to Lands thereabout, and rivers with wandering Moss and corrupt Water, is within less than a Mile of Morleys. And yet by Morleys, as in Hegges Row and Grovettes, is mightely good Plenty of Wood, but good Husbandmen keep it for a Jewel . . . Morleys standeth in Leigh Parish a Mile and more from the Church."

The moat, above which the squared stone foundations rose "a VI Foot," was thirty feet wide.

Sir William Leyland, the "Mr. Lelande" of the chronicler, had a son Thomas, who succeeded him in the first or second year of the reign of Edward VI. He married an Anderton, by whom he had a daughter Anne, and she, failing a son of the marriage, became his heiress. As frequently happens with heiresses Anne Leyland fell in love with a penniless young man, Edward Tyldesley, second son of the Thurstan Tyldesley who built Wardley Hall—the "Skull House." In those days, as in our own, younger sons were not regarded as eligible husbands by the parents of young women destined to possess wealth and property. Thomas Leyland and his wife frowned upon the love affair of the young couple. In Tudor days parents exacted a strict obedience from their children, who never addressed them as father or mother, but as "Sir" or "Madam." Having rejected the young man's addresses for their daughter, Thomas Leyland and his wife considered the matter at an end. But not so their daughter. She loved the ineligible Edward Tyldesley, and flouting her parent's orders had stolen interviews with him and carried on a secret correspondence.

The lovers were betrayed, and Anne Leyland was promptly locked up in her room, her father threatening that there she should remain until she had promised to give up her beloved Edward. But Anne would not give the promise, and the door remained securely locked. Never did a lovelorn captive appear so completely imprisoned. Her only means of escape were the window and the door. Below the window stretched a deep moat thirty feet wide; the key of the door was in her father's keeping.

Anne Leyland was an intrepid and determined young woman, but she must have had the help of some sympathising maid, else she could not have obtained the rope which set her free, nor could her lover have been given intelligence of her plan. History gives us none of these important details. All we are told is, "having provided herself with a rope she tied one end of it round her body, and threw the other to her expecting lover on the opposite side of the moat, when casting herself out of the window into the water, which was thirty feet wide, he dragged her to land, and they were married before the adventure was known to the family."

Imagination must supply the missing links in this tale of love—the messages taken backwards and forwards between Anne Leyland and Edward Tyldesley, the smuggling of the rope, which was doubtless given by the lover to the sympathetic go-between, into her bedroom, and then the waiting for a favourable opportunity. It called for no small courage on the part of the lady to cast herself into the water; moats round Tudor manor-houses were not remarkable for their cleanliness. But the lady leapt, the lover pulled vigorously, and in a few moments she was on the opposite side, dripping but triumphant. Swift horses were in waiting and the happy lovers galloped off to be married.

Her father forgave the elopement and when he died, some four years later, Anne Tyldesley and her husband succeeded to Morleys. One of their descendants was the famous Sir Thomas Tyldesley, who lost his life fighting for King Charles I.

STORIES OF A "LANCASHIRE CURATE"

A CLERGYMAN with a sense of humour has more opportunities of collecting amusing stories than anybody else in the parish. A "Lancashire Curate" tells the following :—Visiting has many pitfalls, especially when the parson is not well acquainted with his parishioners and their relations. A Lancashire curate was visiting a sick man, and spoke of a malicious report that had been brought to him. The person who made the report was not to be trusted, and after giving his reasons for disbelieving the story, the curate concluded :—

"But then it was Mrs. —— who told me, and you know the kind of woman *she* is."

"Yes," replied the sick man, "she is my mother. She's been married twice."

Another curate placed himself in an exceedingly unpleasant position through the same kind of ignorance. He was calling on a newly married couple who had just come into the parish. Whether they were young or old, or whether one was old and the other young, he did not know, his only information was that they were newly married. He found a pleasant young woman preparing tea, whilst the sound of splashing in the "back-place" showed that the husband, who was a collier, was having his "wash." By and by the splashing ceased, there were grunts and groans as the man dried himself, then the door opened and a middle-aged man walked in.

"Good evening," said the curate pleasantly, and turning to the young woman said, "I suppose this is your father."

There was an awkward silence. The collier seized a long brush.

"Feyther! Feyther, eh?" he shouted, crimson with anger. "If tha aren't out o' this house in less nor ten seconds, I'll mek thee as tha feyther won't know thee. I've had enough o' that at th' pit. I'll ha' nooan o' thy lip, tha young whippersnapper."

The curate found discretion the better part of valour, and withdrew hastily.

Some years ago a Bishop of Manchester during one of his visitations in the diocese was examining a Sunday school class. The subject was Moses.

"Who was the mother of Moses?" asked the Bishop.

"Pharaoh's daughter," said a small boy.

"Come, come," answered the Bishop, "you know that Pharaoh's daughter found Moses in the river."

"That's what she *said*," replied the boy.

The same Bishop used to tell a good story against himself. When he was a curate in Sheffield his preaching made a great impression both in his own and neighbouring parishes. On one occasion he was asked if he would receive a deputation of wardens from a neighbouring church. This was their request :—

"Good evening, sir. We want to know if you will do us a favour. You see there is a new Unitarian come into our parish, and he says as how there is no devil, and we thought that if you could come and preach they would soon see that there is a devil."

A good many years ago there was rather a heated discussion both in the newspapers and at meetings, about what were declared to be the "needlessly" large incomes of Bishops. During the discussion it was stated that in the case of the Bishop of Manchester the stipend of four thousand a year was not enough to meet the expenses of his position, and that every year he was obliged to make up the heavy difference out of his private income. The statement was made at a meeting, at the close of which a working-man went up to the ecclesiastic who had given the information, and asked—

" Did I understand you to say that our Bishop can't make both ends meet with four thousand a year ? "

" Yes."

" Really ! " Then there was a pause, the working-man apparently turning the matter over in his mind.

" I can't make it out," he said at last. " Do you think he drinks ? "

Speaking of ecclesiastical dignitaries of Manchester, there was a certain Canon who kindness and gentleness were masked by a most severe and commanding appearance. He was walking down Deansgate one day when a tramp accosted him with—

" Please, sir, may I stay in Manchester to-night ? "

" What have I to do with it ? Why do you ask me ? " replied the astonished cleric.

" I thought you looked as if the town belonged to you," was the answer.

The layman is apt to credit very young curates with being extremely simple and innocent, and the following story is still told in a certain town in Lancashire as a proof of clerical ingenuousness. A young, a very young, curate was making his parish round, and having been told that if he wished to make friends, and gain any influence over a woman in one of the houses on his list, he must admire her baby, remembering the advice, after the usual greeting his first words were—

" What a pretty baby ! How old is it ? "

" Six months next Wednesday," replied the pleased mother.

" Dear me ! " said the very young curate. " What a fine baby ! Is it your youngest ? "

A Lancashire clergyman was reading the Bible to an old woman. When he came to the passage which ends, " There shall be weeping and gnashing of teeth," he paused, wishing to let the full effect of the solemn words sink into his hearer's mind.

" Ah ! " said the old woman, " let 'em gnesh 'em as has 'em. I ain't had none these thirty years."

" Woman, they will be provided ! " was the reply in tones of shocked severity.

But it is not always the clergyman who scores. A parson had made an appointment to visit a sick parishioner. When the day came he was laid up with a sick headache and was unable to go. As soon as he recovered he went to the old lady, and apologising for disappointing her explained that he was always subject to bad headaches which came on without any warning.

" Oh, well," said the old lady, " you mustn't mind. You see it always flies to the weakest spot."

Marriages provide an almost unexhaustible fund of humour for the clergyman with a sense of fun and the ludicrous. The ring is the most fruitful source of absurd incidents. It is either missing at the critical moment, or else it proves too small for the bride's finger. " The poor bride is hot and flustered," says a Lancashire curate. " She has spent, say, half an hour, pushing on gloves which are a size too small for her. She has had a hurrying, bustling day. In the cool of the evening, some days previously, with the western breezes playing about their loving forms as they sat on the fence, they tried the ring on. It slipped on beautifully. When they get to church, the ring goes as far as the joint, the skin puckers up, and then the ring sticks. Such is the difference between courtship and marriage. The excited groom tries to be gentle, but knows that force is needful. He generally gives up in despair, and the bride puts it on herself. One occasion I remember very well. The usual useless force had been wasted and the bridegroom gave it up and looked at me with a look that spoke of helpless misery. Not so the bride. She was fierce.

"' Lick it, tha fooil!' she hissed in the broadest dialect.

"No sooner said than done. He soon was sucking her finger, and in ten seconds the difficulty was solved."

One wonders why the bride did not moisten her finger herself, but there seems to be an unwritten law that on these occasions the lady takes the lead, issuing her orders and directions, and receives unquestioning obedience.

At one wedding when it came to the momentous words, "I will," the bridegroom, a collier, was absolutely dumb.

"Now then," said the bride, giving him a sharp poke in the ribs with her elbow. "Go on! Say, 'I will.'" The tone of her voice was unmistakable. It was too late to repent, and urged by another nudge, the bridegroom obeyed.

Not only is the putting on of the ring a serious difficulty, the finding of it frequently causes equal confusion. Nine times out of ten the bridegroom has forgotten where he put it. Some bring the ring to church in the case in which it was bought, some wear it on their watch-chain, others bring it loose in their pocket, or in their purse. It has even been fastened to the bridegroom's braces. But no matter where it may be, the flustered bridegroom generally forgets where he has placed it, and there is a feverish hunt, to an accompaniment of scarcely suppressed mirth on the part of the spectators.

The bridegroom at these humble weddings is generally meek and subservient, if not absolutely tongue-tied, but occasionally there is an exception. A bridegroom with a reputation for wit is sometimes tempted to air it for the benefit of the assembled friends and relations, chiefly in the form of "asides." A man of this type was once neatly caught by a clergyman at Blackburn. It was at the time when that remarkably silly catch phrase "Now we shan't be long" was in vogue. All through the service the bridegroom had been making *sotto voce* remarks which brought suppressed giggling from the pews. The parson tried to show the man the solemnity of the occasion, but in vain. When he was asked for the ring, the bridegroom made a frantic mock-search through his pockets; his feigned distress, his "Where is it?" "Come on out o' that!" and other expressions, causing handkerchiefs to be stuffed into mouths and faces to be hidden in hats. At last he pretended to find the ring, and holding it up turned to the congregation and said—

"Now we shan't be long!"

This was too much for the sorely strained people in the pews. There was one loud yell of laughter.

"My dear young man," said the clergyman to the grinning bridegroom. "You are mistaken—you will be just a week! Come again next Saturday."

Laughter gave place to tears, but the clergyman, and rightly so, was inexorable. There was no joking on the part of the chastened bridegroom on the next occasion.

ST. CHAD'S CHURCH, ROCHDALE

AFTER the conquest of England by the Normans, the Anglo-Saxon thane, Gamel, Lord of Recedham or Rochdale, made his submission to William the Conqueror, and in consequence was allowed to remain in possession of all his lands and baronial privileges. Some years later he was "minded for the fear of God and the salvation of his immortal soul to build a chapel unto St. Chadde," close to the north bank of the river Roach—then called Rache—and a low, sheltered spot, now called The Newgate, was chosen. Architects were summoned, and building material, stone and wood collected in vast quantities. With all due religious observance the foundations were laid, stakes being driven into the spongy ground and several courses of rubble laid upon the top of them, upon which in turn the cement or "grouting" was to be placed. But when the workmen came the next morning to carry out the "grouting," there was no sign of the foundations, or of the piles of timber and huge stones which had been strewn about the site; everything had disappeared in the night. Foundations, stones and timber were all found on the top of a steep hill on the opposite side of the river; nothing was missing.

The hauling of huge stones and great baulks of timber across a river and up a steep hill could not have been achieved without marks being left upon the river bank and the hill-side. But there were no signs of the passage of this mass of material from one side of the river to the other. The peasantry believed that human agency had no share in the work, and some of them were convinced that the old pagan deities, whom their forefathers had worshipped and whose altars had been thrown down and their rites and sacrifices forbidden, had burst from the thraldom in which they had been held by the Christian priests and were now preparing to revenge themselves. Thane Gamel, however, did not share this belief. He regarded the removal of the building material for his chapel as an outrage upon his authority by some of his own serfs and vassals, an outrage which called for instant vengeance and punishment. He issued a proclamation therefore, stating that unless the offenders were immediately given up, he would fine heavily all his serfs and vassals, and that they would also "be subject to such further inflictions as might still seem wanting to assuage their lord's displeasure." The serfs and vassals, terrified at this threat, and ignorant of the perpetrators of this defiance of their lord, decided that the only way by which they could appease his wrath would be to carry the building material from the top of the hill back to the site from which it had been taken. With infinite labour this heavy task was accomplished, but to their horror and consternation on the following morning the site by the river was bare; all the material had once again been transported by some mysterious agency to the top of the hill. Even Thane Gamel was now satisfied that some supernatural means were at work, for it had required fifty strong men to remove the material on the previous day, and one hundred could not have carried it back up the steep hill in darkness. He therefore sought counsel from the priests, and they argued that some unknown spirits, angered by the choice of the site near the river, might be appeased by the chapel being built upon the hill to which the material was removed. The chapel of St. Chad was therefore built upon the site occupied by the present church, and a hundred and twenty-four steps were cut in the hill-side to enable the good people to get to their prayers.

These legends of the mysterious removal of building materials for churches from the proposed site to another at some considerable distance away, are not uncommon, but in most instances the removal was attributed to the saint in whose honour the church was being built. It was believed that the saint thus indicated his or her preference for another spot. But in the case of St. Chad's Church there seems to have been no suggestion or belief that he was concerned in the removal, the conviction being that the task had been accomplished by evil spirits.

PLAGUE STONES

IN the days when the plague was an ever-recurrent scourge, vinegar was practically the only disinfectant known. The ravages of the plague, which was probably a form of cholera, and made its appearance in this country after the First Crusade, were terrible, three thousand people dying of it in Lancaster alone in the year 1348–49. Money was believed to be a source of infection, especially in towns. The country folk therefore, bringing their produce to sell on market-days during the time of plague, were fearful of the money of the townspeople; they were fearful likewise of entering a town. The buyers met the sellers outside the walls, and the purchase being completed, put their money into a hole made in a large stone, filled with vinegar, from which it was taken by the buyer. These stones were called Plague Stones, and sometimes Penny Stones, because pennies most frequently represented the amount of the purchase.

There were two plague or penny stones at Lancaster, one on the road from the south, near the site of the Ripley Hospital, which led into Penny Street, the name of which is believed to owe its derivation to this fact. The other plague stone was upon the north road, and may still be seen in Ridge Lane, which was part of the old Roman road from Lancaster to Caton. The stone is twelve inches square, with a circular hole in the top about three inches in depth and four inches in diameter. The bottom of the hole, into which the vinegar was put, is shaped exactly like the inside of a cup.

SOME HOGHTON EPITAPHS

OUR ancestors were prone to floweriness in their epitaphs and never failed, where it was possible, to introduce an allegory. In the chancel of Walton-le-Dale church the virtues of a daughter of the house of Hoghton are thus recorded:—

Here lyeth
the body of a pure virgin, espoused
to the Man C⁵ Jesus,
Mrs. Cordelia Hoghton whose
honourable descent you know.

Know now her ascent.

"While in that hall this virgin did remain,
To which this antient chappell doth pertain,
Christ by his friends prov'd her affection kind,
By pore, sick, sore, diseas'd and blind;
And hourely finding at his mercy seat
So many prayers both from and for her met,
Kindly invites her, by his servant Pale,
To the hill country from this lower dale.
She knew his face: with heart and soul most free,
Behold the hand-maid of the Lord, said shee.
So fits her for th' ascent, which proving steep,
And shee not well in breath, stopt here to weep.
But call'd on to make speed by hasty Death,
Left her tir'd body here to gather breath.
Her soul, sound in this faith rehears'd above,
And constant in her, vow'd pure virgin love:
Mounts Sion Hill, loos'd from corruption's band,
A Maid of Honour with the Lamb to stand."

A.H.P.   Sepult May 29. 1685.

Upon a plain brass plate is this inscription:—

"By the appointment of Sir Charles Hoghton Bart., deceased, this plate of brass is here affixed to intimate to all persons whatsoever, that it was his desire, nobody for time to come should be buried under this seat and pew, belonging to the Hoghtons, where his remains are interred, except the Lady Hoghton, his relict, if she so desire. Anno Domini 1710."

Lady Hoghton did "so desire," these being the epitaphs of husband and wife—

Underneath this seat lies the body
of Sir Charles Hoghton, Bart. He was a
gentleman of exemplary piety and
extreme usefulness.

Died the 10th of June 1710
Aged 66
Also the body of Dame Mary Hoghton
eldest daughter of John Lᵈ Viscount
Masereene
in the kingdom of Ireland,
and relict of Sir Charles Hoghton, Bart.
She was a lady sincerely religious,
and valuable in every relation;
remarkable for humility ·
and diffusive in charity,
died the 30ᵗʰ of April 1732
They lived desired
and died lamented.
"The memory of the just is blessed."

The manor of Walton passed into the possession of the Hoghtons in the reign of Elizabeth, being given to the widow and family of Richard Hoghton by the Baron of Newton after Richard Hoghton had been slain.[1]

[1] See "A Manor for a Murder."

LOOK OUT FOR NEW TITLES FROM

PRINTWISE PUBLICATIONS LIMITED

Coming soon:

MANCHESTER 100 YEARS AGO

THE MANCHESTER SHIP CANAL
— 100 Years of History

TRADITIONS, & SUPERSTITIONS OF LANCASHIRE

THE COMPLETE LANCASHIRE COOKBOOK

THE STORIES
AND TALES SERIES

Stories and Tales Of Old Merseyside
(Frank Hird, edited Cliff Hayes)
Over 50 stories of Liverpool's characters and incidents PLUS a booklet from 1890 telling of the city's history, well illustrated.
ISBN 1 872226 20 5   £4.95

Stories & Tales Of Old Lancashire
(Frank Hird)
Over 70 fascinating tales told in a wonderful light-hearted fashion. Witches, seiges and superstitions, battles and characters all here.
ISBN 1 872226 21 3   £4.95

Stories and Tales Of Old Manchester
(Frank Hird, edited Cliff Hayes)
A ramble through Manchester's history, many lesser known stories brought to life, informative yet human book. Over 50 stories.
ISBN 1 872226 22 1   £4.95

Stories Of Great Lancastrians
(written Frank Hird)
The lives of 24 great men of the county, told in easy reading style. Complete with sketches and drawings, a good introduction to the famous of Lancashire and Manchester. John Byrom, Arkwright, Tim Bobbins, Duke of Bridgewater.
ISBN 1 872226 23 X   £4.95

More Stories Of Old Lancashire
(Frank Hird)
We present another 80 stories in the same easy, readable style, very enjoyable, great. With special section for Preston Guild 1992.
ISBN 1 872226 26 4   £4.95

Have you seen . . .

LANCASHIRE 150 YEARS AGO

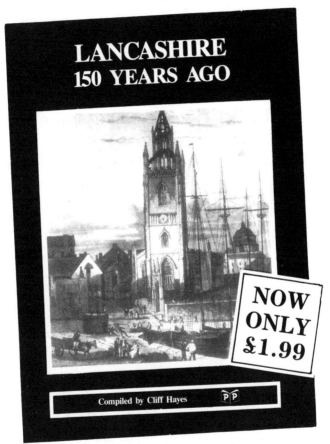

A great addition to the
collection of any lover of
Lancashire's history

ONLY £1.99

NORTHERN CLASSIC REPRINTS
— *POETRY COLLECTION* —

NOW £2.50

Poems & Songs of Lancashire

(Edwin Waugh)

A wonderful quality reprint of a classic book by undoubtedly one of Lancashire's finest poets. First published 1859 faithfully reproduced. Easy and pleasant reading, a piece of history.

ISBN 1 872226 27 2

£4.95

The Best of Old Lancashire
— Poetry & Verse

Published in 1866 as the very best of contemporary Lancashire writing, this book now offers a wonderful insight into the cream of Lancashire literature in the middle of the last century. Nearly 150 years later, edited and republished, the book now presents a unique opportunity to read again the masters of our past.

ISBN 1 872226 50 7

£4.95

Songs of a Lancashire Warbler

(Lowell Dobbs)

A friendly and humorous book of new Lancashire poetry, very much in keeping with the best of the past masters of the dialect and helping to keep alive the heritage of the Lankysheer twang. A book written with insight and compassion, by Lowell Dobbs, winner of many awards for his art and a rising master of dialect prose.

ISBN 1 872226 49 3

£4.95

NORTHERN CLASSIC REPRINTS

The Manchester Man
(Mrs. G. Linnaeus Banks)

Re-printed from an 1896 illustrated edition — undoubtedly the finest paper-back edition ever. Fascinating reading, includes Peterloo. Over 400 pages, wonderfully illustrated.

ISBN 1 872226 16 7   £4.95

The Lancashire Witches
(W. Harrison Ainsworth)

A beautiful illustrated edition of the most famous romance of the supernatural.

ISBN 1 872226 55 8   £4.95

NOW £2.50 — BARGAIN!!!

The Manchester Rebels
(W. Harrison Ainsworth)

A heady mixture of fact and fiction combined in a compelling story of the Jacobean fight for the throne of England. Manchester's involvement and the formation of the Manchester Regiment. Authentic illustrations.

ISBN 1 872226 29 9   £4.95

Hobson's Choice (the Novel)
(Harold Brighthouse)

The humorous and classic moving story of Salford's favourite tale. Well worth re-discovering this enjoyable story. Illustrated edition. Not been available since 1917, never before in paperback.

ISBN 1 872226 36 1   £4.95

The Dock Road
(J. Francis Hall RN)

A seafaring tale of old Liverpool. Set in the 1860s with the American Civil War raging and the cotton famine gripping Lancashire. Period illustrations.

ISBN 1 872226 37 X   £4.95

Getting to Know...

also **THE RIBBLE VALLEY, PENDLE, PEAK DISTRICT & SECRET LANCASHIRE**

OTHER LOCAL PUBLICATIONS

also *Greetings from ...*
ECCLES, AROUND MANCHESTER, OLD SALFORD, YORKSHIRE COAST, LIVERPOOL, THE WIRRAL

OTHER LOCAL PUBLICATIONS

The History of Lancashire Cookery

Tom Bridge takes us deep into Lancashire's culinary past to reveal the classic dishes of the region.

ISBN 1 872226 25 6 £4.95

Includes a facsimile reprint of the U.C.P. Tripe Recipe Book from 1934.

Cammell Laird — The Golden Years

(Dave Roberts)

Well illustrated. A fully history of this great shipyard.

ISBN 1 872226 48 5 £4.95

For The Children

Poems & Stories by well-known authors and personalities. Produced for the Tay Sachs Society.

ISBN 1 872226 14 0 £4.95